W9-BCO-728

DATE DUE

11794

DESIRE AND LOVE IN HENRY JAMES
A STUDY OF THE LATE NOVELS

MCWHIRTER, DAVID BRUCE

PS2127.L65M39 1989

DISCARD
SE

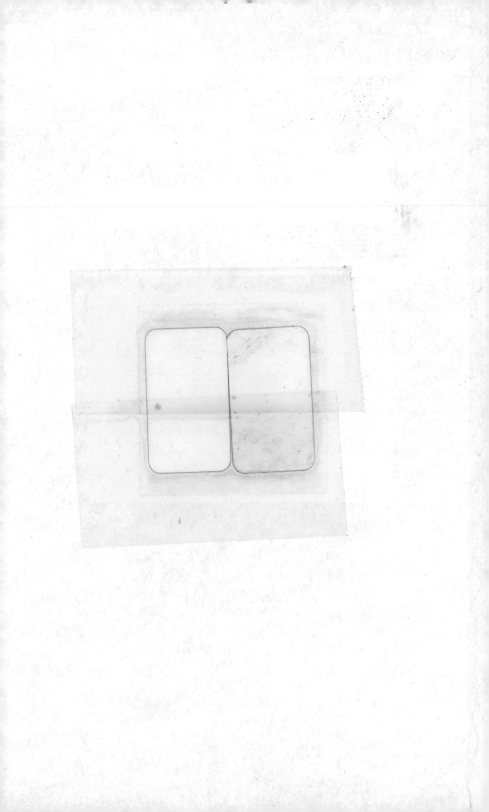

DESIRE AND LOVE
IN HENRY JAMES

A Study of the Late Novels

"The Doctor's Door"   "The Venetian Palace"

These photographs, taken by Alvin Langdon Coburn, were chosen by Henry James to accompany the text of the New York Edition of *The Wings of the Dove* (see the discussion on pp. 10–12).

DESIRE AND LOVE IN HENRY JAMES

A Study of the Late Novels

DAVID McWHIRTER

Assistant Professor of English,
University of Pennsylvania

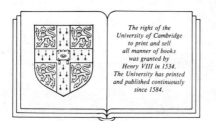

The right of the
University of Cambridge
to print and sell
all manner of books
was granted by
Henry VIII in 1534.
The University has printed
and published continuously
since 1584.

CAMBRIDGE UNIVERSITY PRESS

Cambridge
New York   New Rochelle
Melbourne   Sydney

Published by the Press Syndicate of the University of Cambridge
The Pitt Building, Trumpington Street, Cambridge CB2 1RP
32 East 57th Street, New York, NY 10022, USA
10 Stamford Road, Oakleigh, Melbourne 3166, Australia

© Cambridge University Press 1989

First published 1989

Printed in Great Britain at the University Press, Cambridge

British Library cataloguing in publication data
McWhirter, David
Desire and love in Henry James: a study
of the late novels.
1. Fiction in English. American writers.
James, Henry, 1843–1916 – Critical
studies
I. Title
813′.4

Library of Congress cataloguing in publication data
McWhirter, David Bruce.
Desire and love in Henry James: a study of the late novels /
David McWhirter.
    p.   cm.
Bibliography.
Includes index.
ISBN 0–521–35328–9
1. James, Henry, 1843–1916 – Criticism and interpretation.
2. Love in literature. 3. Desire in literature. I. Title.
PS2127.L65M39 1989
813′.4 – dc 19   88–27437   CIP

ISBN 0 521 35328 9

GG

for Ellen

"What an immense number of words . . . to say you want to fall in love! I've no doubt you've as good a genius for that as any one if you would only trust it a little more."

Henry James, *Roderick Hudson*

CONTENTS

PREFACE AND ACKNOWLEDGMENTS

This project grew most directly – and has been most consistently nourished – out of a deep fascination with the humanly interesting story embodied in James's unfolding career. My first comprehensive reading of James's fiction proved to be a strangely discomforting experience. Increasingly, I found my admiration for his technical virtuosity tempered by reservations about his peculiarly limited sensibility, and particularly by my frustration with his apparent inability to write positively about love, or to grant his characters the power to fulfill their often intensely passionate desires. But in James's last three novels – *The Ambassadors, The Wings of the Dove,* and *The Golden Bowl* – I discovered an unexpected yet unmistakable movement towards a more affirmative vision of life, a movement crowned in the unprecedented embrace of enacted love which he attains with the renewal of Maggie Verver's marriage in *The Golden Bowl*. My book is essentially an exploration of the sources and implications of James's belated acceptance of the reality – as opposed to the imagination – of loving. More specifically, I argue that James's changing conception of love in the late novels is linked to broader shifts in theme and formal strategy which involve a fundamental recasting of his moral and aesthetic assumptions.

In his prefaces to the New York Edition of his work, James repeatedly characterizes his *œuvre* as very much "a *living* affair" (*AN*, 342), as "a thrilling tale" and "a wondrous adventure" (*AN*, 4) in which he could "retrace the whole growth of [his] 'taste'" – "a blessed comprehensive name," he explains, "for many of the deepest things in us" (*AN*, 340). And he invites us to join him in exploring "the manifold delicate things, the shy and illusive, the inscrutable, the indefinable, that minister to deep and quite confident processes of change" (*AN*,

344). But the particular "process of change" which I see unfolding in the pages of James's late novels is likely to trouble some readers, most profoundly, I think, in its discernment of a deliberate and in some senses limiting movement towards closure in texts valued primarily in recent years for their openness and indeterminacy. Post-structuralist critics have increasingly valorized James's fiction as the locus of an autotelic, self-generating, endlessly interpretable *écriture*, blissfully detached from the authority of nature, history, and even of the novelist himself. James has thus been celebrated for his exemplification of a "literality" which is "essentially impermeable to analysis and interpretation" (Felman, 207); for his achievement of an "unresolved ambiguity" through which "the possible is rendered impossible" and "the possible becomes impossible" (Rimmon, xii, 235); and for his capacity "to conceive even of time and death as merely our most privileged fictions" (Bersani, *A Future for Astyanax*, 141). But while I believe, as my reading of *The Ambassadors* will attest, that James *was* drawn toward this radical ideal of an art liberated from the contingencies of a reality he saw as fatally limiting, I also believe that, in the novels of his maturity, he came to understand that the value of a literary work is bound up, inseparable, in fact, from its value, inevitably moral, as an act of life. In *The Wings of the Dove* and *The Golden Bowl*, through a remarkable drama of realization and self-realization, James consciously withdrew from − or perhaps more accurately moved beyond − an aesthetic which emphasized uncertainty, ambiguity, and textual play to arrive at a recognition of the real, binding, but ultimately empowering choices involved in the act of artistic creation. For fictions, as James would insist in his preface to *The Golden Bowl*, are also "literary deeds," embedded, like all our "innumerable acts," in "the conditions of life." And "to 'put' things is very exactly and responsibly and interminably to do them. Our expression of them, and the terms on which we understand that, belong as nearly to our conduct and our life as every other feature of our freedom" (*AN*, 347).

It is only candid of me to acknowledge that my own convictions about the purpose, value and affect of literature closely resemble those which I see James embracing at the end of his career. My most consistent intention and effort throughout this study has been to grant the fullest depth and power and value to the myriad choices − thematic, technical, stylistic, and above all human − enacted by Henry James in these novels, and to root the "illusive," often "inscrutable" surfaces of his texts in the psychological and moral realities of the man who made them. Perhaps the closest analogy to my method is Sartre's concept of "existential psychoanalysis," which searches in "each example of human conduct" for the contours of an "original choice" – a "choice of position in the world" through which the individual "makes himself a person" and confirms "the human meaning of freedom" (568–70). If this reading of James's late fictions admittedly restricts the abstractly infinite possibilities for interpreting them – for every human choice, by realizing some possibilities, renders others inauthentic – it does so in order to find in them the expression of a richer and more meaningful freedom.

In tracing the changing parameters of James's vision of his art, I have found it helpful to draw on a variety of theoretical perspectives – deconstructive, structuralist, phenomenological, psychoanalytical, and Marxist. No one of these approaches should be conflated with my own. As will be readily apparent, I have benefitted greatly from the extra-ordinary wealth of prior criticism devoted specifically to James. But if I wished to locate my contribution amongst the welter of critical voices contending for the elusive turf known as Henry James, I would unhesitatingly align myself with those commentators – critics like Laurence Holland and Leon Edel, or more recently, like John Carlos Rowe, Carren Kaston, and Mark Seltzer – who have worked in various ways to free this great novelist from the myth of the master, and from the life-denying retreat into a refined but sterile art which that myth has always implied. While the terms of my discussion here are primarily ethical and psychological, any attempt to restore James's art to "the conditions of life" – to the social, political, historical and personal contexts in which it was produced – is a project implicitly validated by my own.

Many friends, teachers, colleagues and students have helped make my work possible and rewarding. I can only mention a few here: Kenny Marotta, whose seminar on James at the University of Virginia provided the initial impetus for this study; David Wyatt, whose friend-ship and sympathetic criticism encouraged me throughout its develop-ment; and Robert Langbaum, whose high standards of precision in thought and elegance in expression are, I hope, reflected in these pages. I would also like to thank Robert Lucid, for his confidence in my work and for his support and advice at a crucial juncture, and John

Gontowicz, for his professional and good-humored assistance in preparing various versions of this manuscript.

My deepest debt is to my family, especially to my wife Ellen, whose sustaining love is woven deeply into the fabric of this book.

ABBREVIATIONS

Works by Henry James frequently cited in the text are referred to according to the following abbreviations:

AN   *The Art of the Novel: Critical Prefaces by Henry James*, ed. Richard P. Blackmur. New York: Charles Scribner's Sons, 1937

CT   *The Complete Tales of Henry James*, ed. Leon Edel, 12 vols. Philadelphia: Lippincott, 1964

L   *Letters*, ed. Leon Edel, 4 vols. Cambridge, Mass.: Harvard University Press, 1984

LC   *Literary Criticism*, 2 vols. New York: The Library of America, 1984

N   *The Notebooks of Henry James*, ed. F. O. Matthiessen and Kenneth B. Murdock. University of Chicago Press, 1981

NSB   *Notes of a Son and Brother*. New York: Charles Scribner's Sons, 1916

SBO   *A Small Boy and Others*. New York: Charles Scribner's Sons, 1913

Volume and page citations (i.e. *22*, 186) refer to *The Novels and Tales of Henry James: The New York Edition*, 26 vols. New York: Charles Scribner's Sons, 1907–09.

1 Introduction: Desire, love, and the question of Henry James

The lover's discourse is today *of an extreme solitude.* This discourse is spoken, perhaps, by thousands of subjects (who knows?), but warranted by no one; it is completely forsaken by the surrounding languages: ignored, disparaged, or derided by them, severed not only from authority but also from the mechanisms of authority (sciences, techniques, arts). Once a discourse is thus driven by its own momentum into the backwater of the "unreal," exiled from all gregarity, it has no recourse but to become the site, however exiguous, of an *affirmation.*

Roland Barthes, A Lover's Discourse

> The self's a fine and private place
> But none I think do there embrace.

F.W. Dupee on Henry James

In the preface to his seminal study of Henry James's late fiction, F. O. Matthiessen describes the incident which led him to designate the three novels of James's maturity – *The Ambassadors, The Wings of the Dove*, and *The Golden Bowl* – as their author's "major phase". As he neared the completion of his work on James, Matthiessen recalls,

a distinguished professor asked me what I was doing, and forgetting that he was uneasy with any literature since Trollope, I told him, only to be asked: "What are you going to call it? *The Old Pretender?*" I had forgotten that once bright, if long since hoary, wise-crack, but that conversation gave me my title. I realized more clearly than before that though James' later evolution had involved the loss of an engaging lightness, he knew what he was about, and that if we want to find the figure in his carpet, we must search for it primarily in the intricate and fascinating designs of his final and major phrase. (xiv-xv)

Since the publication of *Henry James: The Major Phase* in 1944, Matthiessen's thesis that the late novels are James's greatest and most

1

essential fictions has gained widespread acceptance. The idea that James began, with *The Ambassadors*, "to do work of a greater depth and richness than any he had approached before" (xiii) has in fact become something of an article of faith amongst his critics. While a few commentators have continued to support the view of earlier readers like Van Wyck Brooks and Vernon Parrington that the late novels represent a falling-off in James's achievement,[1] the figure of "the old pretender" has for the most part given way to that of "the master." And despite the considerable diversity of their assumptions, methods, and conclusions, critics since Matthiessen have almost universally followed his lead in seeing these three novels as both the summit and key to James's *oeuvre*. The most influential overviews of James's career – I am thinking especially of the work of Laurence Holland and Dorothea Krook, but also of Leon Edel's massive biographical study – consistently echo Matthiessen's high valuation of the late fiction, both in the disproportionate attention they devote to the major phase novels, and in their tendency to read James's earlier work largely as a prelude to his final achievement. In addition, important reappraisals of James by such critics as Sallie Sears, Ruth Bernard Yeazell, and Leo Bersani have focused exclusively on the late novels. Matthiessen's own reading of *The Ambassadors*, *The Wings of the Dove*, and *The Golden Bowl* emphasizes what he sees as fundamental resemblances in their style, form, and subject matter. Citing the novelist's return to the "international theme," his increasing preoccupation with characters of highly refined consciousness, and the unique qualities of his late style – as well as the remarkably brief period in which the three novels were composed – Matthiessen argues that James's final works constitute a distinct and basically homogeneous "phase" in his development. And the extent of Matthiessen's influence on James criticism is demonstrated once again by the fact that his view of the late novels as formally and thematically unified has, in the years since his pioneering study, gone largely unchallenged. James's major phase has provoked what can only be described as a startling array of responses: the novels have been interpreted as Swedenborgian allegory, as the embodiment of a "demonic" vision of a "morally absurd" universe, and as the locus of an autotelic art concerned mainly with its own aesthetic processes. Yet for all their varied and conflicting readings of the figure in James's fictional carpet, the critics have almost without exception treated the late novels as though they reflected a consistent set of purposes and techniques – even, in some cases, as though they constituted a single, continuous text. The trend toward apprehending these novels as a kind of literary triptych has only been reinforced by the increasingly theoretical orientation of recent criticism and its emphasis on intertextuality.

My own approach to James's late fiction involves a recognition that *The Ambassadors*, *The Wings of the Dove*, and *The Golden Bowl* are in many respects as different from each other as they are from James's earlier works. More specifically, my questioning of Matthiessen's concept of a unified major phase is rooted in my belief that *The Golden Bowl*, in its unusually positive representation of achieved love, occupies an entirely unique place in the Jamesian canon. The extraordinary and, for James, unprecedented affirmation of love that emerges in the final pages of his last completed novel signals a dramatic departure from the pattern of thwarted and renounced passion which had always dominated his fiction. With the renewal of Maggie Verver's marriage, emblematized in the embrace, given and accepted by husband and wife, which concludes the novel, James arrives at a vision of realized and reciprocated love which in fact reverses both the unfulfilled solipsism depicted in *The Ambassadors* and the tragic failure of love explored in *The Wings of the Dove*. As Stephen Spender sensed many years ago, *The Golden Bowl* is the creation "of a person who, profoundly with his whole being, after overcoming great inhibition, has accepted the idea of people loving" (194).

James's affirmation of love in *The Golden Bowl* has troubled many of his critics, and has been ignored by more than a few, not only because it undermines the supposed unity of the major phase, but also because it comes at the end of a long career in which the novelist consistently denied his protagonists the experience of fulfilled passion. Indeed, any extended immersion in James's *oeuvre* tends to become an adventure in sustained frustration. For in novel after novel, he constructs situations in which his fictional men and women – by virtue both of the circumstances which surround them and of their own characteristic responses to those circumstances – are unable to consummate their desires in the achievement of love. James's status as a major novelist has long been secure, and his brilliance as a technical innovator and theoretician are almost universally acknowledged; yet it is not difficult to discern, in the profusion of critical discourse devoted to his work, a persistent undercurrent of uneasiness, centered on the disturbing but inescapable fact that his art is seemingly unable to accommodate the representation of mature, fulfilled love.

James himself never married, and in all probability remained celibate throughout his long life. The problematical nature of love in his fiction clearly has its roots deep in his personal experience. "I am unlikely ever to marry," James once explained to a friend:

One's attitude toward marriage is a fact – the most characteristic part doubtless of one's general attitude toward life. If I were to marry I should be guilty in my own eyes of inconsistency – I should pretend to think quite a little better of life than I really do. (*L*, 2: 314)

This remarkable if rather appalling admission ought to encourage us to approach the theme of love in Henry James within a broad context of ethical and ontological, as well as psychological concerns. Yet James's critics have typically been content simply to point to the painfully obvious facts contained in his biography, and to dismiss him out of hand as constitutionally incapable of understanding or even acknowledging the actuality of love – especially of sexual love. Here is George Moore, writing in 1886:

The interviewer in us would like to ask Henry James why he never married; but it would be vain to ask, so much does he write like a man to whom all action is repugnant. He confesses himself on every page, as we all do. On every page James is a prude. (in Gard, 172)

Only the terminology has changed when Maxwell Geismar, some seventy-five years later, vituperatively asserts that James suffered from an "infantile-pubescent . . . thwarted sexuality" (436). As in Geismar's case, biographical readings of James have all too frequently resulted in reductive, unprofitable speculations about the novelist's sexuality. Indeed, James has been diagnosed not only as prudish, but as pedophilic, homosexual, impotent, sexually "underdeveloped," and – with reference to his notoriously "obscure hurt" – literally castrated.

One need not to go to these extremes to recognize that something in James's personal psychic economy makes loving, and writing about love in any positive or affirmative way, profoundly difficult for him. But James's attitudes about love are historically as well as psychologically determined. And I think that his critics, at least in part because of the easy availability of psychobiographical explanations, have generally neglected the task of evaluating his problematical treatment of love in terms of the historical context in which he wrote. Many of James's contemporaries – one thinks especially of Hardy, Conrad, and Meredith – share his sense that the enactment of love *is* a problem in a world stripped of the religious and social orthodoxies which had anchored the moral realism of their Victorian predecessors. The happy marriages which typically conclude Victorian novels assert the value of love in a universe that is morally coherent and meaningfully ordered. But modern love, cut off from any transcendent or even transpersonal structures of authority, is no longer sure how to affirm itself. Love for James is centrally a moral question – in *Roderick Hudson*, Rowland Mallet forgoes an opportunity to declare his passion for the woman he loves because, as James puts it, "he felt that it was physically possible to say, '. . . I love you!' but it was not morally possible" (*1*, 470) – but it is a question asked in a moral landscape that is itself increasingly decentered. Paul Armstrong quite correctly sees James's fiction as "a prolonged inquiry into the status of ethics in a world where norms have no foundation deeper than existence itself" (206). Not surprisingly, some of the most judicious commentary on the theme of love in James has come from critics like Sallie Sears, Stuart Hutchinson, and Naomi Lebowitz, who have recognized James's position as a transitional figure who, for all his superficial adherence to the Victorian sexual mores of his audience, nevertheless embodies "the ferocious contradictions of his age." As Sears puts it, James is in many respects "the first 'modern' novelist in English," especially in his "upending of traditional moral categories" (46–51).

Love is made problematical in James's fiction, not by its peripheral importance or absence – as some critics have suggested – but by its insistent and often painful centrality. His approach to love revolves around two antithetical conceptions of its nature and value, the dialectic between which is, I believe, crucial to understanding his evolving vision in the late fiction. The two poles of this dialectic, which I will henceforth call *desire* and *love*, may be roughly characterized as imaginative and active; they imply two fundamentally opposed modes of experience, two ways of encountering life and transforming it into art, the tension between which informs every aspect of the major phase novels. The mode of desire – what James means when he speaks of "the imagination of loving" (*3*, 54) – closely resembles Stendhal's romantic conception of love as a process of imaginative "crystallization" (45–47). Stendhal's "love" is essentially a narcissistic fantasizing activity of the mind, which seeks not to know and affirm the existence of another person (or of any reality outside the self), but to see in the other an absence in which imagination is free to deploy itself, and around which the endlessly proliferating fantasies projected by desire can cluster or crystallize. Rather than engage with the real presence of its object, the desiring consciousness seeks to save the object from life's poverty and finitude by loading it with a rich, multiplicitous, potentially infinite value that is ultimately in excess of its limited reality. Desire is necessarily unrequited, for the reciprocation of passion would bring a true knowledge of the other – a knowledge that inevitably destroys the beautiful but illusory figures of desire's free imagining. Similarly, desire must by definition remain unfulfilled, for it only wants to perpetuate itself *as* desire (as wanting and therefore as lacking), and so perishes in the act of consummation, just as sexual desire "dies" in the discharge of satisfaction. We are very close here to Denis de Rougemont's notion of "Eros": "a desire that never relapses, that nothing can satisfy, that even rejects and flees the temptation to obtain its fulfillment in the world, because its demand is to embrace nothing less than the All" (62). By fleeing fulfillment, the desiring consciousness condemns itself to a decentered wandering, and effectively bars itself from achieving the definite identity attainable only through the concrete realization – the choice and enactment – of a particular desire. Caught in the solipsistic labyrinth of its own endless wanting, desire pursues an impossible dream of escape from the limitations and imperfections of life, especially from the facts of time and death. It thus purchases its rich imaginative freedom at the cost of divorcing itself from reality and from the power to make and alter reality.

Love, in contrast, is a mode not of consciousness or imagination, but of action. Ortega y Gasset's definition of love (explicitly opposed to Stendhalian "love") as a "centrifugal act of the soul" that "goes toward the object uniting with it and positively affirming its being" (20) suggests how, in contradistinction to the centripetal narcissism of desire, love insists on the reality and presence of the other. Instead of projecting onto the other the infinite variety of what *might* be, love embraces the other's limited and imperfect reality, and invites and accepts the binding and defining embrace offered by the other. The notion of unrequited love – so central to Stendhal's theorizing – is here entirely oxymoronic, for love can only come into being through the lovers' mutual acceptance and unillusioned knowledge of each other's reality. Since the primary goal of love is to affirm another's being (and thus the existence of a world outside the self), the lover must choose *an* other, must abandon the "free," decentered mobility of the desiring mode (which affirms only its own wanting) and direct his love toward a specific object. The ability to love thus involves a willingness to give up the multiplicitous possibilities of desire's infinite but abstract imagining for the comparatively restricted but nevertheless concrete reality of an identity defined through choice, action, and fulfillment. Hence the lover determines and makes a reality, instead of merely seeking to escape or evade one. Moreover, though desire is necessarily a part of love, the lover wills the death of his desire in the discharge of satisfaction; indeed, only through repeated acts of intercourse and consummation – sexual, moral, and spiritual – can he keep faith with love's defining purpose: to know and affirm the ever-changing presence of the other. Thus love, unlike desire, accepts the cycle of want and fulfillment through which desire continually perishes that it might be born again: accepts, in other words, its own finitude, and its fundamental nature as a becoming in time. So conceived, love is analogous to de Rougemont's "marriage," where desire is bound by reality and transformed into love through "an entirely carnal eros" (302).

Desire and love thus define not only differing conceptions of passional and erotic relationship, but more generally, two opposed modes of human experience. They imply as well on James's part two radically divergent ways of thinking about the purpose, value and affect of his novelistic art. The desiring mode – manifested formally in James's practice of narrating events through the point of view of a single "center of consciousness" – clearly constitutes the main line of his development. Early Jamesian protagonists like Isabel Archer in *The Portrait of a Lady* and Christopher Newman in *The American do* seek the enacted fulfillment of their desires. But the disastrous results which attend their efforts – Isabel's destructive marriage and Newman's thwarting at the hands of the Bellegardes are symptomatic of the way in which the attempt to love *always* meets with disaster in James – suggest the motive for the novelist's growing fascination with the kind of passion we encounter in another character from *The Portrait of a Lady*, Ralph Touchett. Cut off by illness, and by his response to that illness, from any active participation in life, Ralph withdraws into the desiring mode, and pursues a wholly imaginative "romance" with Isabel. As James puts it, "the imagination of loving – as distinguished from that of being loved – had still a place in his reduced sketch" (*3*, 54). Ralph's way of loving increasingly preoccupies James in the works which follow, especially in the fiction of the so-called "experimental period" which immediately precedes the major phase.[2] *What Maisie Knew*, *In the Cage*, and *The Turn of the Screw* are all fictions intensely focused on themes of sexuality and romantic love. But in each case, this fascination is filtered through the consciousness of a character who can express and enact passion only through an obsessive vicarious concern with the passional lives of others. In *The Sacred Fount*, the novelist reaches a kind of self-parodying apotheosis of the desiring mode. This strange text – the only long fiction, intriguingly, in which James abandoned his usual third-person center of consciousness technique to adopt the first person – presents an unnamed narrator who possesses what we might characterize as an excess of erotic imagination, which he obsessively projects onto everyone and everything he encounters *except* the woman – May Server – who is presumably the real object of his passion. Living as he does entirely inside the fantasizing processes of his desiring imagination, this solipsistic, possibly insane figure has reached a stage where he appears to be literally unaware of the other's presence.

A number of critics have discerned a kinship between the narrator of *The Sacred Fount* and James's most famous hero of excessive imagination, Lambert Strether. And in my reading of James's career, *The Ambassadors* stands as his culminating and most eloquent defense of his commitment to desire. This first of the major phase novels is in fact more closely linked to his earlier work, especially to the experimental novels of the 1890s, than to *The Wings of the Dove* and *The Golden Bowl*. *The Ambassadors* favorably contrasts Strether's free imaginative expansion of life's possibilities to Woollett's rigid and reductive utilitarianism. But this deceptively easy antithesis – reinforced by the novel's immersion of writer and reader in the unbroken process of Strether's consciousness – obscures the more disturbing implications of desire: its powerlessness to effect its vision, its refusal of knowledge, and its profound fear of ends – even when the end is love. For all his imaginative intensity, Strether remains a willing prisoner of his own infinite wanting, and is incapable of responding to the act of love proffered by Maria Gostrey at the novel's close; moreover, James, through his own formal choices, validates the kind of living which his protagonist exemplifies.

The Wings of the Dove, though begun by James just a few months after he completed *The Ambassadors*, embodies a developing critique of desire. This is a less evasive work, both in the hard truths of its tragic plot, and in its surprisingly direct evocation of James's own youthful relationship with Minny Temple. The novel's multiple-consciousness form invests its characters with an unmistakable reality – the reality of subjects – apart from their figurative existence as objects of any single consciousness. By thus locating and binding each character's desire within a concretely, dramatically defined reality, James arrives at a new kind of novelistic art capable of affirming the individual's power and responsibility to choose his own fate. On this basis, James tentatively affirms Milly Theale's heroic but thwarted effort – rooted in her tragic acceptance of her own mortality – to realize her desire in love.

In *The Golden Bowl*, James completes and confirms his progress from desire to love. The heroine of this last novel, Maggie Verver, desires as intensely as Strether; but she also demonstrates a capacity to make the painful, sometimes cruel choices – including the choice between her father and her husband – which necessarily limit and ultimately destroy desire's infinite imaginings in the satisfaction of a specific want. In thus allowing Maggie to move beyond the facile Strether/Woollett antithesis towards a unitary perspective that embraces fulfillment *and* loss, imagination *and* action, James succeeds in transforming the vain freedom of desire into the bound fullness of enacted love. The breakthrough embodied in *The Golden Bowl* reflects not only the triumph of a new kind of Jamesian protagonist, but also a fundamental change in the novelist's conception of his art. James returns to the multiple-consciousness form of *The Wings of the Dove*, with the clear intention of exploiting the positive representational possibilities he had discovered in writing the earlier novel. Moreover, Maggie's freely and powerfully undertaken act of love is adumbrated in James's unprecedented willingness to exercise his own authorial power to manipulate his fictional world towards a positive end.

Forty years ago, Matthiessen rescued James's late fiction from the misconceptions and disregard implied by the "old pretender" rubric. Perhaps it is now time to liberate these great novels from the myth of the master. For James's major phase embodies not the unified, valedictory summation of a perfected art, but an heroic struggle – undertaken at a point when most artists have ceased to grow and change – toward a self- and life-affirming vision that had long eluded him, and toward an art capable of expressing that vision. James, particularly the James of the late fiction, has long been seen as the votary of a refined art divorced from the concrete realities of human experience. His "destiny," as John Carlos Rowe has written, "always seems to end in the intricacies of the late style and its retreat from life into the palace of art" (28). But James's struggle towards love in the late novels, and the ethical and aesthetic revaluations which accompany that struggle, suggest that the myth of the master conceals a courageous embrace of life, made all the more moving by its belatedness, and by the difficult personal and historical conditions in which it unfolded.

Near the end of his preface to *The Golden Bowl*, James offers a brief but suggestive meditation on the Alvin Langdon Coburn photographs which serve as frontispiece illustrations for the twenty-four volumes which comprise the New York Edition of his novels and tales. James uses the occasion to denounce the traditional practice of illustrating specific scenes from fictional works – to decry the attempt, as he puts it, "to graft or 'grow' . . . a picture by another hand on my own picture" – and goes on to warn that such representational illustration, or "anything that relieves responsible prose of the duty of being, while placed before us, good enough, interesting enough and, if the question be of picture, pictorial enough, above all *in itself*, does it the worst of services." In contrast, James asserts, the Coburn photographs fulfill the proper function of illustrations,

the reference of which to Novel or Tale should exactly be *not* competitive and obvious, should on the contrary plead its case with some shyness, that of images always confessing themselves mere optical symbols or echoes, expressions of no particular thing in the text, but only of the type or idea of this or that thing. (*AN*, 331–33)

In terms that reflect his own special sense of novelistic realism, James praises Coburn's photographs for providing "a concrete, independent, vivid instance" of the real, while simultaneously offering "an image distilled and intensified" of "the author's projected world, in which objects are primarily related to each other, and [are] therefore not 'taken from' " reality in any direct way.

James's perceptive appreciation of photography as an art at once vividly realistic and profoundly symbolic is especially interesting in connection with the two pictures, chosen by the novelist in collaboration with Coburn, which accompany the text of *The Wings of the Dove* in the New York Edition, and which I reproduce here as my own frontispiece. For these two photographs, entitled by James "The Doctor's Door" and "The Venetian Palace," evoke in some immediate sense the central Jamesian opposition between fact and symbol, between the real and the image, between the limited actuality of human experience and the infinite imaginings which constitute our "projected worlds." The textual idea "echoed" by "The Doctor's Door" is, of course, Milly Theale's unalterable doom, the sentence of death which, once announced by her physician, hangs over her and our experience throughout James's great tragic novel. The solitary, solid, unadorned Georgian door, firmly grounded in the London pavements, reflects the single, hard fact – the fact of her dying – that Milly must and will face; it adumbrates the strait gate through which she will inevitably pass to complete her destiny, and suggests as well the terrible limits – this door, like so many doors in James, is closed – imposed by life on a passionate young woman who wants only to live. But if this stark image embodies what James surely saw as the central fact of his novel – "that of a young person conscious of a great capacity for life, but early stricken and doomed, condemned to die under short respite" (AN, 288) – then "The Venetian Palace" must be understood as an image of Milly's "unsurpassable activity of passionate, of inspired resistance" to her doom (AN, 289). With its multiple, ornate, and open windows, its elaborate gothic beauty, and its emergence, not from the immovable earth, but from the shifting waters of the Venetian lagoon, the palace symbolizes Milly's desire, her creative and courageous exploration of the possibilities still resident within her grimly narrowed lot: it embodies the same "pervasive mystery of Style" (20, 203) through which she fashions herself into the magnificent princess esconced in the "great gilded shell" (20, 203) of the Palazzo Leporelli, and provides a singular instance of what Merton Densher recognizes as "the mere aesthetic instinct of mankind" – and of its capacity for constructing "beautiful fictions and priceless arrangements" (20, 299).

But the "beautiful fiction" of "The Venetian Palace" cannot effectively alter or remove "the great smudge of mortality" (20, 298) figured by "The Doctor's Door." And over the years, James's critics have tended to follow the novelist's own lead in positing the split between "the fatal futility of fact" (AN, 122) and the rich, free potentiality of art and desire as a profound and unbridgable gap, a radical antinomy of two realms, between which no meaningful commerce is possible. This extreme dualism has become an essential element of "the myth of the high modernist James" (Rowe, 28). In the pages which follow, however, I will argue that The Ambassadors, The Wings of the Dove, and The Golden Bowl enact a progressive disenchantment with, rejection of, and movement beyond these rigid dualities of life and art, reality and imagination, which James himself so often and so persuasively asserted. For I believe that James, at the end of his long career, and through a difficult, often painful reevaluation of his art *and* life, belatedly came to understand that "The Doctor's Door" and "The Venetian Palace" are really the intersecting axes of a unitary, wholly human vision. The two images in fact imply, evoke, and require each other. The single, unadorned arch of the doctor's door constitutes, after all, the basic structure which, repeated, multiplied, and elaborated, empowers the intricate beauty of the Venetian Palace. The complexity of Milly's "great gilded shell" – like that of James's late style – is ultimately only an expansion of possibilities inherent in the simple form which images the central fact of her and her creator's common humanity. Milly discovers the potentiality for her "projected world" in the knowledge she gains by walking through the doctor's door. And taken together, the two photographs suggest how James finally came to envision his art: not as a retreat from or futile resistance to the ugliness and poverty of life, but as an embrace of those inescapable realities – of "those things we cannot possibly *not* know, sooner or later, in one way or another" – which alone can provide a basis for love, and for the exploration and enactment of "the things that can reach us only through the beautiful circuit and subterfuge of our thought and our desire" (*AN*, 31–32).

2 *The Ambassadors* (I): Strether, James, and the figuration of desire

My strong point is those little things which are more important than big ones, because they make up life. It seems that big ones do not do that, and I daresay it is fortunate.

Ivy Compton-Burnett, A Family and a Fortune

> So it is that I have been slow in accomplishment
> through excess of desire.

Jean-Jacques Rousseau, Confessions

At the beginning of *A Small Boy and Others*, Henry James announces the simple yet extraordinary basis upon which he intends to confront the task of autobiography: "I think," he writes, "I shall be ashamed, as of a cold impiety, to find any element altogether negligible" (*SBO*, 2). In the *modus operandi* proposed here, as in so many other respects, James closely resembles that most autobiographical of all his characters, Lambert Strether. Strether, like his creator, is one of those for whom no facet of experience is without import: what James once said of himself in *Notes of a Son and Brother* – that he possessed "an imagination to which literally everything obligingly signified" (*NSB*, 360) – is perhaps even more fundamentally true of Strether. Strether responds with the same mysterious urgency and intensity to even the most superficial and evanescent phenomena. As a man of "monstrous" imagination (*22*, 241), he is unwilling or unable to discount any sensation or perception, no matter how slight; he is acutely conscious at every moment, and as a result is always poised to react to "the quiet instants that sometimes settle more matters than the outbreaks dear to the historic muse" (*21*, 132).

As *The Ambassadors* unfolds, this fundamental *inability not to respond* increasingly constitutes both the principle of Strether's genius and the root of his error. In the initial stages of his European adventure, a nervous Strether still senses the need to repress and control his reactive impulses; thus in London, "the smallest things so arrested and amused him that he repeatedly almost apologized" (*21*, 39). Just a few weeks later, however, Strether, now in Paris, is ready to give himself up to the most infinitesimal sensations without a hint of shame or apology:

> he had attached himself to sounds and suggestions, vibrations of the air, human and dramatic, he imagined, as they were not in other places, that came out for him more and more as the mild afternoons deepened – a far-off hum, a sharp click on the asphalt, a voice calling, replying, somewhere and as full of tone as an actor's in a play. (*22*, 24)

Strether is repeatedly forced to "recognize the truth that wherever one paused in Paris the imagination reacted before one could stop it" (*21*, 96). In Paris, as Miss Barrace puts it, "Everything, every one shows" (*21*, 207). And because everything signifies, Strether is subjected to an unremitting "assault of images" (*21*, 196), all of them capable of evoking "perpetual reactions" (*21*, 96). Gloriani's garden-party, for example, becomes an occasion "not a note of which failed to reverberate" (*21*, 196); it produces in Strether at every juncture "the sense of names in the air, of ghosts at the windows, of signs and tokens, a whole range of expression, all about him, too thick for prompt discrimination" (*21*, 196). In such an atmosphere, even the most meager of impressions evokes intensities of reaction. Thus while Strether cannot hear a word of the polite pleasantries exchanged by Gloriani and an unknown duchess, he nevertheless responds with "absurdities of the stirred sense, fruits of suggestion ripening on the instant" (*21*, 219); and if his encounter with Gloriani himself is of the most perfunctory nature – a mere exchange of glances – Strether still has "the consciousness of opening to it, for the happy instant, all the windows of his mind" (*21*, 196).

Strether's excessively intense reaction to his altogether casual meeting with Gloriani demonstrates the extent to which he can discover value in the tiniest fragment of his experience. In his moment with Strether, Gloriani exercises only a superficial social politeness; his greeting of the man from Woollett really amounts to nothing more than "a single sustained look and a few words of delight at receiving him" (*21*, 196). Yet Strether senses in the artist's simple glance

the deepest intellectual sounding to which he had ever been exposed. He was in fact quite to cherish his vision of it, to play with it in idle hours; only speaking of it to no one and quite aware that he couldn't have spoken without appearing to talk nonsense. Was what it had told him or what it had asked him the greater of the mysteries? Was it the most special flare, unequalled, supreme, of the aesthetic torch, lighting that wondrous world forever, or was it above all the long straight shaft sunk by a personal acuteness that life had seasoned to steel? Nothing on earth could have been stranger and no one doubtless more surprised than the artist himself, but it was for all the world to Strether just then as if in the matter of his accepted duty he had positively been on trial. The deep human expertness in Gloriani's charming smile – oh the terrible life behind it! – was flashed upon him as a test of his stuff. (*21*, 197)

All this is a great deal to have been found in the *pro forma* civility of a man whom Strether acknowledges he is unlikely ever to meet again; he recognizes as much when he admits that Gloriani really knows nothing about "the matter of his accepted duty" – that of bringing Chad home to Woollett – concerning which he imagines he is being tested. And yet the full extent of Strether's reaction to this encounter only emerges several pages later in his famous outburst – "Live all you can" – to little Bilham.

Strether's inordinately intense response to Gloriani's merely perfunctory politeness bears a suggestive resemblance to James's own excited reaction – described in *Notes of a Son and Brother* – to an equally banal meeting with Charles Dickens (*NSB*, 253–56). James was twenty-four when, in 1867, he participated – "restrictedly yet exaltedly" – in a reception for Dickens given by Charles Eliot Norton at his home in Cambridge. As in Strether's meeting with Gloriani, James's actual contact with Dickens was virtually negligible:

the confrontation was but of a moment; our introduction, my companion's and mine, once effected, by an arrest in a doorway, nothing followed, as it were, or happened. . . our hero neither shook hands nor spoke, only meeting us by the barest act, so to say, of the trained eye.

Just as Strether's intensity stems from "the manner in which, while they stood briefly, in welcome and response, face to face, he was held by the sculptor's eyes" (*21*, 197), so the aspiring novelist was riveted by the way in which Dickens "met my dumb homage with a straight inscrutability, a merciless *military* eye"; it was, James insists, a glance "the penetration of which, to my sense, revealed again a world." It is not feasible to reproduce here the fullness of that "world"; for James's reaction, like Strether's to his meeting with Gloriani, is entirely out of proportion to the scanty stimulus which elicited it. In truth James's response finds its warrant not in the perfunctory actuality – the "barest act" – itself, but in "the light of an intense emotion," in the magnitude of passion his consciousness projected (and projects) onto that actuality. In each of these situations the encountered individual presents what James calls an "exquisitely complicated image" of the responsive party's most essential desires: Strether, in Gloriani, sees the artist he might have been and the personal acuteness he lacks; James, in Dickens, the artist he hopes to become and the popular success he sought but never achieved. Thus Strether hints to little Bilham that Gloriani is, of all men, the one "whom *I* should enjoy being like" (*21*, 220); while James writes that

on the evening I speak of . . . it was as a slim and shaken vessel of the feeling that one stood there – of the feeling . . . all unfathomably, undemonstrably, unassistedly and, as it were, unrewardedly, proper to one's self as an already groping and fumbling, already dreaming and yearning dabbler in the mystery, the creative, that of comedy, tragedy, evocation, representation, erect and concrete before us there as in a sublimity of mastership.

Strether is aware that his urgency at meeting Gloriani is largely "nonsense," that the moment he experiences so intensely is in truth rather ordinary; and James too is willing to concede that no other "young person of my then age, and however like myself" would have been "so ineffably agitated, so mystically moved" by Dickens's presence. But James nevertheless asserts that "since the question was of personal values so great no faintest fraction of the whole could succeed in *not* counting for interest." Indeed, he concludes his account of this episode by insisting that his purpose in recounting it has been to provide an "illustration of the force of action, unless I call it passion, that may reside in a single pulse of time."

For James and for Strether, however, every moment seems to involve great "personal values"; nothing ever succeeds in not counting. James's own preoccupation and fascination with the minute details of human experience occupy a central place in his aesthetic virtually from the beginning of his career. Even in his early manifesto, "The Art of Fiction," James already indicates a need to defend his apparent over-attentiveness to superficial phenomena:

Experience is never limited, and it is never complete; it is an immense sensibility, a kind of huge spiderweb of the finest silk threads suspended in the chamber of consciousness, and catching every air-borne particle in its tissue. It is the very atmosphere of the mind; and when the mind is imaginative – much more when it happens to be that of a man of genius – it takes to itself the faintest hints of life, it converts the very pulses of the air into revelations. (*LC*, 1:52)

James wrote this famous passage in 1884, and over the next thirty years he came increasingly to believe in and rely upon what he was to call, in *The Golden Bowl*, the "possible heroism of perfunctory things" (*24*, 288). Strether, while perhaps not a "man of genius," possesses a mind that is highly imaginative; and I can think of no Jamesian character more attuned to the meaning and value of the perfunctory. But the notion that even "the faintest hints of life" and "pulses of the air" can be transformed into "revelations" through the medium of a highly responsive consciousness is perhaps most thoroughly explored in those two volumes – *A Small Boy and Others* and *Notes of a Son and Brother* – which constitute, to my mind, one of the strangest autobiographical ventures in English letters.

The uniqueness of James's memoirs lies in the fact that they are centrally informed by their author's odd and acute consciousness that the events of his life offer to present memory little or nothing of actual personal importance – an assessment confirmed by the persistently peripheral role James assigns himself in structuring what is in effect the story of his own childhood and youth. James emphasizes his own secondary role in the titles he gives to these volumes; and it is indeed always a father or a brother – always one of the "others" – who occupies center stage, while James himself habitually stands aside and merely, though with ferocious intensity, observes. Again and again, with an almost painful frequency, James pictures himself as a marginal or even unnecessary figure in the events of his own life. Of his relationship with his famous father James writes: "My part may indeed but have been to surround his part with a thick imaginative aura" (*SBO*, 74). Similarly, his constant "sense of William's major activity . . . always made the presumption of any degree of importance or success fall, with a sort of ecstasy of resignation, from [his] own so minor" (*NSB*, 13). James's envy of the lives of others is a pervasive theme in the memoirs; even his younger brother Wilkie, with his "successful sociability, his instinct for intercourse, his genius . . . for making friends," evokes in James the perception that he himself is only an "adjunct" moving in "the trail of [Wilkie's] sociability," feeling its "weight on my comparatively so indirect faculty for what is called taking life" (*SBO*, 287–88). Throughout his childhood and youth, James is forced to recognize, the others "all enjoyed, in fine, while I somehow but wastefully mused" (*SBO*, 384).

Yet as he was composing this strangely self-effacing record of his life, James in some sense knew that his real autobiography – the New York Edition of his Collected Works – had already been written. James stands wholeheartedly with the narrator of "The Death of the Lion" (1894) when he asserts that "the artist's life's his work, and this is the place to observe him" (*15*, 119). Thus the dramatic essence of James's life – his lifelong struggle to transform, by a miraculous alchemy, the "fatal futility of fact" (*AN*, 122) into the freedom and triumph of art – finds its record in the series of Prefaces he wrote to accompany the New York Edition. The Prefaces

represent, over a considerable course, the continuity of an artist's endeavour, the growth of his whole operative consciousness . . . Addicted to 'stories' and inclined to retrospect, he fondly takes, under this backward view, his whole unfolding, his process of production, for a thrilling tale, almost for a wondrous adventure. (*AN*, 4)

The Prefaces recount the artist's "luxurious immersion" in "the effort of labor" and "the torment of expression"; such effort and torment may, James knows, "leave him weary and worn; but how, after his fashion, he will have lived!" (*AN*, 29–30)

But this high drama, this "inveterate romance" (*AN*, 287) of the artist's labor in which James, far from being peripheral, is the sole hero, is not the story James must represent in his memoirs. *A Small Boy and Others* and *Notes of a Son and Brother* comprise a kind of negative image of the more passionate and fulfilling "adventure" described in the Prefaces. James's memoirs unfold a life so poor in outward circumstance and dramatic event as to seem almost unlived; at moments one feels that this autobiography is, like James's famous story, "The Beast in the Jungle," the tale of "the man of his time, *the* man, to whom nothing on earth was to have happened" (*17*, 125). What James once wrote of Emerson seems even more applicable to himself:

letters surely were the very texture of his history. Passions, alternations, affairs, adventures had absolutely no part in it. It stretched itself out in enviable quiet – a quiet in which we hear the jotting of the pencil in the notebook. It is the very life for literature . . . the daily addition of sentence to sentence. (*LC*, 1:250–51)

James's regret for the "passions," "affairs" and "adventures" he had missed colors every page of his memoirs. Indeed, the substance of this strange autobiography is the sum of everything James felt he had lost, abandoned and sacrificed in his personal life in order that he might exist as an artist. The two volumes tell a story of things not done, or at best, as we have seen, of things done by others. Thus his "participation" in the Civil War, which was, James insists, "a more constituted and sustained act of living, in proportion to my powers and opportunities, than any other homogeneous stretch of experience that my memory now recovers" (*NSB*, 243), took only the form

of seeing, sharing, envying, applauding, pitying, all from too far-off, and with the queer sense that, whether or no they [the direct participants] would prove to have had the time of their lives, it seemed that the only time I should have had would stand or fall by theirs. (*NSB*, 379–80)

James's own role in the war would be restricted, "in a peculiar degree, alas, [to] that of living inwardly – like so many of my other cases" (*NSB*, 243). What we have in these memoirs, then, is the tale of wars not fought and passions – notably James's romantic attraction to Minny Temple – left unpursued and unconsummated. Thus in confronting his memories, James repeatedly evinces a painful awareness of how meager his history must seem by any normal measurement of substance and vitality and achievement. From his childhood on, James cannot escape recognizing, his excessive imagination – as "monstrous" as Strether's – has had the effect of "cutting [him] off from any degree of direct performance, in fact from any degree of direct participation, at all" (*SBO*, 194). His life is palled by "the chill, or at least the indifference, of a foreseen and foredoomed detachment" (*SBO*, 226), by a resigned knowledge "that the only form of riot or revel ever known to [him] would be that of the visiting mind" (*SBO*, 25). In the face of such a life, pursued in such an indirect fashion, James on occasion stands appalled: "I lose myself in wonder at the loose ways, the strange process of waste, through which nature and fortune may deal . . . with those whose faculty for application is all and only in their imagination and their sensibility" (*SBO*, 10).

Like the James of the autobiography, Lambert Strether is a "man who hasn't 'lived,' hasn't at all, in the sense of sensations, passions, impulses, pleasures" (*N*, 226), and much of what we have just discerned in James can be perceived in Strether as well. James conceived of Strether as a man who feels tired . . . without having a great deal to show for it; disenchanted without having known any great enchantments, enchanters, or, above all, enchantresses; and even before the action in which he is engaged launches him, is vaguely *haunted by the feeling of what he has missed*. (*N*, 375) [my emphasis]

Once again we are in the presence of a man whose life can be substantially defined by the range and extent of what he has missed, lost, and left undone. Strether perceives himself as a "perfectly equipped failure" (*21*, 44) who hasn't "had the gift of making the most of what he tried" (*21*, 85), and who consequently has "*never* made a good thing" (*21*, 66). He cannot examine his life in retrospect without finding everywhere "the wreck of hopes and ambitions, the refuse-heap of disappointments and failures" (*21*, 65). By the time he arrives in Paris, Strether "had ceased even to measure his own meagerness, a meagerness that sprawled, in . . . retrospect, vague and comprehensive, stretching back like some untapped Hinterland from a rough coast-settlement" (*21*, 87). Moreover, Strether's sense of failure and his acute awareness of what might have been are not confined to the realms of career and worldly success; at the heart of Strether's resignation lies the memory of the greatest waste of all:

the young wife he had early lost and the young son he had stupidly sacrificed. He had again and again made out for himself that he might have kept his little boy, his little dull boy who had died at school of rapid diptheria, if he had not in those years so insanely given himself to merely missing the mother. It was the soreness of his remorse that the child had in all likelihood not really been dull – had been dull, as he had been banished and neglected, mainly because the father had been unwittingly selfish. This was doubtless but the secret habit of sorrow, which had slowly given way to time; yet there remained an ache sharp enough to make the spirit, at the sight now and then of some fair young man just growing up, wince with the thought of an opportunity lost. Had ever a man, he had finally fallen into the way of asking himself, lost so much and even done so much for so little? (*21*, 84)

This meditation – the only point in the novel at which Strether directly confronts and assesses the full extent of his loss – occurs during the leisurely but crucial hour of reverie he spends in the Luxembourg Gardens, an hour which issues in Strether's first attempt to visit Chad Newsome. And it is of course Chad who is foreshadowed in Strether's musings about "some fair young man just growing up." As Mrs. Newsome's husband-to-be, and as the ambassador representing both her personal authority and the moral and cultural authority of Woollett in general, Strether arrives in Paris with the intention of functioning as a surrogate father for Chad; the young man, in his turn, will replace Strether's lost son.

But the longer Strether remains in Paris, the more his relationship with Chad comes to be dominated by another dimension, one that is both fruitful and troubling. Noting that James uses the resonant phrase "son and brother" to designate Chad, Laurence Holland characterizes Strether's double role in this way:

> Strether looks on Chad, as James was later to look on himself [in the autobiography], in the role of son and in the role of close and competitive brother, directing towards Chad the aspirations and expiatory sense of responsibility he felt for his own lost son and projecting onto Chad the unfulfilled aspirations of his own experience. (238)

This second aspect of Strether's relationship to Chad – the older man's use of the younger as a vehicle for the vicarious enacting of thwarted desires – is another key element in the resemblance between Strether and the James of the memoirs. When James reaches the rather rueful conclusion about his relationship with William "that what I probably most did, all the while was but to pick up. . . the crumbs of his feast and the echoes of his life" (*NSB*, 13), he grasps the fundamental truth of Strether's bond with Chad as well.

Strether is well aware that he never, as he says to Maria Gostrey, "had the benefit [of youth] at the proper time – which comes to saying that [he] never had the thing itself" (*22*, 50); as he admits to little Bilham, it is in point of fact "too late" for him to have the life he has missed (*21*, 217). But like James himself, Strether lives – in a manner – through his imaginative adjacency to and appropriation of the direct participation of others. One's youth, he tells Miss Gostrey, "has to come in somewhere, if only out of the lives, the conditions, the feelings of other persons. . . The point is that [Chad and Madame de Vionnet are] mine. Yes, they're my youth; since somehow at the right time nothing else ever was" (*22*, 51). Thus just as James was able to participate in the Civil War only through an imaginative apprehension of others' direct actions, just as he was able to form boyhood friendships only by placing himself in the wake of Wilkie's more effective sociability, so Strether can live out the romantic fantasies of his youth and enact his present suppressed love for Madame de Vionnet only through the mediating figure of Chad – by picking up, in the final analysis, the crumbs of Chad's feast and the echoes of his life.[1] Curiously, though he is the central consciousness of *The Ambassadors*, Strether, like James, becomes a peripheral actor in his own story. While he witnesses everything that transpires in the novel, it is always the others who *do* things, who in effect *live*; Strether remains the passive observer, living indirectly through the "doings" of others. And Strether's propensity for living vicariously does not restrict itself to Chad. Strether to some extent projects his unfulfilled desires onto every masculine figure whom he encounters. We have already noted Strether's envious identification with Gloriani's artistic achievement and personal authority; his excessive reaction to his meeting with the sculptor can be understood as his attempt to garner for himself, however indirectly, some of "the terrible life" he sees in Gloriani's smile. Even little Bilham's bohemian life, with its "romantic" innocence and its "legend of good-humoured poverty" (21, 127), provides Strether with an achieved image of the youth he wishes he had had.

But if Strether, like his creator, achieves a sense of selfhood through his vicarious attachment to other more masculine figures, there is, of course, one crucial difference. For the novelist is possessed of another life: the active, fulfilled, achieved life of the artist which finds its true autobiography in the Prefaces to the New York Edition and its substance in James's fictional *oeuvre*. Of the artist, we remember, James wrote: "how, after his fashion, he will have lived!" James was tempted by the idea of making Strether an artist, but rejected the possibility because an artist, like a journalist, a lawyer or a doctor, "WOULD in a manner have 'lived' " (*N*, 226–27). This verbal echo emphasizes James's conviction that he *had* lived a full life, albeit one of a highly specialized nature.[2] As I suggested earlier, however, this other life – the romance of the struggle towards expression – is not really an available resource for the story James must tell in his memoirs. Now while this is true in the sense that James reserves for a separate occasion the story of how his novels and tales were conceived and composed, it is misleading in another and perhaps more important sense. For on every page of *A Small Boy and Others* and *Notes of a Son and Brother*, present simultaneously with the waste and loss of James's personal history, there exists that very "effort of labour" and "torment of expression," that very process of writing which for James is the most intense form of living. This dual mode of existence is the key to understanding the thematic and compositional structure of James's memoirs. Through acts of memory, attention and expression performed in the literary present – through writing – James seeks to redeem the losses of the past, losses defined not only by the peculiarly unfulfilled nature of James's life, but also by the very pastness of the events involved. James responds to the inconsequence of his own past through a present effort of expression which at every moment insists on the "possible heroism of perfunctory things," on searching out "the force of action, unless I call it passion, that may reside in a single pulse of time." The heroism and the passion are really a function of present memory – of James's writing – rather than of the meager events of the past themselves. Thus when James regrets that his participation in the "immense and prolonged outwardness . . . at the very highest pitch" that marked the Civil War "had to be in a peculiar degree, alas, that of living inwardly," he immediately goes on to

add that my 'alas' just uttered is in the key altogether of my then current consciousness, and not the least in that of my present appreciation of the same. . . My appreciation of what I presume at the risk of any apparent fatuity to call my "relation to" the War is at present a thing exquisite to me, whereas it had to be at the time a sore and troubled, a mixed and oppressive thing. (*NSB*, 243–44)

By emphasizing the strangely unlived quality of his life, with its litany of things missed, lost and left undone, James creates both the need and the opportunity for a strategy that places a high valuation on trivial details. The smallness, superficiality, and inconsequence of James's memories determine his pervasively felt need to surround these objects of "the poor actual" (*SBO*, 175) with an expansive and transforming imaginative attention; if he is to redeem "the fatal futility of fact," he must systematically invest small things with large values, discover depths in the merest surface, and find meaning in things that don't appear to matter. But James clearly believes that the frustration and failure he experienced in life not only made necessary his expansive, inspiring art, but made it possible as well. In the first place, it is only the small and perfunctory things – those things without an obvious intrinsic significance of their own – that will allow themselves to be appropriated by the imagination and invested with whatever meaning and value the writer's consciousness conceives. This is the realization that lies behind that "practical plea for the superficial" (*SBO*, 96) that James makes on every page of his memoirs. The large things, on the other hand, the achieved successes, the inherently important objects and events, have less worth for the imagination, for they come pre-equipped with a finality and a meaning of their own. "I like ambiguities and detest great glares" (*NSB*, 106), insists James, for it is the great glare of the important achievement, of the completed "thing done and dismissed," that "has ever, at the best, for the ambitious workman, a trick of looking dead, if not buried" (*AN*, 99). The smooth surfaces of such large finalities offer no openings through which the artist's transforming imagination can enter and engage the event; his only responsive option is passive documentation or reproduction, a kind of art which is for James no art at all: "strange enough the 'aesthetic' of artists who could desire but literally to reproduce" (*SBO*, 113).

But there is another way, related but perhaps more crucial, in which James's lack of fulfillment in life makes possible the intense kind of living he achieves in his art. Unconsummated desire, cut off from successful enactment in the past, does not cease to exist; rather, it becomes the essence of James's passionate and hyper-responsive imagination – becomes the force behind his writing. Desire returns as present attention and expression, as what Freud calls a "freely mobile cathectic energy" (18:62), capable of infusing even the most negligible fragments of the past with a value and significance they never originally possessed. The man "who feels desire," Socrates explains in *The Symposium*, "desires what is not in his present power or possession, and desire and love have for their object things or qualities which a man does not at present possess but which he lacks" (Plato, 77). Desire is always a lack; if the lack is filled desire is erased. Thus if James's life – the life of actions and events narrated in his memoirs – had been marked by success instead of failure, fulfillment instead of want, direct action instead of indirect "participation," presence instead of absence, then James would have been incapable, by his own standards, of that specialized kind of living he calls art. By having failed to live enough, or by convincing himself that he has so failed, James is belatedly able to infuse his writing with the full strength and passion of his unfulfilled desires, and thus to live again, profusely, in imagination. Life is undoubtedly, and in one sense tragically, "a tale of assimilations small and fine." But it is precisely such "small and fine" things which, unlike the large successes of the past, invite the deployment of desire; and James finds delight and compensation in the knowledge that "out of [this] refuse, directly interesting to the subject-victim only, the most branching vegetations may be conceived as having sprung" (*SBO*, 182).

It is perhaps this belated conversion of "refuse" into "the most branching vegetations" – of the dross of the lived past into the gold of the past remembered and expressed – that James has in mind when he suggests, in *A Small Boy and Others*, that "success in life may perhaps be best defined as the performance in age of some intention arrested in youth." If success *can* be so defined, James asserts, then "I may frankly put in a claim to it" (*SBO*, 84–85). And Lambert Strether, with his "strange outbreaks" and "belated uncanny clutches at the unusual, the ideal" (*22*, 119), has by this definition at least an equal claim. James rejected the possibility of making Strether an artist, but he nevertheless did conceive of his protagonist as "*fine*, clever, literary almost" (*N*, 226). And if Strether is unable, like his creator, to redeem the failures and the losses of his life through the romance of expression, he nevertheless possesses an intensely desiring imagination that closely resembles James's, and that also serves, at least in part, to redeem. Strether too achieves a kind of romance of labor – woven, as he recognizes, out of "elements mild enough" (*22*, 245) – through the quality and urgency of his responsiveness. Like James, Strether channels all the force of his unfulfilled aspirations into the intensity of his present attention – though that attention is not, in Strether's case, directed towards the remembered details of the past, but towards the facts, however perfunctory, of the Parisian present.

Strether's life in Paris is really a twofold process similar to James's dual mode of existence in the autobiographies. *The Ambassadors* relates the unfolding of a certain set of concrete events, but it also embodies the movement of Strether's "freely mobile cathectic energy" through the field created by those events. Philip Weinstein has illuminated this duality by noticing that while Strether exhorts little Bilham to "live all you can," he somehow "betrays his own advice and fails to 'live all he can,' that the kind of living he finally exemplifies, with its sacrifices and deprivations, contrasts fundamentally, if obscurely, with what he urges upon little Bilham." In seeking to define the difference "between Strether's advice and his example, between 'living' as he urges it and 'living' as he embodies it," Weinstein draws a useful distinction between direct experience, for the most part manifested "by Chad and his circle" in the "attainment of intimacy and passion" and in the "sense of having realized one's potential identity through active immersion in the world," and imagination, embodied in Strether's "protean inner vision," with all its "multiple facets – artistic, idealistic, innocent, vicarious, obsessive . . . " (1–2).[3]

Like James, Strether seems ill-equipped for the life of active immersion; but Strether's desiring imagination, mirroring the achievement of James's writing, finds a compensatory abundance in dancing across the surface of life, and in transforming that surface into an arena for another kind of "action." Near the end of Gloriani's garden-party, an occasion, as we have seen, marked for him by a veritable "assault of images" yet by very little of intrinsic depth or importance, Strether himself momentarily recognizes the distinction which Weinstein elucidates:

> Strether's impressions were still present; . . . but he was to ask himself afterwards, that evening, what really *had* happened – conscious as he could after all remain that for a gentleman taken, and taken for the first time, into the "great world" . . . the items made a meagre total. It was nothing new to him, however, as we know, that a man might have – at all events such a man as he – an amount of experience out of any proportion to his adventures. (*21*, 227)

In terms of what James here calls "adventures," Strether's entire Parisian sojourn, like his afternoon at Gloriani's, is merely a continuation of the meager past. Strether remains what he always will be: the man who ruefully stands on the periphery and watches while others achieve success, intimacy and fulfillment. Strether's only real opportunity for successful direct performance resides in his role as Mrs. Newsome's ambassador; the embassy offers Strether a unique chance to exercise the authority he so admires and envies in others, and promises a kind of worldly achievement – in the form of marriage with Mrs. Newsome – he regrets he has been unable to attain in the past. But Strether's commitment to another mode of living, to that interior "process of vision" (*AN*, 308) which he understands as "experience," persistently undermines his ability to proceed effectively toward the completion of his ambassadorial task. In a duplication of the pattern delineated by James's memoirs, the two kinds of "living" defined by Weinstein are seen to be not simply different, but mutually incompatible. In other words, the disproportion perceived by Strether – "that a man might have . . . an amount of experience out of any proportion to his adventures" – is not descriptive but proscriptive. The richness of Strether's experience depends upon the poverty of his adventures, and vice-versa.

In the famous "house of fiction" passage from the Preface to *The Portrait of a Lady*, James explains that observers of varying sensibilities garner different impressions from inspections of the same "human scene": all "are watching the same show," writes James, "but . . . one seeing big where the other sees small, one seeing coarse where the other sees fine" (*AN*, 46). James's work, I believe, implies a necessary link between these two ways of seeing – big and coarse, small and fine – and the two modes of living embodied in both *The Ambassadors* and the autobiographies. To achieve success in the realm of direct performance and full immersion requires a perspective that grasps life almost exclusively in its "big" and "coarse" aspect. Fulfillment comes most easily to the man who ignores everything but his goal, who responds to a task as to something already completed – to the man, in other words, who refuses to be distracted by particulars from his direct progress toward the finalized success he has conceived in advance. This is the kind of man John Dewey had in mind when he observed that "it is possible to be efficient in action and yet not have a conscious experience. The activity is too automatic to permit a sense of what it is about. . . Obstacles are overcome by shrewd skill, but they do not feed experience" (38). Though we speak of him – justifiably – as fully immersed, the efficient man is not conscious of his immersion, does not, in James's sense, experience what he moves through. Intent on the completion of an end, he is blind to the ambiguities and possibilities lodged in the specific objects and individual moments of which his adventure is comprised. For the man who moves authoritatively toward fulfillment, details lack the attractions which they hold for the desiring imagination; they are meaningful or valuable only insofar as they can be subordinated to the achievement of the action as a whole. George Eliot defines the type in describing Tom Tulliver in *The Mill on the Floss*: "a character at unity with itself – that performs what it intends, subdues every counteracting impulse, and has no visions beyond the distinctly possible – is strong by its very negations" (V. ii).

To this essentially masculine figure Dewey opposes "those who are wavering in action, uncertain, and inconclusive like the shades in classical literature" (38-39). This more feminine figure is Lambert Strether.[4] If Strether is, as he tells little Bilham, "unfit for [his] job" (*21*, 177), it is because he is incapable of seeing his embassy in large terms, as a totality encompassing intention, execution and achievement. In contrast, Mrs. Newsome, with her "stiff general view" (*22*, 91) of life and her distant moral and geographical perspective, comprehends the embassy as a single massive entity, as a coherent block of action the results of which are already determined. She is efficient without even being there; for she possesses a broad pre-existent overview, a plan, "drawn up," as Strether unhappily perceives, "in complete ignorance of all that, in this last long period, has been happening to [Chad]" (*22*, 42). That plan, Strether increasingly objects, "took no

account whatever of the impression I was here on the spot immediately to begin to receive from him – impressions of which I feel sure
I'm far from having had the last" (22, 42). The longer Strether remains
in Paris and the more he sees of Chad and Madame de Vionnet, the
less he can accommodate himself to Mrs. Newsome's scheme;
everything his consciousness touches – perhaps especially the superficial things – distracts his attention from Woollett's all-inclusive,
systematic approach. But precisely because it embodies a vision that
sees "big" and "coarse" and which is blind to immediate impressions,
Mrs. Newsome's plan provides a failsafe blueprint for success. When
Sarah Pocock arrives in Paris to take over the ambassadorial reins from
Strether, she does so with the "high firm definite purpose" (22, 70) of
adhering strictly to Mrs. Newsome's plan. Scrupulously avoiding
seduction by or even contact with the details and ambiguities of Chad's
situation – those small things to which Strether's desiring imagination
so insistently and passionately attaches itself – Sarah conscientiously
sees the affair only in its largest, most clichéd, and most fatal aspect:
Chad must and will be retrieved from the corruption of Paris to the
safety of Woollett. And Sarah – "as prompt to act as the scrape of a
safety-match" (22, 73) – naturally succeeds where Strether fails.

We have already noticed that Strether's loyalties are at first still divided
between the two ways of seeing. In the initial stages of his embassy he is
wary of his own tendency to see small and fine, nervous about his propensity to digress and dally, and from time to time he attempts to summon up
a high firm definite purpose of his own. Thus when Chad first tries
to glean from Strether some sense of what Woollett has imagined his
Parisian life to be, the older man can only demure: "Oh we've never
pretended to go into detail. We weren't in the least bound to that" (21,
155–56). But if Strether initially shares Woollett's nervous avoidance of
details, he also exhibits from the beginning a barely suppressed
dissatisfaction with the rigidity and comprehensiveness of Mrs.
Newsome's plan. In an early scene that hints at his incipient revolt
against Woollett, Strether accompanies Maria Gostrey – a woman he
scarcely knows – on a somewhat impetuous but nevertheless conventional sight-seeing tour of the medieval city of Chester. Despite the
inconsequence of the occasion, Strether begins to overreact in his
habitual Parisian manner. An "assault of images," akin to that which will
transform Gloriani's party, starts to unfold: "all sorts of . . . pleasant
small things – small things that were yet large for him – flowered in

the air of the occasion" (*21*, 15). The process by which Strether attaches himself to the slightest details is enacted by his gaze as it traces the course of Chester's "tortuous wall," wandering

in narrow file between parapets smoothed by peaceful generations, pausing here and there for a dismantled gate or a bridged gap, with rises and drops, steps up and steps down, queer twists, queer contacts, peeps into homely streets and under the brows of gables, views of cathedral tower and waterside fields, of huddled English town and ordered English country. (*21*, 15–16).

But at this early stage of his embassy, Strether is uneasy about his own proclivity for seeing small and fine. He worries that his preoccupation with momentary impressions and trivial objects – his attraction to "rises and drops, steps up and steps down, queer twists, queer contacts" – will distract him from the duty that provides the sole justification for his European venture. Strether thus represses his own responsiveness; the embarrassing multiplication of reactions is abruptly terminated. Strether does not yet feel free to attach himself wholeheartedly to the momentary and superficial things he encounters, is afraid to loose his desiring imagination. For he is troubled by a guilty sense that this spontaneous excursion with Miss Gostrey (who is herself a "queer contact") diverges, in an obscure but potentially ruinous way, from what has been planned – specifically from his prearranged rendezvous with Waymarsh. Strether betrays his resistance to his own reactions by repeatedly glancing at his watch, a gesture that elicits from Maria Gostrey the shrewd observation that he is "doing something that [he] thinks not right." Maria goes on to identify Strether's uneasiness with what she defines as the general "failure of Woollett" – namely, "the failure to enjoy" (*21*, 16). And a few minutes later, Strether himself elaborates on her observation:

"You did put your finger on it a few minutes ago. It's general ['the failure to enjoy'], but it avails itself of particular occasions. That's what it's doing for me now. I'm always considering something else; something else, I mean, than the thing of the moment. The obsession of the other thing is the terror. I'm considering at present for instance something else than *you*." (*21*, 19)

The "other thing" which so effectively and unfortunately blots out "the thing of the moment" is literally Mr. Waymarsh himself. But the idea of Waymarsh's formidable patriarchal presence evokes Mrs. Newsome's equally massive figure, and by extension the determined immobility of Woollett as a whole. Strether's nervousness about meeting Waymarsh manifests his troubled and reluctant allegiance to Woollett's all-encompassing plan for his embassy. He is, in fact, "not wholly disconcerted" when Waymarsh fails to meet his boat at Liverpool; on the very first page of the novel, Strether acknowledges the existence within himself of a "secret principle . . . that had prompted [him] not absolutely to desire Waymarsh's presence at the dock" (*21*, 3). Serving as a counter to his anxiety about departing from what has been mapped out in advance, this "principle" whispers to Strether, perhaps insidiously, that

his business would be a trifle bungled should he simply arrange for Waymarsh's countenance to present itself to the nearing steamer as the first "note" of Europe. Mixed with everything was the apprehension, already, on Strether's part, that it would, at best, throughout, prove the note of Europe in quite a sufficient degree. (*21*, 3-4)

Strether, in other words, if he worried about straying from his plan, is even more fearful that Waymarsh and the airtight, end-oriented arrangement he symbolizes will prevent him from experiencing Europe in the fullest and freest sense.

Strether's unwarranted excursion with Miss Gostrey can thus be understood as a tentative protest against Waymarsh and Woollett. Longing for escape from the restrictive finalities of Woollett's big and coarse prevision, he cannot conceal his growing openness to seduction by the tantalizing ambiguities of things immediate, small and fine. As little for Strether as for James, in fact, will "the finer, the shyer, the more anxious small vibrations, fine and shy and anxious with the passion that precedes knowledge, succeed in being negligible" (*AN*, 149). More than any other Jamesian character, Strether will come to adopt a mode of thinking that is, in Georges Poulet's elegant formulation, "ready every hour to conceive a passion for the event that hour brings" (22). Strether thus increasingly attempts to convert his ambassadorial adventure into an experience through the alchemy of his desiring imagination. Like James, he intuitively understands that the vision which *knows* life only in its totality – "I know Paris," Sarah Pocock confidently exclaims (*22*, 91) – is blind to precisely those "vibrations of the air" which are of greatest value to "*the passion which precedes knowledge*" [my emphais] and which are therefore most receptive to imaginative incursion and envelopment: to those particulars, in other words, that produce by their openness to the transformations of desire the richest and most abundant experience. Because he grasps this paradox, Strether adopts a strategy which seeks to explode Mrs.

Newsome's totalizing vision into many distinct particles, small and fine, of immediate perception and sensation. Strether's mode of encountering people and things begins by shattering reality – Woollett's authoritative vision of a unified reality that is systematically meaningful – into a thousand shards of potential experience. Refusing to accept his embassy as something pre-determined in its meaning and implications, Strether proceeds to splinter the single, solid entity of Mrs. Newsome's plan and of the world-view from which it stems into a multiplicitous array of small ambiguities. In effect, Strether exchanges Woollett's confident *statement* about the meaning of Chad's Parisian sojourn into a bristling bundle of rapidly proliferating *questions*. Every object or person Strether encounters is ripped loose from the meaningful context provided by Woollett's "arrangement." Everything, as we have seen, signifies, but the significance of each particular is no longer bound by the demands of the overall scheme. Strether perceives every detail in the freedom of its isolation. For it is the singleness, the unity of Mrs. Newsome's plan that he cannot accept; the only "unity" he will acknowledge is that of his experience, the fine, unbroken thread he trails behind as he wanders through the labyrinth created by his own desire.

The intricate twists and turns of that thread, however, could never have been predicted in advance. And so when Sarah Pocock bluntly accuses Strether of being willing to "sacrifice mothers and sisters to [Madame de Vionnet] without a blush," Strether responds by insisting that his actions have been free of the taint of intention: "I don't think there's anything I've done in any such calculated way as you describe. Everything has come as a sort of indistinguishable part of everything else" (22, 200–01). Having cut himself off from the authority of Mrs. Newsome's plan, Strether in no way substitutes any all-embracing purpose of his own. Rather, the process of his experience emerges from his peculiar way of approaching each fragment of reality as though it were absolutely disconnected from any context whatsoever. For Strether, every moment is a beginning, every object the point of departure for a new perspective on life, or for many such perspectives. Because his sense of reality is liable to undergo a fundamental transformation at any moment, he is the least complacent of characters. Unlike Mrs. Newsome, who "doesn't admit surprises" (22, 239), Strether seems almost to seek out the unpredictable. Crossing the lawn of his Chester hotel on his way to join Maria Gostrey for their spontaneous excursion, Strether has a sudden "sense of himself as at that moment launched in something of which the sense would be quite disconnected from the sense of his past and which was literally beginning then and there" (21, 9). Strether's odd feeling that the moment is in some way radically *original* typifies his reaction to almost everything he confronts, and suggests as well a fundamental tenet of the *modus operandi* he will adopt for his embassy as a whole: his persistent urge to free the present from the past. Everything, for Strether, is "new." When he first meets Miss Barrace, he feels himself "in the presence of new measures, other standards, a different scale of relations" (21, 114). His initial encounter with Chad provides an even greater shock: the young man appears as "a phenomenon of change so complete that his imagination, which had worked so beforehand, felt itself, in the connexion, without margin or allowance" (21, 136–37). Even Sarah Pocock, whose mannerisms "were all elements with which intercourse had made him familiar," strikes Strether, upon her arrival in Paris, "almost as if she had been a new acquaintance" (22, 73).

Strether repeatedly finds himself "in presence of new facts," facts which, he discovers, are "less and less met by [Woollett's] old reasons" (22, 43). No matter how ordinary a perception may appear to be, there is always "something in it that touche[s] him to a point not to have been reckoned before-hand" (22, 146). Having freed himself from the emotional and epistemological determinants projected by the past, Strether begins to experience life as a series of what Paul de Man has called "moments of genuine humanity . . . at which all anteriority vanishes, annihilated by the power of an absolute forgetting" (147–48). Strether, moreover, does not abandon his Woollett origins (and their concomitant purposes) in order to substitute a new origin that implies a new set of goals; what Strether really wants is *to be always at the beginning*, at that point where everything is new and lacks definition. Edward Said has posited an important distinction between two elements that are present in any "point of departure":

One leads to the project being realized: this is the transitive aspect of the beginning – that is, beginning with (or for) an anticipated end, or at least expected continuity. The other aspect retains for the beginning its identity as *radical* starting point: the intransitive and conceptual aspect, which has no object but its own constant clarification. (*Beginnings*, 72–73)

Said associates the transitive aspect of beginning – which "foresees a continuity that flows from it" (76) – with the nineteenth-century realistic novel, while modern writers, he theorizes, have elevated in importance the intransitive aspect which willingly accepts "the risks of rupture and discontinuity" (34). In these terms, *The Ambassadors* may be said to embody the transition to modernism: Strether makes himself into a modern character by replacing his initial transitive beginning – his departure for Europe with the express object of bringing Chad home to Woollett – with a succession of intransitive beginnings that prefigure no particular end. Having shattered Woollett's coherent world into a multitude of disconnected fragments, Strether proceeds to treat each object and moment as a radical beginning; he places no limits on the free play of consciousness and imagination that such points of departure may engender.

An analogous concern with the nature of beginnings is manifest in James's frequent discussions – mostly in the Prefaces to the New York Edition – of the genesis of his own fictions. He locates the origin of *The Spoils of Poynton*, for example, in a slight anecdote overheard "one Christmas Eve when I was dining with friends: a lady beside me made in the course of talk one of those allusions that I have always found myself recognizing on the spot as 'germs.' " The growth of his novel from this merest bit of gossip about a lady "at daggers drawn with her only son" over the ownership of some furniture reminds James that most of his fictions "have sprung from a single small seed, a seed as minute and windblown as that casual hint . . . dropped unwittingly by my neighbor, a mere floating particle in the stream of talk." For James, as for Strether, it is the small things – "the stray suggestion, the wandering word, the vague echo" – "at touch of which the . . . imagination winces as at the prick of some sharp point: its virtue is all in its needle-like quality, the power to penetrate as finely as possible." "This fineness," James continues,

communicates the virus of suggestion, anything more than the minimum of which spoils the operation. If one is given a hint at all designedly one is sure to be given too much; one's subject is the merest grain, the speck of truth, of beauty, of reality, scarce visible to the common eye. (*AN*, 119)

In order to preserve the radical intransitivity of his germ, the novelist must isolate "the first step of the actual case" from its context, "reduce almost to nought the form, the air as of a mere disjointed and lacerated lump of life, in which we may have happened to meet it" (*AN*, 120). For the "ten words" in which James recognizes "all the possibilities of the little drama of my 'Spoils' " also constitute a beginning in the transitive sense, a point of departure for a story with its own continuity and end in the actions actually taken by the mother and son. But to this "rest" of the story, James shuts his inner ear:

For the action taken, and on which my friend, as I knew she would, had already begun all complacently and benightedly further to report, I had absolutely, and could have, no scrap of use; one had been so perfectly qualified to say in advance: "It's the perfect little workable thing, but she'll strangle it in the cradle, even while she pretends, all so cheeringly, to rock it; wherefore I'll stay her hand while yet there's time." I didn't, of course, stay her hand – there never *is* in such cases "time"; and I had once more the full demonstration of the fatal futility of Fact. . . It was not, however, that this in the least mattered, once the seed had been transplanted to richer soil. (*AN*, 121–22)

The original "vital particle," if it is to be allowed to retain its intransitive freedom, must be ripped from the circumstances which actually surround it, must be made utterly discontinuous with the actuality from which it is drawn.

James's desire to avoid knowing the rest of the story adumbrates Strether's own efforts to suppress or evade knowledge. In truth, Strether can no more forget Mrs. Newsome's plan – that purpose for which he has been sent out – than he can Mrs. Newsome herself; his ability to disjoin an object or a moment from its context is really a willful suppression of what he already knows. And the advice he proffers to Madame de Vionnet in respect to Mrs. Newsome – "Don't know – don't want to know" (*21*, 276) – informs his own mode of managing his embassy throughout. Strether's habitual reevaluations of the meaning of his embassy and of his own position therein – his readiness to change his entire framework for looking at things on a moment's notice – are derived from his conviction that any scheme of knowledge, whether it be Mrs. Newsome's plan or some "arrangement" of his own, runs the risk of limiting or even deadening the individual object by seeing in it only a confirmation of what it has conceived in advance. Knowledge, the big and coarse vision, with its sure sense of the fulfillment toward which action moves, *explains* details by restricting their potential significance to that single meaning which confirms the pre-defined context: things mean only insofar as they can be integrated into a coherent continuity that is already determined. The particular object is thus reduced to the measure of its usefulness towards an end – whether it serves to enable progress toward that end or stands as an impeding obstacle to be overcome. Simply put, knowledge – the basis for direct action – sees things as means to an end; while Strether's preferred mode of approach, characterized by the "passion which precedes knowledge," sees things as points of departure unencumbered by any *a priori* definition of goals.

In a short paper, "Formulations on the Two Principles of Mental Functioning," Freud draws a relevant distinction between the ego as dominated by the reality principle and as determined by the pleasure principle: "Just as the pleasure-ego can do nothing but wish . . . so the reality-ego need do nothing but strive for what is useful and guard itself against damage" (12:223). The striving for what is useful is thus opposed to the dynamics of desire. But while Freud understands the unmediated wishing of the pleasure-ego as an illusory, deceitful activity, ultimately harmful when allowed free rein, James – or more specifically in my reading, the James of *The Ambassadors* – would see desire's escape from the criterion of usefulness as a liberating movement which may save reality from its own poverty. In a critical piece written in 1902, James investigates this duality as it is manifested in Balzac's fictional *oeuvre*, which according to James repeatedly shows "the artist of the *Comedie Humaine* . . . half smothered by the historian." There exists a "perpetual conflict" between "the originator" and the "reporter" in Balzac, between "two laws" which "can with no sort of harmony or congruity make, for the finer sense, a common household." A further clarification makes James's own preference clear:

the irreconcilability of the two kinds of law is, more simply expressed, but the irreconcilability of two different ways of composing one's effect. The principle of composition that his free imagination would have, or certainly might have, handsomely imposed on him is perpetually dislocated by the quite opposite principle of the earnest seeker, the inquirer to a useful end, in whom nothing is free but a born antipathy to his yoke-fellow. (*LC*, 2: 94–95)

"The originator" cannot, James knows, exist in entire independence from "the reporter"; but to reduce even fictional things to the value of their use – however noble the purpose – strikes James as a murderous reductivity. The free desiring imagination may be yoked to "a useful end," but the law of the artist requires a willful suppression of the knowledge of that end. James's critique of George Eliot's work reveals the same assumptions. Though Eliot's characters "are deeply studied and massively supported," James regrets that "they are not *seen*, in the irresponsible plastic way." The "philosophic door is always open, on her stage," and too often "we are aware that the somewhat cooling draught of ethical purpose draws across it." (*LC*, 1: 1003). Strether learns to resist those "explanations" that stem from ethical purpose or certain knowledge; indeed, his heart, as James tells us, "always sank when the clouds of explanation gathered. His highest ingenuity was in keeping the sky of life clear of them." Explanations, for Strether, are "mostly a waste of life" (*21*, 141), a deadening extension of the past into the present which makes it impossible to begin. As a means of avoiding explanations, Strether adopts and expands the method he discerns in Maria Gostrey's determined disinterest in identifying the "small, trivial, rather ridiculous object of the commonest domestic use" manufactured in Woollett; Maria, he observes, prefers "a positive cultivation of ignorance" in regard to the article's identity, for "in ignorance she could humour her fancy, and that proved a useful freedom" (*21*, 61). Miss Gostrey's "abstention" (*21*, 61) from knowledge – even at the end, when Strether offers it as "a great commentary on everything," she "not only had no wish to know, but she wouldn't know for the world" (*22*, 322) – defines his approach to every aspect of his embassy, from the smallest details to the largest mysteries. The ironies of an operational method which cultivates ignorance are explored in an amusing scene during which Strether, having encountered little Bilham at Chad's apartment, reports to Waymarsh on what he has "sniffed" out. Waymarsh, always literal-minded, seeks useful facts:

"Do you mean a smell? What of?"

"A charming scent. But I don't know."

Waymarsh gave an inferential grunt. "Does he live there with a woman?"

"I don't know."

Waymarsh waited an instant for more, then resumed. "Has he taken her off with him?"

"And will he bring her back?" – Strether fell into the enquiry. But he wound it up as before. "I don't know."

The way he wound it up . . . seemed to produce in his companion a slight irritation. "Then what the devil *do* you know?"

"Well," said Strether almost gaily, "I guess I don't know anything!" His gaiety might have been a tribute to the fact that the state he had been reduced to . . . was somehow enlarging, and the air of that amplitude was now doubtless more or less – and all for Waymarsh to feel – in his further response. "That's what I found out from the young man."

"But I thought you said you found out nothing."

"Nothing but that – that I don't know anything."

"And what good does that do you?"

"It's just," said Strether, "What I've come to you to help me to discover." (21, 105–06)

While Waymarsh, with his utilitarian Woollett perspective, becomes increasingly annoyed with Strether's litany of I don't knows, Strether sees his own ignorance as "somehow enlarging." Waymarsh's question – "And what good does that do you?" – is by Strether's standards the only question one should not ask, for it ignores the positive value of ignorance, the freedom for fancy and imagination which accompanies a lack of knowledge.

Strether's desire not to know informs his encounters with everyone and everything. It is at work even in such a superficial matter as his wandering, during the celebrated country excursion of Book XI, by the banks of a river "of which he didn't know, and didn't want to know, the name" (22, 247). But Strether evades knowledge and avoids explanations in more crucial matters as well; indeed, his entire "experience" is constructed through acts of what de Man calls "deliberate forgetting" (148). Thus when Strether at long last recognizes the sexual liaison that lies at the heart of Chad and Madame de Vionnet's relationship, he is simultaneously forced to acknowledge just how studied his ignorance has been. Foreseeing Maria Gostrey's question – "What on earth – that's what I want to know now – had you then supposed?" – he admits "at last that he had really been trying all along to suppose nothing" (22, 266).

I have already suggested that Strether's project implies an effort to convert Woollett's statement about the meaning of Chad's relationship with Madame de Vionnet into a multiplicity of questions which extend, modify and even overturn that meaning. And the pattern we have just been tracing – Strether's method of suppressing knowledge in order that he might grasp every object and moment as an unrestricted point of departure – evinces itself nowhere more persistently than in his instinctive conversational habit of responding to others' statements by questioning elements within those statements. The meaning of a sentence depends upon its end, upon the sentence's ability to reach syntactical closure; a statement achieves meaning by imposing a limit on the possible significances inherent in the sentence's beginning. Questions, on the other hand, unless they are purely rhetorical, are focused not on the end of a single meaning, but on opening up the ambiguities implied by certain elements within the sentence. A question *begins* a mental process; a statement brings one to a close. Strether's conversion of statements into questions is particularly manifest in his almost literally "endless" conversations with Maria Gostrey; in one such scene, Strether is discussing with Maria the possible implications of little Bilham's remark that Chad's relationship with Madame de Vionnet is "a virtuous attachment." Strether challenges Miss Gostrey:

"You don't believe in it!"
"In what?"
"In the character of the attachment. In its innocence."
But she defended herself. "I don't pretend to know anything about it. Everything's possible. We must see."
"See?" he echoed with a groan. "Haven't we seen enough?"
"*I* haven't," she smiled.
"But do you suppose that little Bilham has lied?"
"You must find out."
It made him almost turn pale. "Find out any *more?*"
He had dropped on a sofa for dismay; but she seemed, as she stood over him, to have the last word. "Wasn't what you came out for to find out *all?*" (*21*, 188–89)

In an incisive analysis of this and other similar passages, Ruth Bernard Yeazell has characterized the mode of such conversation as one in which "Maria and Strether continually echo and qualify each other's words, as the language which one chooses evokes in turn new insights in the other" (69). The interchange in fact enacts the same configuration we have seen elsewhere. Strether refuses to take Maria's statements as completed finalities; he prefers instead to shatter their syntactical unity by isolating a single element – a word or phrase – and disconnecting it from the statement's end-oriented continuity. The word, once freed from the duty of participating in the sentence's overall coherence, functions as a point of departure for a mental process which escapes from the limitations of the sentence as statement. The whole dialogue hinges on certain words – "it", "see," "find out" – which Strether pries loose from the context of a statement and proceeds to employ as beginning questions. Meaning in the ordinary sense depends upon the rapid and more-or-less direct progress of a sentence (an action) toward a pre-determined significance (a goal). Employed in this manner, words are only important insofar as they are useful in efficiently and successfully completing the sentence's transitive syntactical structure. Just as particular elements "do not feed experience" for Dewey's man "efficient in action," so words lack the possibilities of intransitivity when they are used in everyday language: they are only means to the end of meaning. In contrast to this essentially metonymic conception of language, Strether uses language in a more poetic or metaphoric sense, one which disengages words from their contextual limits and which resists restricting them to their function in the sentence.

The "syntax" of Woollett's plan is fixed and clear: Chad will be made to break off his "hideous" connection with Madame de Vionnet (*22*, 205); he will be brought home to Woollett to marry Mamie Pocock and assume command of the family business. What Strether comes to hate and to resist is the blind, headlong progress of Woollett's statement towards an end which, he fears, will reduce Chad himself to the status of that "small, trivial, rather ridiculous object of the commonest domestic use" on which Woollett's manufacturing empire is built. James employs the linguistic analogy in describing Strether's hypothesis that the Pococks have come to Paris "to reduce Chad to the plain terms in which honest minds could deal with him" (*22*, 81). And indeed, Woollett measures everyone, as it does everything, according to the reductive standard of utility. The syntax of its plan rushes past the unique possibilities of individuals much as ordinary language speeds by the potentiality of particular words. Chad is useful only insofar as he will give up the woman he loves and his own pursuit of pleasure in favor of family duty and a businessman's career; Mamie, only because she will marry Chad, whatever her own desires – and it is only Strether who dreams that she might have any – may be. Not surprisingly, the act of utilitarian reduction which most appalls Strether is that inflicted on Madame de Vionnet; refusing to budge from her original preconception – "Do you consider her even an apology for a decent woman?" she bluntly asks Strether – Sarah perceives in Chad's lover only an obstacle to be overcome or pushed aside. "It was so much – so much," Strether muses, "and she treated it, poor lady, as so little" (*22*, 202). Ultimately, Strether comes to understand that he himself has been and is being used. There is no room, in his role as Mrs. Newsome's ambassador, for him to develop and express his own intelligence and style and taste. He is not supposed to see for himself; Mrs. Newsome, he tells Miss Gostrey, has imagined "horrors," and "I was booked by her vision . . . to find them; and that I didn't, that I couldn't, that, as she evidently felt, I wouldn't – this evidently didn't at all, as they say, 'suit' her book" (*22*, 241). Woollett expects Strether to squash his identity into the compact space allotted his function in the overall plan. Even Waymarsh, in a rare metaphorical mood, can sense what is being done to Strether: "You're being used for a thing you ain't fit for. People don't take a fine-tooth comb to groom a horse" (21, 109).

Perhaps the most "used" character in The Ambassadors is Sarah Pocock's long-suffering husband Jim – though he seems blissfully unaware of how he has been victimized. Strether, at least, with his name on the cover of Woollett's Review, possesses "one presentable little scrap of an identity" (21, 65). But Woollett's "determination of [Jim's] fate" has left him "perfectly usual"; and the "perfectly usual," Strether knows, means Jim's being "normally and consentingly though not quite unwittingly out of the question." So completely has Jim submerged his own desires and individuality in Woollett's scheme, "he would have been practically indistinguishable hadn't his constant preference for light-grey clothes, for white hats, for very big cigars and very little stories, done what it could for his identity" (22, 82–83). Such are the meager pleasures proper to the man totally dominated by the Woollett reality-principle. Yet it is to this, to Jim's "extravagantly common" status (22, 88), that Chad, Strether fears, is destined to be reduced. He wonders if "what Sally wanted her brother to go back for was to become like her husband" (22, 84); and when he contemplates "that whole side of life" on which Jim is "out of the question," he begins to fear his own intended fate: "he asked himself if this side of life were not somehow connected, for those who figured on it, with the fact of marriage. . . Should he ever know himself as much out of the question for Mrs. Newsome as Jim knew himself – in a dim way – for Mrs. Jim" (22, 82)?

Though Woollett sometimes seems as utilitarian in its approach as Mr. Gradgrind's school, Mrs. Newsome and her representatives are not alone in their willingness to use others. Though their ultimate purposes may be less vulgar than Woollett's, may indeed be beautiful and noble, Chad and Madame de Vionnet are equally adept at using Strether in an effort to achieve their aims. For Chad, Strether functions as a protective buffer against both his mother and his lover. And Madame de Vionnet – despite Strether's interior yearning – sees him largely as a tool to be grasped in her desperate struggle to hold on to Chad; only belatedly does she recognize the superiority of Strether's non-utilitarian mode of relating to others:

"What I hate is myself – when I think that one has to take so much, to be happy, out of the lives of others, and that one isn't happy even then. One does it to cheat one's self and to stop one's mouth – but that's only at the best for a little. The wretched self is always there, always making one somehow a fresh anxiety. What it comes to is that it's not, that it's never, a happiness, any happiness at all to *take*. The only safe thing is to give. It's what plays you least false." (*22*, 282–83)

Madame de Vionnet's outburst goes to the heart of what William Gass has called the central theme of all the works of James's maturity: "the evil of human manipulation." Gass refers us to Kant: "So act as to treat humanity, whether in thine own person or in that of any other, in every case as an end withal, never as a means only" (181). But Strether believes that the only way to fulfill Kant's imperative – the only way to treat others as ends-in-themselves – is to see in them all the possibilities of an unfettered, intransitive beginning.

The moral superiority Madame de Vionnet discerns in Strether takes the form of a steady refusal to substitute his own system or syntax for those that others have sought to impose. If people are the syntactic elements of Woollett's statement, then Strether's constant effort is to free them from the "penal form" (*22*, 272) of that syntax – or of any other. And he can do this because his only plan, as he tells little Bilham, is "to have none" (*22*, 168). It is not simply that he can see in Madame de Vionnet the variety of "fifty women" (*21*, 265). So determined is Strether to liberate others from imprisoning arrangements that he sees even in the Pococks "a quantity as yet unmeasured" (*22*, 63). While Woollett views Mamie Pocock as nothing more than "the pretty girl of the moment" – and as a bait to tempt Chad back to Massachusetts – Strether discovers in her a "remarkable" woman. Refusing to relate to her as to a mere cipher in Woollett's already bound "book," Strether becomes conscious of "something odd and ambiguous" in Mamie, something that

represented the possibility between them of some communication baffled by accident and delay – the possibility even of some relation as yet unacknowledged. There was always the old relation, the fruit of the Woollett years; but that – and it was what was strangest – had nothing whatever in common with what was now in the air. . . She had in fine more to say to him than he had ever dreamed the pretty girl of the moment *could* have. (*22*, 147–48)

Strether here goes beyond a simple rejection of Woollett's plan for Mamie; for he is also overturning and thereby enriching the syntax of his own previous relationship with her. Instead of mentally squeezing her into the clichéd role of the young American girl, instead of seeing her as a ready-made, manufactured wife for a young man who shows no signs of appreciating her value, Strether finds in her the beginning of possibilities as yet unformulated.

One of those possibilities is, Strether wants to believe, a romance with little Bilham. And Strether's imaginative revaluation of Mamie can be seen as yet another attempt to recover, through a vicarious relationship, something of the youth he never had. Strether's liberating revision of Mamie in fact adumbrates in a minor key his changing conception of Chad Newsome. For Strether, Chad's is "a case of transformation unsurpassed" (21, 137): "there was no computing at all what the young man before him would think or feel or say on any subject whatever" (21, 150). The syntax by which Strether has heretofore understood Chad – his sense of him as the "wretched boy" who has "worried" his mother "half to death" (22, 55) – simply breaks down: "you could deal with a man as himself – you couldn't deal with him as somebody else" (21, 137). And though he is initially alarmed and dismayed, Strether quickly comes to see in Chad's "absolutely *new* quantity" (21, 150) a value that has "quintupled" (22, 312): every aspect of this new Chad – every word he utters and every gesture he makes – harbors for Strether "an implication of possibilities" (21, 198).

The discontinuity in Chad's personality – this remarkable "sharp rupture of an identity" (21, 137) – evinces itself particularly in the elements of his appearance; Strether observes, in fact, that "it would have been hard for a young man's face and air to disconnect themselves more completely than Chad's at this juncture from any discerned, from any imaginable aspect of a New England female parent" (21, 240). Strether's imaginative rupture of Chad's genealogical link to Woollett is subtle but crucial; it suggests the degree to which he wishes Chad – and through Chad, himself – to be utterly, radically free from the past. It also reminds us that the Woollett plan Strether so hates is genealogical or dynastic both in its basic quality – in the way it uses the present as a means to a future that is itself bound by the past – and in its ultimate goal of retrieving Chad to carry on the family business and name. Said associates his concept of the transitive beginning with "the set of relationships linked together by familial analogy: father and son, the image, the process of genesis, a story. In their place," Said writes, the intransitive beginning substitutes the brother, discontinuous concepts, paragenesis, construction. The first of these series is dynastic, bound to sources and origins, mimetic. The relationships holding in the second series are complementarity and adjacency; instead of a source we have the intentional beginning, instead of a story a construction. I take this shift to be of great importance in twentieth-century writing. (*Beginnings*, 66)

Strether's adoption of the intransitive mode can thus be linked to a widespread initiative in modern literature that seeks to overthrow the dynastic authority of the father. If the typical Victorian romance is centered around the search for the true father, and posits the achievement of identity as being dependent upon a reaffirmation of the family, the modern novel often revels in the condition of rootlessness and orphanhood, seeing in the absence of the father the ground of all authentic existence.[5]

Now Woollett, though it is a society run by women, is essentially a culture built on concepts rooted in paternal authority; Mrs. Newsome seems less a mother than a father, and the "big brave bouncing business" (*21*, 59) to which Chad is expected to return represents the direct legacy of his father. The business, Strether tells Miss Gostrey,

has so developed that an opening scarcely apparent three years ago, but *which the father's will took account of* as in certain conditions possible and which, under that will, attaches to Chad's availing himself of it a large contingent advantage – this opening, the conditions having come about, now simply awaits him. (*21*, 70) [my emphasis]

The particular manner in which his father's will manifests itself for Chad adumbrates, moreover, the more general prevalence of patriarchal structures in the puritan society of New England. The duty owed to Woollett is the duty owed to the father, in both a social and a religious sense. But oddly enough, Chad, for all Strether's vicarious investment in him, is by no means sure that he wants to break with his Woollett inheritance. Though Strether admires Chad because "he has done what he liked most" (*21*, 169), it is he, and not Chad, who chooses to see the Parisian present as discontinuous with the paternally determined past. Strether's ultimate betrayal of Woollett's plan through his charge to Chad to remain with Madame de Vionnet measures his own desire – not Chad's – to free himself from the past's authority.

Ironically, both Woollett's scheme and James's plan for the novel assign to Strether the role not of the son – the typical rebel of modern literature – but of the father. Strether's embassy in fact constitutes a test of his capacity as a father: if he succeeds in bringing Chad home to roost, he will prove himself worthy of becoming Mrs. Newsome's husband – and Chad's step-father. Initially, and partly because he fears his own unmasculine tendency to dawdle and delay, Strether determines on a method of dealing with Chad according to which the "necessity of the first order was not to lose another hour, nor a fraction of one; was to advance, to overwhelm, with a rush" (*21*, 142–43). His first words to Chad are appropriately direct: "I've come, you know, to make you break with everything, neither more nor less, and take you straight home" (*21*, 147). This is Strether trying, with limited success, to adapt himself to Woollett's syntax. Yet even as he addresses Chad in these terms, Strether is acutely aware that they simply don't apply to a Chad who is "so totally different" (*21*, 149). Long before he confronts Chad face to face, Strether has grown uncomfortable with the scheme that defines his role *vis-à-vis* Chad as that of a father to a son. Strether clearly senses that his own enjoyment of Paris, his perpetual reactions to everything he sees, will have the effect of undermining his authority for Chad; and yet, he asks, "was he to renounce all amusement for the sweet sake of that authority" (*21*, 89)? To fatherly "authority" and its syntax of statement Strether opposes the mode of "amusement" or pleasure, that syntax of desire which values everything in free isolation from its paternally determined function, a syntax which, because it is made up of perpetual beginnings, is really no syntax at all, but a series of configurations imaging his desire. And so, having no father against whom he can rebel, Strether chooses, though not without considerable ambivalence, to rebel against his own fatherly identity.

When Strether abdicates his fatherly role, he exchanges a relationship with Chad that is fixed and inflexible for one that is essentially a free and open process. Without the anchor of paternal authority, his position *vis-à-vis* the younger man invites continual reevaluation and redefinition. We recall Laurence Holland's observation that Strether comes to look on Chad not only as a son but also as a "close and competitive brother" of whom he is somewhat envious. But the relationship is really even more fluid, for elsewhere Strether and Chad effectively reverse their "natural" roles, with Chad – who for Strether exudes "some sense of power . . . something latent and beyond access, ominous and perhaps enviable" (*21*, 156) – assuming the mantle of authority over Strether's ephebic sense of inadequacy. With his air of experience – especially sexual experience – and his touch of grey hair, Chad makes Strether feel like a youthful innocent; and "if Strether was to feel young . . . it would be because Chad was to feel old" (*21*, 142). Strether finds himself behaving as if he were Chad's pupil. The authority and man-of-the-world *savoir-faire* with which the younger man enters Miss Gostrey's box at the theater confuses him to the point of making him feel "like a schoolboy wishing not to miss a minute of the show" (*21*, 139).

This odd reversal of roles, culminating in Strether's rejection of Chad's offer to return to Woollett, reflects a persistent pattern in *The Ambassadors*: the man who arrived in Europe in the guise of the father repeatedly thinks of himself as a youth or a child in relation to others. When Sarah Pocock arrives in Paris, Strether imagines himself, "under her direction, recommitted to Woollett as juvenile offenders are committed to reformatories" (*22*, 61). Similarly, Strether compares his anxiety in the face of the "remorseless analysis" offered by Waymarsh – whom Miss Barrace associates with "The Great Father" (*21*, 206) – to "the embarrassment he had known at school, as a boy, when members of his family had been present at exhibitions" (*21*, 172). Strether's frequent identifications of himself with young children barely conceal his wish to evade his parental duties. Just how attractive an escape from fatherly responsibility is for him can be seen in his private fantasy, as he wanders through Notre Dame, that "he might have been a foreign student under the charm of a museum – which was exactly what, in a foreign town, in the afternoon of life, he would have liked to be free to be" (*22*, 5). Strether's daydream involves a tacit admission of the force of personal desire which underlies his exchange of his paternal role for that of the irresponsible son; only by escaping his identity as father can he experience the youth he never had. But such escapism is not without its danger, something Strether realizes when, near the end of the novel, he finally discovers "the deep deep truth of the intimacy" between Chad and Madame de Vionnet:

That was what, in his vain vigil, he oftenest reverted to: intimacy, at such a point, was *like* that – and what in the world else would one have wished it to be like? . . . he almost blushed, in the dark, for the way he had dressed the possibility in vagueness, as a little girl might have dressed her doll. (*22*, 266)

This rather chilling image – "sickening," one critic has called it (Garis, 309) – posits a pathetic end for Strether's project of carefully cultivated ignorance, and provides a measure of the cost he incurs by replacing the certainty of paternal identity with the irresponsible freedom of a childish one. One wonders too whether James does not intend here an oblique comment on the cost of his own strategy, in several of the works which immediately precede *The Ambassadors*, of submerging his authorial identity in the consciousness of a child – often that of a young girl.[6]

The implications of this image – its suggestions of sexual immaturity, powerlessness, and vulnerability to manipulation by others – remind us once again that Strether is, in the realm of direct action and achieved intimacy, largely impotent. But the child's irresponsibility – his freedom to play with all the possibilities implied by the object which he encounters – is more often than not a positive value in James's universe. And Strether, moreover, does not abandon paternal duty *only* to adopt a childish escapism; the role of son, like those of brother and father, constitutes but one element in the fluid process of free relationship into which he falls once he has cut his ties to Woollett's authority. The extent of that fluidity is suggested by the constant shifting of the metaphorical framework through which Strether characterizes his relationship to Miss Gostrey. If at one stage he feels himself a child to Maria's nanny, at another juncture he senses his relation to her as that of "a benign old person who wishes to be 'nice' to a younger one" (*21*, 20); while at still another point Strether thinks that "they might have been brother and sister" (*21*, 10).[7] Strether's image of himself as a little girl in fact suggests yet another component of his newly unanchored self, a feminine aspect which is, I believe, of great importance in understanding the nature of his encounters with other people and with the world that surrounds him. Strether recognizes the feminine quality within his consciousness far less frequently than he does the childish element; and when he does, it is, not surprisingly, a source of acute embarrassment to him. When he discovers himself in the act of admiring "the broad red velvet band with an antique jewel" that Maria Gostrey wears around her throat, he wonders, somewhat sheepishly, what

a man conscious of a man's work in the world had to do with red velvet bands? He wouldn't for anything have so exposed himself as to tell Miss Gostrey how much he liked hers, yet he *had* none the less . . . caught himself in the act – frivolous, no doubt, idiotic, and above all unexpected. (*21*, 51)

The subtlety of Strether's attention to the nuances of Miss Gostrey's toilet is, he feels, profoundly at odds with the masculine aggressiveness required for "a man's work in the world" – specifically for his own work of bringing Chad home to Woollett. This is the scarcely concealed import of Waymarsh's remark that "people don't take a fine-tooth comb to groom a horse." For as we have already seen, Strether's susceptibility to things small and fine, his tendency to dally over the most superficial details, is fundamentally unfitted to the sort of direct action Woollett expects of him. If Woollett's paternally-determined syntax speaks in a direct, hurried, masculine voice, then Strether's dawdling figurations of desire may be understood as a feminine, perhaps even a motherly strategy of expression.

In his meditation on *The Poetics of Reverie* – an intriguing subject in connection with a daydreamer like Strether – Gaston Bachelard offers a suggestive distinction between masculine and feminine approaches to reality:

> To love things for their use is a function of the masculine. They are components (*pièces*) of our actions, of our live actions. But to love them intimately, for themselves, with the slownesses of the feminine, that is what leads us into the labyrinth of the intimate Nature of things. (31–32)[8]

The usefulness of things can only be determined by someone who possesses an unshakeable sense of the end to which such use pertains: someone, that is, like Mrs. Newsome, who never wavers in her progress toward the success she has conceived in advance. The paternal/masculine will values things only insofar as they are useful in validating the meaning it has already determined. But the feminine sensibility, instead of seeking to impose its will or its meaning on the things it encounters, loves them "for themselves," for their uniqueness; the desire with which it invests things insists on no particular direction, only wishing to nurture in a motherly way the multitude of possibilities they imply. Consciousness, James once wrote, "closes maternally round [life]" (*LC*, 2:891); but the mother approaches her child not to impose an end, but to foster a beginning. Speaking of his own mother in *Notes of a Son and Brother*, James describes how he and his siblings

> simply lived by her, in proportion as we lived spontaneously, with an equanimity of confidence... which left us free for detachments of thought and flights of mind, experiments, so to speak, on the assumption of our genius and our intrinsic interest, that I look back upon as to a luxury of the unworried that is scarce of this world. (*NSB*, 177)

The mother assumes the son's "intrinsic interest" apart from any parental design, and therefore leaves him "free for detachments of thought and flights of mind." And if the James children "lived by" Mary James, it was, the novelist insists, only because she "lived in ourselves so exclusively" that she "*was* each of us, was our pride and our humility, our possibility of *any* relationship, and the very canvas itself of which we were floridly embroidered" (*NSB*, 179–80). With his "sense of her gathered life in us, and of her having no other" (*NSB*, 177), James envisions the idealized mother as living – like Strether or like himself as seen in the memoirs – indirectly or vicariously through others.[9]

In contrast, James appears to have been from an early age acutely conscious of his difference in intellect and sensibility from his famous father, who was, like his two eldest sons, a writer, and to have felt that difference as an opposition. Despite his familiarity with "the paternal philosophic *penetralia*," James felt his own imagination drawn to "such *other*, doubtless already opposed, perceptions and conclusions. . ." (*NSB*, 160–61). He speaks of his

detachment of sensibility from everything, everything, that is, in the way of great relations, as to which our father's emphasis was richest. *There* was the dim dissociation, there was my comparative poverty, or call it even frivolity, of instinct: I gaped imaginatively, as it were, to such a different set of relations. I couldn't have framed stories that would have succeeded in involving the least of the relations that seemed most present to *him*; while those most present to myself, that is more complementary to whatever it was I thought of as humanly most interesting, attaching, inviting, were the ones his schemes of importances seemed virtually to do without. Didn't I discern in this from the first a kind of implied snub to the significance of mine? (*NSB*, 171)

The father, who wishes to reproduce in the son a confirming image of himself, sees the son's value as bound up with his own. And James, convinced of the deep "dissociation" or even discontinuity of his own "schemes of importances" from his father's well-defined religious and philosophical beliefs, quite naturally perceived those beliefs as a threat to his own difference. But in his mother, James found an ally and a source of protection against impingements – real or imagined – of the fatherly will:

My father had terms, evidently strong, but in which I presumed to feel, with a shade of irritation, a certain narrowness of exclusion as to images otherwise – and oh, since it was a question of the pen, so multitudinously! – entertainable. Variety, variety – *that* sweet ideal, *that* straight contradiction of any dialectic, hummed for me all the while as a direct, if perverse and most unedified,

effect of the parental concentration, with some of its consequent, though
heedless, dissociations. I heard it, felt it, saw it, both shamefully enjoyed it and
shamefully denied it as a form, though as form only; and I owed thus supremely
to my mother that I could, in whatever obscure levity, muddle out some sense
of my own preoccupation under the singular softness of the connection that she
kept for me, by the outward graces, with that other and truly much intenser
which I was so little framed to share. (*NSB*, 180–81)

James thus saw his mother as a buffer against the aggression of his
father's ideas. For while the elder James never sought to impose his
beliefs on his children, he was, for his novelist son, essentially a man
of ideas, and as such basically a masculine figure. *Ideas* for James –
especially as they are manifested in the systematic thought of
philosophy – are masculine, because they involve an effort to explain
or define life as a fixed and comprehensive totality. In an early essay
on Sainte-Beuve, James distinguishes between "the masculine stamp"
in the French critic – "the completeness, the solid sense, the constant
reason, the moderation, the copious knowledge, the passion for exactitude and for general considerations" – and "something feminine"
which he finds "in his tact, his penetration, his subtlety and pliability,
his rapidity of transition, his magical divinations, his sympathies and
antipathies, his marvelous art of insinuation, of expressing himself by
fine touches and of adding touch to touch." James expresses great
admiration for Sainte-Beuve's androgynous critical voice, and recognizes that the masculine and feminine elements cannot really be
isolated from one another: "it is impossible to keep these things apart. . .
there is scarcely a stroke of his pen that does not contain a little of each of
them." But in summarizing Sainte-Beuve's critical method, James suggests his own high valuation of the feminine aspect, as well as his sense
of the threat implicit in the masculine: "the critic in his conception,
was not the narrow lawgiver or the rigid censor that he is often assumed to be; he was the student, the inquirer, the observer, the interpreter,
the active, indefatigable commentator" (*LC*, 2:681–84). In a letter
quoted by James, his father records *his* own impulse "to seek the *laws*
of these appearances that swim round us in God's great museum, to
get hold of some central facts which make all other facts properly circumstantial and orderly" (*NSB*, 182). Masculine thought, with its
emphasis on "completeness" and "exactitude," attempts to rigidify the
fluidity of experience into a fixed hierarchical system which allows one
to see some facts as central, others as peripheral – as less useful, we

might say. Such laws provide an *a priori* measure of the value of any object or fact: the lawgiver is thus the father, who is always before the son. But as I have already argued, James's and Strether's fascination is precisely with those circumferential facts, those perfunctory things, which are, when freed from the paternally-determined context, of potentially infinite value. The feminine sensibility, with its emphasis on the "sweet ideal" of "variety" rather than on the "narrowness of exclusion" which characterizes the limited dialectic of masculine thought, prefers a lawless immersion in the flux of experience. This is the burden of T. S. Eliot's famous remark that James had "a mind so fine that no idea could violate it" (Dupee, 110). And it is also the sense of Strether's realization, late in the novel, that Woollett's ideas, which had once "possessed him," "had now lost their authority" over him (*22*, 68).

Naomi Lebowitz, one of James's best critics in this regard, has perceived in his work an ongoing struggle between "the masculine will," the "essentially religious or philosophical" nature of which "raises the status of relationship to a religious or romantic ritual," and the "feminine sensibility," which is primarily "social" in character and which "keeps relationship alive by disturbing ritual, by submitting it to the tests of change." According to Lebowitz, Strether gains, in the course of his Parisian adventure, "a working feminine sensibility" which he deploys in opposition to Woollett's "dogmatism of masculine will" (61–67).[10] Some such formulation seems necessary if we are to explain how Strether comes to discover depths of value in a relationship – that of Chad and Madame de Vionnet – which defies both the ritual of marriage and Woollett's rigid moral standards. The father in Strether, who would impose Woollett's ideas on Chad and who would *judge* Madame de Vionnet by the strictest ethical laws, gives way to the mother, whose sympathetic imagination wishes only to protect Chad's difference from Woollett's authority and aggression, and who attempts to nurture and keep alive an intimacy that must, by Woollett's standards, be denied, and that may in fact already be dying. The struggle of the maternal against the paternal is felt as the struggle of life against death. This is why James, present at the birth of one of his fictional progeny, attempts to suppress any foreknowledge of the rest of the story for fear that the infant will be strangled in its cradle. As he writes at one point in his *Notebooks*, even a "small idea" or a "little subject" must be treated as "a little germ – to be possibly nursed" (*N*, 305).

And in discussing his revisions of earlier works for their republication in the New York Edition – an occasion which he imagines as "the reappearance of the first-born of my progeny . . . a descent of awkward infants from the nursery to the drawing-room under the kind appeal of enquiring, of possibly interested, visitors" – James once again assigns himself the maternal functions of "the nurse's part." Revision requires a "tidying-up of the uncanny brood," with all "the common decencies of such a case – the responsible glance of some power above from one nursling to another, the rapid flash of an anxious needle, the not imperceptible effect of a certain audible splash of soap-and-water" (*AN*, 337–38). In a literary tradition that has only recently been freed from the genealogy of father and son, James's motherly relationship to his aesthetic offspring strikes an unusual and revealing note.[11]

Strether has already lost one son because of the mother's absence; and he is determined to avoid the sacrifice of yet another to paternal selfishness. Strether failed his son – the "little dull boy" who "had been dull, as he had been banished and neglected, mainly because the father had been unwittingly selfish" – by failing to provide the nurturing qualities of the mother; and his transformation of his present embassy is, one senses, a kind of penance for that failure, as well as a chance to make it good. So just as Mary James was, for her children, the "possibility of *any* relation, and the very canvas itself on which [they] were floridly embroidered," Strether becomes for Chad and Madame de Vionnet, through an "intervention [that] had absolutely aided and intensified their intimacy," "a common priceless ground for them to meet upon" (*22*, 278). In the strange symbiosis of mother and child, the lovers live through Strether, just as he – however circuitously – lives through them.

3 *The Ambassadors* (II): The point where the death comes in

The road of excess leads to the palace of wisdom.
William Blake, "The Marriage of Heaven and Hell"

And yet nothing has been changed except what is
Unreal, as if nothing has been changed at all.
Wallace Stevens, "As You Leave the Room"

In his effort to protect life from the death paternally-determined meaning portends, Strether is always seeking to subvert, to halt or at least to delay, the forward rush of aggressive masculine action toward fulfillment of its purpose. And so with the full tenderness and force of his unfulfilled desire, Strether's consciousness closes around the thing of the moment, not to use it or to imprison it in any particular meaning, but to protect its status as an intransitive beginning, and to invest it with the potential for all meaning. To the utilitarian reductionism of those whom James calls "the gross fools, the headlong fools, the fatal fools," Strether opposes the "consciousness . . . subject to fine intensification and wide enlargement" (*AN*, 67), a consciousness which envelops each object in a womblike maternal warmth, a fostering air in which the object is free to grow in whatever direction and to whatever extent it chooses. In this nurturing atmosphere, growth is luxuriant, uncontrolled, unpredictable; the object, however trivial, proliferates an ever-expanding array of significances, is endowed with an exponentially increasing value that seems to reach toward infinity. One might say, alternatively, that Strether's consciousness approaches the object the way a child approaches something he has never before encountered. Because he does not know the object's use, the child is free to play with its potential, to posit for it all kinds of functions and significance, to discover in it, through an "active, contributive close-circling wonder (*AN*, 149–50), an always larger imaginative realm.

Regardless of whether we see in Strether the nurturing protectiveness of a mother or the irresponsible playfulness of a child, the resultant process of repeated unwarranted expansions constitutes the fundamental rhythmic structure of his experience. Nothing is more typical of *The Ambassadors* than the way in which both Strether's consciousness and the text itself are liable to expand – suddenly, unpredictably, excessively – upon the most limited and unpromising of grounds: in response, as we have seen, to phenomena as slight as a polite greeting or a lady's neckband. Everything Strether sees becomes a source of "perpetual reactions," a point of departure for an astonishing dilatory activity that investigates, with "the slownesses of the feminine," a continually enlarging field of speculation. At any given moment Strether can experience the sensation of "truth spreading like a flood" (*21*, 243), a process, described by James in *A Small Boy and Others*, in which "the limits of reality . . . seemed ever to recede and recede" (*SBO*, 243). Like James himself in the autobiographies, Strether seems always to be "treating an inch of canvas to an acre of embroidery. Let the poor canvas figure time and the embroidery figure consciousness – the proportion," James suggests, "will perhaps then not strike us as so wrong" (*NSB*, 481). But the proportion *has* struck many critics as perplexingly wrong: Yvor Winters is far from alone in his complaint that James's characters exhibit a "marked tendency . . . to read into situations more than can be justified by the facts as given" (331). Strether responds so excessively, however, precisely in order that he might move beyond what is "justified"; how else can the poor facts be freed from their "fatal futility?" Only in the protective warmth and irresponsible freedom of Strether's desiring consciousness do things have a chance to live beyond their use, and only through them can he achieve his "experience."

Strether's gradual abandonment of his Woollett-inspired preconceptions about Chad and Paris hinges upon a series of such expansive moments of inordinate response. The first occurs even before Chad's initial appearance when Strether pauses in the street outside the young man's flat, enthralled and imaginatively carried away by his glimpse of its spacious balcony:

Many things came over him here . . . Poor Strether had at this very moment to recognize the truth that wherever one paused in Paris the imagination reacted before one could stop it. This perpetual reaction . . . piled up consequences till there was scarce room to pick one's steps among them. (21, 96)

The "piling up" of "consequences" continues when Strether first confronts Chad himself during a "stretch of decorous silence" at the Comédie-Francaise, a half hour in which his immediate impression of the younger man – a fleeting visual sensation garnered as Newsome unexpectedly enters Maria Gostrey's box – explodes into a crisis "that occupied his whole mind." Strether's sudden recognition of the intruder's identity "had been quite one of the sensations that count in life; he certainly had never known one that had acted, as he might have said, with more of a crowded rush" (21, 135–36). Among the "abounding results" (21, 140) generated by this encounter is the planting of the seed of Strether's conviction that Chad's is "a case of transformation unsurpassed." This seed, in its turn, burgeons and blossoms in yet another expansive moment. As Strether and young Newsome walk home from the theater, Chad pauses momentarily in the light of a street lamp, where the sudden impression of his illuminated visage launches Strether into a whole new and voluminous speculative excursion. Seeing in Chad's aspect "a kind of demonstration" of "some sense of power," he once again begins to multiply insights at a breathtaking rate. "In a flash" he understands Chad as "an irreducible young Pagan" – "perhaps . . . the thing most wanted at Woollett" – and before Chad turns away from the lamp, Strether's luxuriantly unfolding vision has already "prefigured and accompanied the first appearance there of the rousing personage" (21, 156–57).

This fundamental pattern of disproportionate response and perpetual crisis recurs persistently on every level of the text and in every facet of Strether's experience. Like the young Henry James, he is sustained by a "felt need that everything should represent more than what immediately and all too blankly met the eye" (SBO, 411). And Strether does see more; everywhere he goes, the air, as it was at Gloriani's party, is positively thick with "signs and tokens." In his desire to liberate things from their obvious use or meaning, Strether again and again allows them to generate "sudden flights of fancy" (21, 86), to set in motion "a thousand unuttered thoughts" (22, 161). Every stray glance becomes "a look into which he could read more than one message" (22, 78); every detail welcomes his "impulse to overcolour"

(*21*, 104). This impulse calls to mind James's defense, in his Preface to *The Awkward Age*, of his own often-criticized method of "appreciable, or more exactly perhaps . . . almost preposterously appreciative, over-treatment" in handling the seemingly simple situations around which his novels are constructed. James answers such criticism by insisting on "the wonder of what 'over-treatment' may, in the detail of its desperate ingenuity, consist of" (*AN*, 114–15). The compositional method set forth in the Prefaces is, like Strether's responsive mode, one which seeks out "the lurking forces of expansion" (*AN*, 42) in the most superficial details, and which subjects each fleeting moment to "the law of entire expression" (*AN*, 144). The novelist's essential duty, according to James, lies in his "office of expressing *all that is in* the hour" (*AN*, 323). But any attempt to define the extent or the nature of that "all" in advance is in some way a violation of "the expansive, the explosive principle in one's material" (*AN*, 278). James thus arrives at

the truth of the vanity of the *a priori* test of what an *idée-mère* may have to give. The truth is that what a happy thought has to give depends immensely on the general turn of the mind capable of it, and on the fact that its loyal entertainer, cultivating fondly its possible relations and extensions, the bright effloresence in it . . . is terribly at the mercy of his mind. That organ has only to exhale, in its degree, a fostering tropic air in order to produce complications almost beyond reckoning." (*AN*, 101)

The novelist's original "germ" – be it a character or a situation – becomes itself, when it is protected from the "*a priori* test" of the father, a kind of mother. And it is in this rich brood of "complications almost beyond reckoning" that James locates the essence of his own experience as a writer.

One of the more astonishing examples of Strether's expansive method unfolds during an early scene from the novel – one we have already glanced at – which describes his evening engagement, for dinner and the theater, with Maria Gostrey. Seated opposite Maria in the dining room of his London hotel, Strether, still on the threshold of his European adventure, notices only a few scattered details of his companion's generally unremarkable physical appearance: the "soft fragrance of the lady," her dress " 'cut down,' as he believed the term to be, in respect to shoulders and bosom," and especially the "broad velvet band with an antique jewel" which encircles her throat. Typically, Strether concentrates his attention on each detail in isolation, and when at last his consciousness closes in on the velvet band, he provides us with a dazzling demonstration of the depth and wealth and profusion of meaning to be found in a single inconsequential fact:

It would have been absurd of him to trace into ramifications the effect of the ribbon from which Miss Gostrey's trinket depended, had he not for the hour, at the best, been so given over to uncontrolled perceptions. What was it but an uncontrolled perception that his friend's velvet band somehow added, in her appearance, to the value of every other item? . . . What, certainly, had a man conscious of a man's work in the world to do with red velvet bands? He wouldn't for anything have so exposed himself as to tell Miss Gostrey how much he liked hers, yet he *had* none the less not only caught himself in the act − frivolous, no doubt, idiotic, and above all unexpected − of liking it: he had in addition taken it as the starting point for fresh backward, fresh forward, fresh lateral flights. The manner in which Mrs. Newsome's throat was encircled suddenly represented for him, in an alien order, almost as many things as the manner in which Miss Gostrey's was. (*21*, 50−51)

As a "starting point," Maria's neckband is clearly a case of radical intransitivity. Such passages have undoubtedly fueled critical charges that James's characters − and by implication James himself − respond to facts in a manner wholly disproportionate to anything really justified by those facts. Like Gloriani's perfunctory greeting, this minor detail possesses in and of itself little apparent significance. It tells us next to nothing about Miss Gostrey or about anything else, being what James's father would have called a circumstantial rather than a central fact. For a character of a less imaginative cast than Strether, or for a more traditionally realistic novelist than James, Maria's velvet band would at best − and then only in aggregation with other similar details − provide some small insight into the lady's taste, or perhaps an obscure hint of her social and financial status; it would mean, in other words, metonymically, only in conjunction with its surrounding context. All facts need not be central, as H. G. Wells's famous critique suggests: "All true stories are a felt of irrelevances. But James," Wells impatiently continues, "sets out to make his novels with the presupposition that they can be made continuously relevant" (106). Nothing, we remember, not even the most negligible fact, will succeed in not counting.

And yet Strether − despite James's remarkable indulgence − has barely scratched the surface of what Miss Gostrey's simple ornament has, for him, to give. For before the scene shrinks back to the proportions of reality − Strether and Maria now in their box at the theater −

James has expended several pages of increasingly urgent and elaborate prose in tracing the circuit of rapidly multiplying ramifications in which Strether's desiring imagination envelops the velvet band. If the first of Strether's uncontrolled perceptions are linked more or less directly with various aspects of the immediate concrete situation, it is not long before his mind and his desire move on to "fresh backward, fresh forward, fresh lateral flights." In effect, metaphor replaces metonomy as the dominant mode through which Strether appropriates reality.[1] For as he "[sits] there and [lets] his imagination roam," the moment, intensely concentrated in this single detail, becomes a kind of vortex, into which facts, thoughts, emotions, hopes and memories begin to rush. Maria's neckband evokes many places for Strether: London, Woollett, Boston, Paris. And even more strikingly, he discovers in it an opening that allows him to reach beyond the present into the rich vastness of time. Thus in the present moment and immediate object Strether discovers the recent past of his life with Mrs. Newsome, the more distant "period of conscious detachment occupying the center of his life," and "the far-away years" when his wife and son were still alive (21, 52) – as well as the future that awaits him in Paris. Indeed, Strether widens the moment's time frame still further when he compares Mrs. Newsome and Miss Gostrey – through a simile "no gentleman of his age at Woollett could ever have embarked on!" – to those heroines of another age, Queen Elizabeth and Mary Stuart (21, 51–52). What begins for Strether as a modest tête-à-tête with a woman he scarcely knows expands in intensity and scope to the dimensions of a sumptuous banquet attended by figures of memory (his dead wife and son), anticipation (that other son, Chad Newsome), and history.

But don't Strether's "backward" and "forward" flights – his expansions of the moment to include both past and future – conflict in some way with his effort to protect the present object from domination by its context? Isn't he once again "considering something else; something else," that is, "than the thing of the moment?" A crucial distinction needs to be reemphasized here. For in Strether's expansive moments, the past returns not as knowledge but as yearning, not as presence but as absence, not as a defining fullness but as a lack. What Strether remembers as he sits with Maria Gostrey at dinner are unfulfilled desires, missed chances, irreparable losses. The occasion reminds him, for example, that he had been to the theatre, even to the opera, in Boston, with Mrs. Newsome, more than once acting as her escort; but there had been no whiff of vague sweetness, as a preliminary: one of the results of which was that at present, widely rueful, though with a sharpish accent, he actually asked himself *why* there hadn't. (*21*, 50)

Miss Gostrey's appearance, her dress "cut down" and her velvet band, elicits from Strether not a judgment of the lady based on Woollett's standards of propriety, but a realization that Mrs. Newsome's dress "was never in any degree 'cut down' " and that "she never wore round her throat a broad red velvet band" (*21*, 50). Similarly, the romantic "publicity" of the occasion recalls to Strether that "he had married, in the far-away years, so young as to have missed the time natural in Boston for taking girls to the Museum; and it was absolutely true of him that . . . he had never taken any one anywhere" (*21*, 52). Strether thus remembers not what he has done, but what he has wanted to do; not the banal reality of his relationship with Mrs. Newsome, but the romance and intimacy he has yearned for; not, in essence, what has been, but *what might have been*. This is what Strether means when he muses that "it was the way of nine tenths of his current impressions to act as recalls of things imagined" (*22*, 6) − of "things imagined," not of things actually achieved or possessed. Again and again Strether brings to the present moment the unfulfilled desires of his lost youth. An afternoon on a park bench in the Luxembourg Gardens is filled for him with "a recognition . . . of the promises to himself that he had after his other visit [to Paris] never kept" (*21*, 85). A lady sitting in "supreme stillness" in a chapel at Notre Dame − Madame de Vionnet, Strether will soon discover − reminds him "of some fine firm concentrated heroine of an old story, something he had heard, read, something that, had he had a hand for drama, he might himself have written" (*22*, 6–7). Chad himself becomes "a kind of link for hopeless fancy, an implication of possibilities − oh if everything had been different!" (*21*, 198).

Strether invests the present object with his desire not in order to fulfill that desire but in order to reexperience it, to feel again the yearnings of his youth; the moment is not a means toward satisfying desire, but a way of intensifying and expressing the desire itself. And desire is always a lack, a wanting. This is the perversity and genius of Strether's approach. He does not really want to consummate his desires, to fill the lack he feels. And it is not only that it is "too late" for such direct fulfillment: more importantly, Strether knows that fulfillment would erase desire, would eliminate the very force which

allows him to live so luxuriously in the indirect mode. For this reason
he adopts a strategy the effect of which "is fairly to make him want
things that he shouldn't know what to do with," indeed, "*to make him
want more wants*" (*21*, 40) [my emphasis]. Haunted by the feeling of
what he has missed, Strether comes to Paris not "to dip, to consume
– he was there to reconstruct. He wasn't there for his own profit –
not, that is, the direct; he was there on some chance of feeling the brush
of the wing of the stray spirit of youth" (*21*, 94). The "freedom" with
which he approaches the thing of the moment is, Strether comes to
realize, intimately bound up with

> the youth of his own that he had long ago missed . . . the main truth of the
> actual appeal of everything was . . . that everything represented the substance
> of his loss, put it within reach, within touch, made it, to a degree it had never
> been, an affair of the senses. That was what it had become for him at this
> singular time, the youth he had long ago missed – a queer concrete presence,
> full of mystery yet full of reality. (*22*, 211)

Thus while it is certainly true that "the fact that he had failed . . . in
everything, in each relation and in half a dozen trades," has made for
"an empty present" and "a crowded past," we must understand that
the past is "crowded" with absences, with unsatisfied desires that can
be read into the "empty present" to give it a new kind of fullness. The
complex alchemy by which absence is converted into "a queer concrete
presence" finds a precise image when Strether pauses at the former site
of the palace of the Tuileries: "The palace was gone, Strether
remembered the palace; and when he gazed into the irremediable void of
its site the historic sense in him might have been freely at play. . . He
filled out spaces with dim symbols of scenes . . ." (*21*, 79). Just as Maria's
ability to "humour her fancy" depends on her "ignorance" of the
Woollett article's identity, so Strether's opportunity to fill the empty
"spaces" of the present with the substance of his desire hinges on the
"irremediable" lostness of the past; if the present were anything other
than a "void," it would not be open to his imaginative play. The excess of
Strether's responsiveness is an excess of desire; and in his expansive
moments, the past returns only as wanting, as an absence that exerts no
authority over the present. Desire expands the moment so that it might
live, if only for a brief time, beyond its uses in the syntax of Woollett's
doom; desire gives everything and takes nothing, nothing, that is, except
the opportunity to feel again the power of its own wanting.

In its motherly aspect, consciousness protects the moment from the aggression of the father's meaning; in its childish nature, it plays freely with the moment's possibilities. But it is as desire – as a wanting that wants only more wants – that consciousness is able to posit each object, person or moment as potentially infinite. Because he can never be satisfied, Strether can transform even so slight an object as Maria's neckband into a whole imaginative world without bounds, into a veritable hothouse of intellectual and emotional variations and permutations. And just as Strether's varied and multiplicitous reactions exceed anything authorized by the object in which they originate, so the quantity of writing James devotes to this momentary perception seems utterly disproportionate to the miniscule duration actually involved. In light of such abundance and superfluity, it is rather astonishing to find James expressing frustration at his inability to allow Strether's consciousness to treat the neckband even more expansively: "all sorts of things," he writes, "now seemed to come over [Strether], comparatively few of which this chronicler can hope for space to mention" (*21*, 52). The response which appears so disproportionate to critics like Winters and Wells is, as far as James is concerned, disappointingly if necessarily limited by the requirements of the novel as a whole.

This is not James's only expression of regret at having to cut short the expansive motion of Strether's desiring consciousness. In describing Strether's excursion through Chester with Miss Gostrey, James notes the multiplying array of "pleasant small things" which "flowered in the air of the occasion" for his hero; but then, in a rare authorial intrusion, James goes on to explain that "the bearing of the occasion itself on matters still remote concerns us too closely to permit us to multiply our illustrations" any further (*21*, 15). James is admitting here that he cannot, as a responsible author, allow Strether's expansions to pursue an infinite course. For he can only pretend to share Strether's ignorance of the context in which things exist. As an author, he speaks with the author's authority, as one who knows the novel's overall plan and who sees from the perspective of the end to which the novel's action is leading. No matter how intensely he wishes to avoid restricting the potential value of the moment, he must inevitably measure it according to its usefulness in attaining the completion he intends – according to its "bearing . . . on matters still remote." The freedom of *the writer* – for whom writing is a form of desiring – is countered by the responsibility of *the author*. The feminine, which rejects as "vanity" any *a priori* test of what an object has to give, is opposed by the masculine, which values the object only for its function in the novel's pre-determined scheme. "The author," writes Michel Foucault, "is the principle of thrift in the proliferation of meaning" ("What Is an Author?" 159).[2] And despite his conviction that "no imaginative response *can* be disproportionate . . . to any right, any really penetrating, appeal" (*AN*, 260), James recognizes that the author must finally exercise his authority to restrict "the proliferation of meaning":

> Any real art of representation is, I make out, a controlled and guarded acceptance, in fact a perfect economic mastery, of that conflict: the general sense of the expansive, the explosive principle in one's material thoroughly noted, adroitly allowed to flush and colour and animate the disputed value, but with its other appetites and treacheries, its characteristic space-hunger and space-cunning, kept down. The fair flower of this artful compromise is to my sense the secret of "foreshortening." (*AN*, 278)

The theoretical compromise James outlines here was never, in practice, an easy achievement for the novelist. In the letters and *Notebooks* of his late phase James repeatedly acknowledges the difficulty of keeping the expansive principle in check. Writing to Howells in regard to *The Sacred Fount*, James admits that the novel, despite "*the tenuity* of the idea," had grown "by a rank force of its own into something of which the idea had, modestly, never been to be a book" (*L*, 4:251). In another letter, James explains to a publisher why a story contracted for 10,000 words has inordinately doubled in size: "I have too much manner and style, too great and invincible an instinct of completeness and of seeing things in all their relations, so that *development*, however squeezed down, becomes inevitable. . . " (*L*, 4:22). As a writer – as one who understands writing as a mode of desiring – James wants always to see and say more; just as desire wants only to go on wanting, so writing looks always for a way to continue its own productive existence. Thus the *writer* in James insists "that to treat even one of the most ambiguous subjects with due decency we must for the time, for the feverish and prejudiced hour, at least figure its merit and its dignity as *possibly* absolute" (*AN*, 309). But this *writer* – the representative of Freud's pleasure-ego or of Bachelard's feminine principle – must find a way of coexisting with the masculine ego of the *author*, which has for its main concern the completed work of art, and which speaks with the authority of foreknowledge. The clash between these two forces usually results in a dynamic alternation of impulses rather than in any consistent or peaceful compromise. Thus we find James regretting "the scant space for illustration of Mrs. Bradham," a minor character in *The Ivory Tower*:

> wherewith indeed of course I reflect on the degree to which my planned compactness, absolutely precious and not to be compromised with, must restrict altogether

the larger illustrational play. Intensities of foreshortening, with alternate vividnesses of extension: that is the rough label of the process. (25, 326)

James's late style embodies a constant dialogue between *writer* and *author*; it oscillates between an impulse of deliberate forgetting, which allows for the free expansive growth of the germinal idea or perception, and a necessity of inevitable remembrance, which acts to limit that growth and to direct it toward a specific and pre-determined end.

This fundamental pattern informs every facet of James's later work; indeed, the special quality of the late Jamesian sentence lies precisely in its marriage of the desire to add and elaborate *ad infinitum* with the need to preserve a strict syntactical integrity. But the alternation of *writer* and *author* is perhaps nowhere more evident than in James's memoirs, the distinctive rhythm of which is really nothing more than a give and take between his desire to dilate endlessly around the tiniest particles of memory and his felt duty to stick, as he puts it, to "the straighter line of [his] narrative" (*NSB*, 53). In recalling his childhood walks home from school, for example, James focuses his attention on a house – a "romantic...countryplace" left standing through some odd chance amidst the bustle of downtown New York – that he remembers as being especially stimulating to his inveterate "practice of wondering and dawdling and gaping." Despite an admitted sense of "perhaps making too much of these tiny particles of history," James permits the moment – imaged for him in the young boy peering through the house's "tall brown rails" – to expand into a lengthy contemplation of his own characteristic detachment:

He is a convenient little image or warning of all that was to be for him. . . . For there was the very pattern and measure of all he was to demand: just to *be* somewhere – almost anywhere would do – and somehow receive an impression or an accession, feel a relation or a vibration. He was to go without many things, ever so many – as all persons do in whom contemplation takes so much the place of action; but everywhere, in the years that came soon after, and that in fact continued long, in the streets of great towns, in New York still for some time, and then for a while in London, in Paris, in Geneva, wherever it might be, he was to enjoy more than anything the so far from showy practice of wondering and dawdling and gaping: he was really I think much to profit by it. (*SBO*, 25–26)

Like Strether's reaction to Miss Gostrey's neckband, this response – of which the above passage represents only a small portion – is a signal instance of James's impulse, "innate and inbred, of seeing the whole content of memory and affection in each enacted and recovered moment, as who should say, in the vivid image and the very scene; the light of the only terms in which life has treated me to experience" (*SBO*, 3). And yet, even such a moment, which seems potentially to contain the infinity of all experience, must be brought to an end by the *author*. James abruptly terminates the expansion, recognizing and repressing in his writing the very "practice" he saw in himself as a child: "But I positively dawdle and gape here − I catch myself in the act; so that I take up the thread of fond reflection that guides me through that mystification of the summer school, which I referred to a little while back . . ." (*SBO*, 27).

As the author of the autobiographies, James's task is simply to record the events of his personal history in the order in which they occurred; no single event can be allowed to disrupt or delay for long the progress of "the straighter line of [his] narrative." The mimetic author seeks only to reproduce the series of facts which comprise the record of his direct experience; he willingly accepts the "myth of filiation" − the phrase is Roland Barthes's − through which authority is conferred on a "reality" (history) that exists prior to the work, and which is understood to determine it ("From Work to Text," 77–78).[3] But James, as we have noted, finds "strange . . . the 'aesthetic' of artists who could desire but literally to reproduce." Largely because his own life − in the direct sense − sounds a litany of failures and losses and unfulfilled desires, James cannot understand the artist who refuses to fight against "the fatal futility of fact":

How can one consent to make a picture of the preponderant futilities and vulgarities and miseries of life without the impulse to exhibit as well from time to time, in its place, some fine example of the reaction, the opposition or the escape? (*AN*, 223)

The place where James indulges his impulse to "react" and "oppose" is the place of *writing*, where he relives the "futilities and vulgarities and miseries" in a manner which transforms them into an experience of great value. *Writing* "converts the very pulses of the air into revelations," and thus "escapes" the poverty of the *author*'s merely reproduced "picture."

Strether too lives a dual existence. His excessive responses to people and things are to him what writing is to James: a living reaction to or escape from the poor actualities which define his direct experience. But his perpetual reactions can provide only momentary respites from the reality of what he knows − despite his determined "cultivation of ignorance" − to be happening. When James allows Strether to go on reacting, he is deliberately suppressing his knowledge of the novel's overall plot and plan: he is only postponing what he knows must come. And for Strether too the expansive mode is essentially a way of delaying the inevitable. Though he knows his Parisian experience must come to some end – "I can't myself, you know," he tells Chad, "at the best, or at the worst, stay for ever" (22, 34) – his entire approach to his embassy is one that pretends the experience *will* last forever. Indeed, *The Ambassadors* has been characterized by more than one critic as a single long delaying action.[4] From the novel's opening pages, where he is conscious of having "enjoyed extremely the duration of delay" before meeting Waymarsh (21, 5), to its last, where he acknowledges his indulgence in "the sweetness of vain delay," Strether's project is governed by "the impulse to gain time" or more precisely, by the desire to stop time. For Strether's expansive reactions are also "responsive arrests" (21, 20) which temporarily halt the onward flow of time in order to protect each moment's innocence, freedom, and potential infinitude. The aggressive masculine syntax founded on the authority of knowledge merely uses or ignores or pushes aside the things it encounters, all the while moving beyond them with the greatest possible speed. But the more feminine figuration of desire attempts to prolong or distend the individual perception, to slow or even stop the forward progress of time, in the hope of saving what it perceives from being swallowed up in the continuity which surrounds it. The maternal consciousness wishes to rescue the moment from history and from the single meaning of completed fatherly syntax. Strether's strategy of fine postponements expresses his desire *to be always at the beginning*, at that moment when everything is possible and nothing is certain. His real enemy is time itself, time as history, as the father. For as soon as it is allowed to pass back into the context of history, the instant of radical beginning takes on a transitive aspect, becomes yet another determining point of origin; it becomes the past which impinges on the present and threatens to control and limit the future – becomes, in effect, still another father.

Strether's overresponsive method of apprehending reality thus embraces an attempt to save each moment – whether it be the prolonged "moment" of his Parisian experience as a whole or one of the tiny particles of time which make up that whole – from the death its passing implies. To protect the moment from history by extending its duration to infinitude and by loading it with all memory and all desire, to see "the whole content of memory and affection in each enacted and recovered moment" – this is Strether's deeply romantic project. The romantic, according to Georges Poulet, tries to envelop his lifelong consciousness in the sphere of the present moment. It is . . . a question of giving the moment all the profundity, all the infinity of duration of which man feels capable. To possess his life in the moment is the pretension or the fundamental desire of the romantic. (26)

But to accomplish such a project, Strether must find a way of ripping the moment away from its historical context, of detaching the individual element from the authoritative syntax of time's deadly statement. Richard Poirier notes that "*The Ambassadors* offers remarkably beautiful instances of the hero's effort to transform the things he sees into visions, to detach them from time and from the demands of nature, and to give them the composition of *objets d'art*." But Poirier recognizes that these moments, while beautiful, are also in some sense sterile:

having, by the very nature of the imagination that engendered them, only a tangential relation to what is really going on, these moments needn't be *made* into anything else, needn't be organic, as the phrase goes, with anything but the creative vision itself. They are, as it were, pure art in being freed from the pressures of any environment but that of the mind from which they issue. (124–27)

Strether's project – to detach the moment from time, to free it from context – is of course an impossible one, as doomed to futility as his efforts not to know what is happening around him. And Strether understands that his "cultivation of ignorance" can only delay the coming of knowledge. When he admits to Maria Gostrey that he has purposefully avoided obtaining from little Bilham the name of the "two particular friends" who constitute Chad's "virtuous-attachment" – "their name," he explains, "was a thing that, after little Bilham's information, I found it a kind of refreshment not to feel obliged to follow up" – Maria proffers a warning: "Oh," she returned, "if you think you've got off –!" But Strether knows better: "I don't think I've got off. I only think I'm breathing for about five minutes. I dare say I shall have, at the best, still to get on. . . . I don't meanwhile take the smallest interest in their name" (*21*, 186). This small postponement allows Strether to pursue with Miss Gostrey's assistance a rich speculative expansion in which the possible identities of the two women in question proliferate in a playful yet almost absurd fashion; by not knowing their name he is free to attribute to them a variety of ages, nationalities and marital situations. But for all the imaginative wealth of his varied imputations, Strether *will* soon know the women's names, will

eventually possess the facts which determine for them particular identities. And when he knows who they are, his beautiful speculations about
who they might be will collapse in ruins. He cannot evade forever the
single knowledge of syntactical completion. In a conversation with
Strether concerning Chad and Madame de Vionnet, little Bilham is
astonished to learn that Woollett's emissary has done an about-face:

"You mean that after all he shouldn't go back?"
"I mean that if he gives her up – !"
"Yes?"
"Well, he ought to be ashamed of himself."
(*21*, 286)

Strether's broken sentence images in miniature his strategy of delay: he
tries to halt the sentence at the moment of its widest potentiality. But
the "if" will be followed by a "then," predication will come, the
sentence must be completed. Roland Barthes, a critic who has written
beautifully on the attractions of delay, pinpoints Strether's dilemma
in the following formulation:

> The Sentence is hierarchical: it implies subjections, subordinations, internal
> reactions. Whence its completion: how can a hierarchy remain open? The
> Sentence is complete. Practice, here, is very different from theory. Theory
> (Chomsky) says that the sentence is potentially infinite (infinitely catalyzable),
> but practice always obliges the sentence to end. (*The Pleasure of the Text*, 50)[5]

Just as the hierarchies of James's father's thought imply the "laws" of
a completed philosophical system, so the hierarchies of syntactical
organization imply the completed sentence.

The delaying which accompanies Strether's dilatory responses thus
signals an attempt to preserve the object perceived at the instant of its
greatest intransitive freedom, at the moment of desire, when nothing
has yet been chosen or determined. But Strether knows that the
possibilities his method creates are ultimately both temporary and illusory. Indeed, it is precisely at those points when Strether is trying
hardest to detach the object and moment from history – to make them
into what Poirier calls "visions-of-reality-as-art" (124) in which
"rewards are immediate and reckonings postponed" (*22*, 59) – that the
impossibility of his project is most forcefully brought home to him.
Two justly celebrated scenes from the novel – Strether's solitary visit
to Notre Dame which becomes an encounter with Madame de Vionnet,
and the famous country excursion of Book XI which culminates in the

recognition scene at the Cheval Blanc – embody this ironic truth: that the moments when the impulse to expand and escape is most determinedly asserted are also the moments when context and knowledge and judgment can least be avoided. Strether dallies in Notre Dame because the church offers him "a refuge from the obsession of his problem": "he was aware of having no errand in such a place but the desire not to be, for the hour, in certain other places." We recall that Strether tries to think of himself for the moment as "a student under the charm of a museum" – a wishful formulation which expresses not only his desire to escape responsibility, but also his longing to be free of the destructive processes of time. As he wanders inside the church, Strether counts himself among "those who were fleeing from justice. Justice was outside, in the hard light, and injustice too; but one was as absent as the other from the air of the long aisles and the brightness of the many altars." In the space created by this deferral of justice – of Woollett's "justice," but also of the doom of time itself – Strether embarks on one of his most unfettered expansions, a dilation centered on the unknown lady who sits in "supreme stillness" in one of the cathedral's small chapels and informed as always by the desire to "reconstitute a past," in this case the imagined romantic past he has derived from his reading of Victor Hugo. As his speculative flights about the mysterious woman multiply, James is forced to admit that "all this was a good deal to have been denoted by a mere lurking figure who was nothing to him." But Strether suffers "the surprise of a still deeper quickening," for the "lurking figure" is none other than Madame de Vionnet (22, 6–7): in a flash his entire romantic expansion of the moment is swept away by the return – with a greater force than ever – of "the obsession of his problem."

The Cheval Blanc episode encompasses an even more determined flight from justice and knowledge, and constitutes the supreme instance in the novel of Strether's effort to transform reality into a vision detached from time and context. The return of the Pococks from Switzerland – an event, Strether knows, that will mean the end of everything – is imminent, and in the face of this "reckoning to come" (22, 293) he orchestrates his most extended expansion: a day utterly irrelevant to his embassy, in a place "selected almost at random," into which he packs all the content of his memory and desire. Realizing that "such days, whatever should happen, were numbered," Strether had gone forth under the impulse – artless enough, no doubt – to give the whole of one of them to that French ruralism, with its cool special green into which he had hitherto looked only through the little oblong window of the picture-frame. It had been as yet for the most part but a land of fancy for him – the background of fiction, the medium of art, the nursery of letters; practically as distant as Greece and well-nigh as consecrated. Romance could weave itself, for Strether's sense, out of elements mild enough; and even after what he had, as he felt, lately "been through," he could thrill a little at the chance of seeing something somewhere that would remind him of a certain small Lambinet that had charmed him, long years before, at a Boston dealer's and that he had quite absurdly never forgotten. It had been offered, he remembered, at a price he had been instructed to believe the lowest ever named for a Lambinet, a price he had never felt so poor as on having to recognize, all the same, as beyond the dream of possibility. He had dreamed – had turned and twisted possibilities for an hour: it had been the only adventure of his life in connexion with the purchase of a work of art. The adventure, it will be perceived, was modest; but the memory, beyond all reason and by some accident of association, was sweet. The little Lambinet abode with him as the picture he *would* have bought – the particular production that had made him for the moment overstep the modesty of nature. He was quite aware that if he were to see it again he should perhaps have a drop or a shock, and he never found himself wishing that the wheel of time would turn it up again, just as he had seen it in the maroon-coloured, sky-lighted inner shrine of Tremont Street. It would be a different thing, however, to see the remembered mixture resolved back into its elements – to assist at the restoration to nature of the whole far-away hour: the dusty day in Boston, the background of the Fitchburg Depot, of the maroon-coloured sanctum, the special green vision, the ridiculous price, the poplars, the willows, the rushes, the river, the sunny silvery sky, the shady woody horizon. (*22*, 245–46)

In this luminous moment all of the motifs we have been tracing come together. Once again Strether is trying to "reconstitute" an *imagined* past: not to repeat a past success – it is only "the picture he *would* have bought" – but to feel again the force of desire which informed the past, to reexperience the past as wanting. Detached from the context of his embassy, Strether's day becomes for a time an alternative world, a space where all places and times flow together in a suspended duration of desire. Just as Notre Dame assumed the timeless aspect of a museum, so the country excursion exchanges the precipitation of the clock for the suspended time of a work of art; "the oblong gilt frame" – a conflation of the remembered Lambinet and his train compartment's window –

disposed its enclosing lines; the poplars and the willows, the reeds and the river . . . fell into a composition . . . it was all there, in short – it was what he

wanted: it was Tremont Street, it was France, it was Lambinet. Moreover he
was freely walking about in it. (22, 247)

"It was what he wanted": what he desires, what he lacks. And so the
day becomes for Strether an elaborate and extended daydream, a protected space in which all kinds of useless and hopeless wishes achieve
a "queer concrete presence." "Walking about" in this liberated other-
worldly air, Strether directs his mental steps toward the woman who
symbolizes everything he desires. Recalling his request to Madame de
Vionnet that she "not talk about anything tiresome," Strether transforms his tentative remark into what is, for all intents and purposes,
a declaration of love:

it had served all the purpose of his appearing to have said to her: "Don't like
me, if it's a question of liking me, for anything obvious and clumsy that I've,
as they call it, "done" for you: like me – well, like me, hang it, for anything
else you choose. So, by the same propriety, don't be for me simply the person
I've come to know through my awkward connexion with Chad – was ever
anything, by the way, *more* awkward? Be for me, please, with all your
admirable tact and trust, just whatever I may show you it's a present pleasure
for me to think you." (22, 251)

The declaration is roundabout, indirect, never spoken; it represents an
attempt to transform a wish into reality, not through action, but
through the sheer force of wanting. It speaks of a desire that cannot
be fulfilled, and emerges only in the safety and sterility of imaginative
excess. But it is there all the same: see in me, it asks, more than my
usefulness, and be for me the thousand things I desire.

But the suspended time of the Lambinet frame cannot last forever.
The stasis of the picture gives way first to the dynamics of drama –
"the picture," he notes, "was essentially more than anything else a
scene and a stage," and "though he had been alone all day, he had
never yet so struck himself as engaged with others and in midstream
of his drama" – and ultimately to a more foreboding, constricted sense
of the real "conditions" in which that drama is unfolding:

Not a single one of his observations but somehow fell into a place in it; not
a breath of the cooler evening that wasn't somehow a syllable of the text. The
text was simply, when condensed, that in *these* places such things were, and
that if it was in them one elected to move about one had to make one's account
with what one lighted on. (22, 253–54)

From painting to drama to text: Strether's dawdling day slips inexorably back into life. The elements of his escapist expansion are also syllables in the "condensed" statement – "that in *these* places such things were" – with which he must make his "account." And the language of this "text" will soon find an echo in Strether's realization that "intimacy, at such a point, was *like* that." For what happened at Notre Dame happens again. Strether's vision undergoes an even "sharper arrest" when, as he sits in the garden of the Cheval Blanc awaiting his dinner, he suddenly sees "exactly the right thing" needed to complete the picture –

a boat advancing round the bend and containing a man who held the paddles and a lady, at the stern, with a pink parasol. It was suddenly as if these figures, or something like them, had been wanted in the picture, had been wanted more or less all day, and had now drifted into sight, with the slow current, on purpose to fill up the measure. (22, 256)

The very thing that completes the picture is also the thing that rips the picture from its frame and restores it to time; the filling of the void in the picture eliminates that space where desire and imagination have lived. For the man and the lady are Chad and Madame de Vionnet, and Strether finds himself face to face once again not only with "the obsession of his problem" but also with the revealed knowledge – so long avoided – of the couple's sexual intimacy. Strether feels his discovery as an awakening from reverie, as a "sharp fantastic crisis that had popped up as if in a dream" (22, 257–58). The pure duration of the moment which, in Poirier's terms, "needn't be organic . . . with anything but the creative vision itself," gives way to the hard realities of knowledge and judgment and time, to a wholly organic connection with the inevitable text from which Strether has attempted to escape, but of which he has only succeeded in postponing the end.

James thus seems to be acknowledging that the rich imaginative multiplicity fostered by Strether's desiring consciousness will inevitably give way to the poverty of single knowledge, and that his intense responses are literally in excess of the real objects and people from which they spring. Strether himself senses that his "sudden gusts of fancy," his "suppositions and divinations," have in truth "no warrant but their intensity" (22, 274). Under the first shock of the Pocock's arrival, he finds himself wondering if the "experience" he has constructed for himself through his delays and dilations is not in fact "fantastic and away from the truth. . . Did he live in a false world, a world that had grown simply to suit him, and was his present slight irritation . . . but the alarm of the vain thing menaced by the real" (22, 80–81)? Indeed, as the novel comes to a close, Strether must acknowledge repeatedly the falseness and vanity of the world he has built. The "virtuous attachment" into which he has read so much beauty is really at base a common sexual liaison: "he was mixed up with the typical tale of Paris" (22, 271). As one critic has aptly noted, "without the mind of Strether, the story of Chad and Madame de Vionnet is essentially conventional" (Lebowitz, 89).

Just as the inflated value Strether has given Chad and Madame de Vionnet's affair suffers an inevitable shrinkage, so the people in whom he has seen so many possibilities are unavoidably reduced in stature. Maria Gostrey, who seemed to hold for him an importance entirely out of proportion to her peripheral function in his "business," becomes at last a minor figure in a hierarchy which must assert itself:

the time seemed already far off when he had held out his small thirsty cup to the spout of her pail. Her pail was scarce touched now, and other fountains had flowed for him; she fell into her place as but one of his tributaries. (22, 48)

Strether's changed estimation of Maria's importance "marked for himself the flight of time" (22, 48); now, for all his detestation of Woollett's a priori, utilitarian judgments, Strether must himself measure the limits of Maria's usefulness – must see the end of what she has, for him, to give. And he must recognize too that he has seen too much in Chad. Like James in Notes of a Son and Brother, Strether is forced to confront his own "wasteful habit or trick of having a greater feeling for people's potential propriety or felicity or full expression than they seemed able to have themselves" (NSB, 39). The sudden reduction of Chad's value comes as "the sharpest perception yet" and "like a chill in the air." Madame de Vionnet

had but made Chad what he was – so why could she think she had made him infinite? She had made him better, she had made him best, she had made him anything one would; but it came to our friend with supreme queerness that he was none the less only Chad. Strether had a sense that he, a little, had made him too; his high appreciation had, as it were, consecrated her work. The work, however admirable, was nevertheless of the strict human order, and in short it was marvellous that the companion of mere earthly joys, of comforts, aberrations (however one classed them) within the common experience, should be so transcendently prized. (22, 284–85)

Strether explicitly links himself here with a feminine principle of desire, which seeks transcendence through an expansion of the loved object to infinite proportions. But the Chad Newsome of the novel's close is of "the strict human order." The reality of the callow young man who is willing to abandon Madame de Vionnet, who indeed may be keeping another woman in London, belies Strether's earlier estimation of Chad's miraculous transformation. The expansive moment centered on Chad's visage illuminated by a street-lamp – a moment in which Chad's potential had seemed limitless – is echoed with devastating irony when Strether meets him for the last time. Chad has just returned from London, where "he had been getting some news of the art of advertising":

> He appeared at all events to have been looking into the question and had encountered a revelation. Advertising scientifically worked presented itself thus as the great new force. "It really does the thing, you know." They were face to face as they had been that first night, and Strether, no doubt, looked blank. "Affects, you mean, the sale of the object advertised?" "Yes – but affects it extraordinarily; really beyond what one had supposed. I mean of course when it's done as one makes out that, in our roaring age, it *can* be done. . . It's an art like another, and infinite like all the arts. . . With the right man to work it *c'est un monde.*" (*22*, 315–16)

The "power" Strether has sensed in Chad will be employed on behalf of the most utilitarian end conceivable: the sale of Woollett's unmentionable product. And Chad's sketch of advertising as an "infinite" art that can create a whole world provides a withering parody of Strether's expansive method. For a man of Strether's sensibility, an "art" which seeks only "the sale of the object advertised" must represent everything he detests – the naked aggression of masculine syntax rushing toward an utterly manipulative and vulgar end.[6]

Even Madame de Vionnet herself, the woman who in Strether's eyes has been as "various and multifold" as Shakespeare's Cleopatra (*21*, 271), and in whom he has invested an infinitude of desire, will take her place in "the strict human order."

> It was actually moreover as if he didn't think of her at all, as if he could think of nothing but the passion, mature, abysmal, pitiful, she represented, and the possibilities she betrayed. She was older for him to-night, visibly less exempt from the touch of time . . . he could see her then as vulgarly troubled, in very truth, as a maidservant crying for her young man. (*22*, 286)

"You're afraid for your life!" Strether exclaims to her during their final encounter (22, 285). And in this recognition of her terror at losing Chad, Strether concedes that her sublimity is the creation of his own consciousness, a romantic projection forged from his lifetime of thwarted desire. Madame de Vionnet is not infinite. Like Chad, she exists "within the common experience," is a child of fatherly time, and a victim of that awful wanting which makes us human. If she is still for Strether "the finest and subtlest creature, the happiest apparition, it had been given him, in all his years, to meet" (22, 286), she is also now a figure of poverty, like him a prisoner of her own needs. "It was almost appalling," Strether thinks, "that a creature so fine could be, by mysterious forces, a creature so exploited" (22, 284). Ageing, trapped in a loveless marriage, at the mercy of Chad and Woollett − "old and abject and hideous" she calls herself (22, 288) − Madame de Vionnet becomes a symbol of the feminine brutalized by the masculine, of the fragile works of the moment swallowed up by the aggression of time.

For the father always returns, as time, as death. Early in the novel, Strether recalls having "read somewhere of a Latin motto, a description of the hours, observed on a clock by a traveller in Spain": "*Omnes vulnerant, Ultima necat*" − "all wound, the last kills" (21, 93). And it is precisely this progress of the hours toward death that Strether has dreamed of halting, but which he has only succeeded in delaying. At certain points − his day in the country, for example − Strether seems almost to believe in the infinite duration of the moment. At such moments he feels as he did on his first day in Chester, when delighted by the unexpected postponement of his rendezvous with Waymarsh, he thinks of himself as "a man who, elatedly finding in his pocket more money than usual, handles it a while and idly and pleasantly chinks it before addressing himself to the business of spending" (21, 5). But this is the time-sense of the beginning, when time remains a rich store to be spent − that one can *imagine* spending − in an infinite plethora of possible ways; it is the time-sense of the moment of desire, when everything can still be dreamed, before choices have been made and consequences incurred, before the moment has been absorbed back into the flow of history. This attitude toward time can be traced in James's work at least as far back as *The Portrait of a Lady*, where Isabel Archer wishes to be free to choose among all the possibilities in the world, and so resists the necessity of actually making any particular choice, for fear of the limiting consequences it will entail.

Strether has a "double consciousness" (21, 5) − of time as well as of life itself. And as his hours in Paris inexorably run out, time's rich store shrinks to nothing more than a poor interval preceding death. Strether wants desperately to believe that he has, "by his own hand," stopped "the swing of Chad's pendulum back . . . toward Woollett": "he had the entertainment of thinking that . . . he had for that moment stopped the clock" (22, 59). But it is the clock that wins in the end, that wounds and finally kills. In his last conversation with Maria Gostrey, Strether lights on the perfect

image of his recent history; he was like one of the figures of the old clock at Berne. *They* came out, on one side, at their hour, jigged along their little course in the public eye, and went in on the other side. He too jigged his little course – him too a modest retreat awaited. (22, 322)

Like Shakespeare's

> poor player
> That struts and frets his hour upon the stage
> And then is heard no more   (*Macbeth*, 5.5.24–26)

Strether's time is up. He is consigned to the oblivion of Woollett and the death of all he has imagined.

How, then, are we to judge Strether's remarkable "process of vision?" Are Strether's intense and expansive responses after all anything more than a vain and irrelevant excess? Does the experience he creates for himself through these responses contain any solid value, or is it merely, like the romantic sublimity of Madame de Vionnet, an "apparition?" Has Strether gained or accomplished anything through his dilations and postponements? Has he made a difference? Such questions are not easily answered: James's best critics are very much divided in their evaluations, and even those commentators who sympathize most with Strether's mode of encountering reality have found it difficult to sustain their enthusiasm for Strether's way. Robert Garis, a more antipathetic commentator, has argued persuasively that James himself adopts, near the end of *The Ambassadors*, a decidedly unadmiring stance in relation to his central character. Garis believes that the novel's last seven chapters turn against and "annihilate" what has come before. He cites the Cheval Blanc episode and in particular its concluding image of "the little girl hiding her doll's nakedness from herself" as evidence of James's own changed attitude toward Strether: "this image destroys at one stroke the validity of his previous imaginative realizations" (309).

Garis's cases is a strong one; for while Strether's desiring consciousness mirrors James's own, the latter does allow his fictional double to wonder whether he has been "fantastic and away from the truth," does have him admit to Chad that he has "moved among miracles. It was all phantasmagoric" (*22*, 301). There is little evidence to suggest that Strether has changed anything: Chad is, after all, "only Chad" – "the son of his father," as Miss Gostrey points out (*22*, 321) – and all signs point to his imminent return to Woollett and the "art" of advertising, to his willingness to abandon Madame de Vionnet. Even while he exhorts little Bilham to "live all you can," Strether recognizes that he is powerless to effect his dreams in the face of an utterly deterministic universe:

"The affair – I mean the affair of life – couldn't, no doubt, have been different for me; for it's at the best a tin mould . . . into which, a helpless jelly, one's consciousness is poured – so that one 'takes' the form, as the great cook says, and is more or less compactly held by it: one lives in fine as one can. Still, one has the illusion of freedom; therefore, don't be, like me, without the memory of that illusion." (*21*, 218)

Strether will go home to Woollett with the memory of that illusion: it is what he has gained. And perhaps he will carry with him as well the memory of another illusion – that of having loved Madame de Vionnet. But because he has not tried to consummate or even express that love in any direct fashion, the only memory he garners is the memory – like all his others – of desire. Strether's love for Madame de Vionnet remains a secret wish, unexpressed and unconsummated. He does not even allow himself the luxury of jealousy toward the unworthy man "ineffably adored" (*22*, 285) by Madame de Vionnet, feels instead only a passive, buried envy. In a passage from *A Small Boy and Others*, James describes his own childhood envy of his cousin, Gus Barker – a romantic, masculine, athletic figure whose life was to be "cut short, in a cavalry dash, by one of the Confederate bullets of 1863" – and remarks

that though in that early time I seem to have been constantly eager to exchange my lot for that of somebody else, on the assumed certainty of gaining by the bargain, I fail to remember feeling jealous of such happier persons – in the measure open to children of spirit. I had rather a positive lack of the passion, and thereby, I suppose a lack of spirit; since if jealousy bears, as I think, on what one sees one's companions able to do – as against one's own falling short – envy, as I knew it at least, was simply of what they *were*, or in other words of a certain sort of richer consciousness supposed, doubtless often too freely supposed, in them. They were so *other* – that was what I felt; and to *be* other, other almost anyhow, seemed as good as the probable taste of the bright compound wistfully watched in the confectioner's window; unattainable, impossible, of course, but as to which just this impossibility and just that privation kept those active proceedings in which jealousy seeks relief quite out of the question. A platitude of acceptance of the poor actual, the absence of all vision of how in any degree to change it, combined with a complacency, an acuity of perception of alternatives, though a view of them as only through the confectioner's hard glass – that is what I recover as the nearest approach to an apology, in the soil of my nature, for the springing seed of emulation. I never dreamed of competing – a business having in it at the best, for my temper, if not for my total failure of temper, a displeasing ferocity. If competing was bad snatching was still worse, and jealousy was a sort of spiritual snatching. With which, nevertheless, all the while, one might have been "like" So-and-So, who had such horizons.

James "scarce know[s] whether to call the effect of this miserable or monstrous. It was the effect at least," he adds, "of self-abandonment – I mean to visions" (*SBO*, 175–76).

This stunning admission of utter powerlessness – of "a platitude of acceptance of the poor actual, the absence of all vision of how in any degree to change it" – could stand as a motto for Strether's situation at the end of *The Ambassadors*. Like James, Strether possesses "an acuity of perception of alternatives" to the stupidity and fatality he sees all around him; but the vision through the confectioner's window is ultimately only a wasteful excess of desire that cannot alter anything, that can at best defer the inevitable. By choosing a life of "self-abandonment . . . to visions," Strether like James confines himself to a role of helpless wanting. For even the protest of jealousy "seeks relief" through "active proceedings," and this is a path Strether has effectively closed to himself. Like all forms of direct masculine action, jealousy involves a kind of violence, a "displeasing ferocity" or "spiritual snatching" – an abhorrent aggression against the other. Every aspect of Strether's method aims at averting or foregoing such violence. But without it – without the aggressiveness of a masculine, success-oriented syntax – nothing can be achieved or won; without some willingness to compete and manipulate and take, to live in a more direct sense, desire can never be transformed into love. Strether is unable to preserve Chad and Madame de Vionnet's love in the face of Woollett's paternal force, let alone to consummate or pursue his own. He "lives" only by feeding the "sprawling meagerness" of his "experience" on the lives of others and on the endless store of his own powerless envy. Which is another way of saying that Strether, for all the intensity of his wanting, can never achieve love. Love requires a conjunction of masculine and feminine, of knowledge and ignorance; it needs both the freedom of imagination and the strictures of reality, both the beginning of desire and the end of desire. In the *Symposium*, Socrates explains that love is "of an intermediate nature" – "half-way between mortal and immortal." Love, being half-god and half-man, is one of those "spirits" whose special function is to "bridge the gap" between the divine and the human and to "prevent the universe from falling into two separate halves" (81). But Strether, for all his labor, can never bridge this gap. Though Madame de Vionnet produces in him an impression "that might have been felt by a poet as half mythological and half conventional" (*21*, 270), the two realms coexist without ever merging. Between the transcendent, infinite duration he desires and the vulgar contingency of the clock he avoids there can be no commerce. For all its magnificence, Strether's desire is helpless, unable – and unwilling – to effect its ends; it cannot change that poor actuality in relation to which it is only a supplementary figure, an excess. The idealizations of Strether's expansive consciousness remain unnecessary to reality's syntax of statement. His figures of desire escape that syntax for a while, and momentarily retard its forward progress by adding to it all sorts of dilatory speculation and dreaming; but in the end the statement completes its intended meaning – nothing fundamental has been changed. Strether knows he has experienced only "the illusion of freedom"; but despite his "sense of moving in a maze of mystic closed allusion" (*21*, 278), he never abandons his road of excess, which leads not to Blake's "palace of wisdom" but to the endlessness of wanting more wants. Strether's two modes of existence thus overlap without ever meshing in a fruitful productivity. In Freud's terms, there is no effective mediation between the reality principle and the pleasure principle: Strether goes on wishing while the world remains unalterably vulgar and fatal.

Love, especially in its sexual aspect, mediates between desire and reality, and in doing so it alters the nature of both extremes. In conjoining imagination and fact, fancy and flesh, love drains and eventually kills desire. For desire is always a lack and never a possession: love realizes desire by using it up, by provoking its death. But love also transforms reality, changes it in a way that desire alone cannot; by investing the real with its desire, love *makes* a difference where desire only *sees* or *dreams* one. And unlike desire, love can triumph over the sterility and the fragility of the "poor actual" – but only if it is willing to sully the purity of desire with the dross of reality, and to limit its wanting in the pursuit of a specific object. Sexual love, of course, is not really an option for Strether: it is too late, and Madame de Vionnet loves another man. But we must reemphasize the dependance of Strether's whole approach to life on a persistent effort to preserve and intensify desire rather than to fulfill it. By cultivating his ignorance of the sexual intimacy embraced by Chad and Madame de Vionnet's love – by dressing up "the bare facts one has to recognize" (*22*, 168) – Strether is able to romanticize the affair, to see in it all sorts of beauty and intensity that evade those facts. And in a more general sense Strether's consciousness, because it seeks to prolong indefinitely the moment of desire, is always working against fulfillment. Desire's potential for infinitude fights against the limitation and completion that consummation represents. We are close here to what Denis de Rougemont calls "the erotic process," which

introduces into life an element foreign to the diastole and systole of sexual attraction – a desire that never relapses, that nothing can satisfy, that even rejects and flees the temptation to obtain its fulfillment in the world, because its demand is to embrace no less than the All. It is *infinite transcendence*, man's rise into his God. And this rise is without return. (62)

Strether's much-discussed aversion to sexuality thus reflects a more pervasive problem inherent in the very rhythm – odd and sometimes exasperating – of his expansive method. It is a rhythm which invests every moment with the intensity of crisis, but which prefers to terminate rather than resolve these crises. James wrote in *Notes of a Son and Brother* that "the play of strong imaginative passion, passion strong enough to *be*, for its subject or victim, the very interest of life, constitutes in itself an endless crisis" (*NSB*, 369). And in the Preface to *The Ambassadors* he locates "the idea of the tale" in "the fact that an hour of such unprecedented ease should have been felt by [Strether] *as* a crisis" (*AN*, 307). As readers of *The Ambassadors*, we in fact experience the novel as "an endless crisis." We seem always to be at *the* crucial moment, but resolution (another word for consummation) is always delayed and deferred. Time and time again we feel ourselves, with Strether, "in presence altogether of truth spreading like a flood"; but the spreading flood never organically subsides – it is only cut off by an arbitrary authorial action and by the exigencies of fate and fact. Truth seems ever imminent, but never achieves a full presence, except as an utter negation that obliterates Strether's intensity without relieving or resolving it. Because he will not make his own ends, Strether must merely suffer those that are imposed on him by the authority of others and of reality itself.

When Strether says, in regard to the "great difference" that awaits him in Woollett, "I shall see what I can make of it" (22, 325), we know that his "making" will unfold in imagination and not in actuality – that Woollett will not constitute for him an end, but only another beginning. We sense that he will experience Woollett the way he has experienced Paris. His desiring consciousness will discover in Woollett's poverty a whole range of new possibilities; and to some extent we admire Strether for his fidelity to his generous "process of vision." But that fidelity and generosity are in a more fundamental sense disturbing, for they disguise a consistent effort to hide from the human reality which lies outside the sterile safety of mere desire. Thus Strether runs away from an opportunity to join with another in really *making* an end to his Parisian adventure. When Maria Gostry declares *her* love for Strether through an "offer of exquisite service, of lightened care, for the rest of his days," Strether refuses on the grounds that it would violate his guiding principle "not, out of the whole affair, to have got anything for [himself]." Maria understands that, as she tells Strether, "with your wonderful impressions you'll have a great deal"; and she instinctively knows that those "impressions" are in truth the substance of his desire for Madame de Vionnet. Strether recognizes Maria's offer as one that

might well have tempted. It built him softly round, it roofed him warmly over, it rested, all so firm, on selection. And what ruled selection was beauty and knowledge. It was awkward, it was almost stupid, not to seem to prize such things. (22, 325–26)

But Strether prefers an illusory quest for the All to even the most beautiful "selection"; he chooses the empty "freedom" of a hopeless imaginative desire rather than be "built . . . round" or "roofed . . . over" by the real intimacy of an active love. He leaves Maria, as Lawrence Holland has suggested in a frequently quoted remark, "in the affair of art, the affair of memory and imagination, rather than in the affair of love which she hopes for" (281).

But it is, of course, Madame de Vionnet and not Maria Gostrey toward whom Strether directs the full force of his immense yearning and unfulfilled desire: she is the "enchantress" who might have been. And though he can never hope to possess her – indeed, though he would not want to were he given the opportunity – Strether does make what must count as at least a gesture of love toward this woman who loves another. In his own inimitably super-subtle and roundabout way, Strether finally brings himself to the assertion of making an end, an end that stands in direct opposition to Woollett's original intention and that finds its truth in the penultimate value of love. When Strether tells Chad, in a final interview, "You'll be a brute, you know – you'll be guilty of the last infamy – if you ever forsake her" (22, 308), he is enacting in a modest way his own love for Madame de Vionnet, while at the same time acknowledging and honoring the beauty and wisdom and pathos of her love for Chad. Strether's direct effort to make Chad stay proves all the more moving in that it recognizes in Madame de Vionnet's love not only the truth of its sexual basis, but also the beauty of its common humanity – that of "a maid-servant crying for her young man" – and the profound wisdom of her knowledge that "the only certainty is that I shall be the loser in the end" (22, 288). For this moment Strether seems to understand that love – which, as Socrates knows, "on one and the same day . . . will live and flourish . . . and also meet his death" (Symposium, 82) – is superior to desire, which always denies death; he seems to glimpse the truth that even Chad, for all his shortcomings, instinctively grasps: "that one can't but have it before one, in the cleaving – the point where the death comes in" (22, 317).

Strether's final encounter with Chad embodies a strange and suggestive irony: in charging the younger man to remain in Paris, in attempting to bend Chad to his purpose, Strether has reassumed the mantle of the father which he earlier cast aside with such determination. The two men revert to their original roles. Addressing Chad in a commanding, authoritative tone, Strether becomes "as grave, as distinct, as a demonstrator before a blackboard," while Chad "continued to face him like an intelligent pupil" (22, 310–11). And Strether asserts his paternal authority not only in the language he uses, but also in the strictness of the accounting he brings to bear on Chad: "You owe her everything. . . . You've in other words duties to her, of the most positive sort; and I don't see what other duties – as the others are presented to you – can be held to go before them" (*22*, 313). Strether's firmness of judgment here – his assertion of a moral hierarchy in which some "duties" are central and others peripheral – marks a striking reversal in a man for whom all systematic or *a priori* judgment has been so abhorrent. It seems also to run counter to his previous effort to allow Chad the greatest freedom and range of possibilities. But Strether's sense of duty has nothing to do with Woollett's genealogical imperatives; born of his desire and his experience, his final judgment locates the highest value in a love that is socially unsanctioned and that is on the verge of collapse. If Strether can be said to make an end at all, it is here. When he issues his authoritative charge to Chad – "You'll be a brute, you know – you'll be guilty of the last infamy – if you ever forsake her" – he achieves his own fatherly syntax of statement; for once he speaks from knowledge as well as ignorance, from belief as well as desire:

That, uttered there at the solemn hour, uttered in the place that was full of her influence, was the rest of his business; and when once he had heard himself say it he felt that his message had never before been spoken. (*22*, 308)

Strether's reassertion of his paternity creates, in Paul Ricoeur's words, "the likeness of the father in accordance with which the giving up of desire is no longer death but love" (549). For perhaps the first time in James's long career, we reach a point where the return of the father – of reality and of time – holds the possibility of something more than mere extinction.

Yet the possibility is really only a very remote one. Though James purposely leaves the question open, Chad's return to Woollett seems assured. Indeed, it is not difficult to find in Strether's charge only one more example of his tendency to overvalue, to see too much in the younger man, and to suppress the facts which invalidate his illusory desire. Can we claim for Strether even the limited success which James, in a luminous passage, attributes to "the great anodyne of art?"

The great thing to say for [artists] is surely that at any given moment they offer us another world, another consciousness, an experience that, as effective as the dentist's ether, muffles the ache of the actual and, by helping us to an interval, tides us over and makes us face, in the return to the inevitable, a combination that may at least have changed. (*LC*, 1:1400)

Strether, in all probability, has changed nothing.[7] Like James as a

small boy, he has "but one success, always – that of endlessly suppos-
ing, wondering, admiring" (*SBO*, 243). And the attempt to resolve the
excess of desire into the fullness of realized love remains an unfinished
project, one that James will take up again in *The Wings of the Dove* and
The Golden Bowl. For Strether, despite his gesture of love, remains a
willing prisoner of his own desire, a denizen of that "homeless
freedom" (*SBO*, 223) in which James located the spiritual residence of
those who, like himself, possess "too much" imagination.

4 *The Wings of the Dove* (I): The contracted cage

But I find myself feeling . . . how much more interesting a writer may be on occasion by the given failure than by the given success. Successes pure and simple disconnect and dismiss him; failures – though I admit they must be a bit qualified – keep him in touch and in relation.

Henry James, Introduction to *Madame Bovary*

Does the imagination dwell the most
Upon a woman won or a woman lost?
If on the lost, admit you turned aside
From a great labyrinth out of pride,
Cowardice, some silly over-subtle thought
Or anything called conscience once;
And that if memory recur, the sun's
Under eclipse and the day blotted out.

W.B. Yeats, "The Tower"

James completed *The Ambassadors* in May of 1901; by mid-July he had already begun dictating a new novel, a love story, he announced, that would be entitled *The Wings of the Dove*.[1] Yet despite the apparent ease with which James stepped from Lambert Strether's story into Milly Theale's, despite, moreover, widespread critical complacency in attributing formal and thematic unity to the "major phase" novels, few readers, I think, will deny that the two fictions offer strikingly different experiences.[2] Our sense of the disparity between these two novels cannot be adequately accounted for simply by observing that the earlier work is a comedy, the later a tragedy. Such a distinction is only partially accurate; and it does little to explain how and why the fluid style and seamless continuity of Strether's "process of vision" could give way so quickly to the clotted, hesitant prose and gap-filled structure

83

of *The Wings of a Dove.* The discrepancy is perhaps best captured by a bald and rather unscholarly comparison: *The Ambassadors,* whatever our final judgment of the novel and its hero, is basically "fun" to read, while *The Wings of a Dove* offers us an experience − trying, often claustrophobic, sometimes infuriating − in repeated frustration.

James's own sense of the profound differences between *The Ambassadors* and *The Wings of a Dove* is clearly evinced in the respective Prefaces he wrote to accompany the novels' republication in The New York Edition. That James felt the two fictions were equally important to any full understanding of his career is certain: in 1913 he included both titles in the "more 'advanced' " course he prescribed for a "delightful young man from Texas" who had sought his guidance in approaching the Jamesian canon (*L*, 4:683).[3] But if James awarded both novels a central status in his *oeuvre,* his comments in the Prefaces suggest that these high valuations were based on variant if not opposed criteria. The Preface to *The Ambassadors* exudes throughout the pride and confidence of an artist revisiting what he judges to be, "frankly, quite the best, 'all round,' of [his] productions" (*AN*, 309). While he does not shrink from acknowledging − as he does elsewhere in the Prefaces − the "inevitable deviation (from too fond an original vision) that the exquisite treachery even of the straightest execution may ever be trusted to inflict even on the most mature plan" (*AN*, 325), James here emphasizes more consistently those "repaired losses," "insidious recoveries," and "intensely redemptive consistencies" (*AN*, 326) that helped him to transform his "original vision" into a successful work of art. James returns repeatedly in these pages to his remembered sense of the relative ease with which this particular "game of difficulty" was "breathlessly played" (*AN*, 311). At every stage of its composition, he asserts, the project gave off "the same golden glow": "nothing resisted, nothing betrayed" (*AN*, 310). The novelist theorizes that even among an artist's most promising subjects,

there is an ideal *beauty* of goodness the invoked action of which is to raise the artistic faith to its maximum. Then truly, I hold, one's theme may be said to shine, and that of "The Ambassadors," I confess, wore this glow for me from beginning to end. (*AN*, 309)

James goes on to compare the facility with which *The Ambassadors* virtually "wrote itself" to the persistent difficulties he encountered in composing *The Wings of the Dove.* In telling Strether's story, James insists,

I recall . . . no moment of subjective intermittence, never one of those alarms as for a suspected hollow beneath one's feet, a felt ingratitude in the scheme adopted, under which confidence fails and opportunity seems but to mock. If the motive of "The Wings of the Dove" . . . was to worry me at moments by a sealing-up of its face . . . so in this other business [*The Ambassadors*] I had absolute conviction and constant clearness to deal with; it had been a frank proposition, the whole bunch of data, installed on my premises like a monotony of fine weather. (*AN*, 309–10)

If *The Ambassadors* sprang from a "frank proposition" and evoked no "resistance" or "betrayal" in the process of its development, the subject of *The Wings of the Dove*, in contrast,

seemed particularly to bristle. It was formed, I judged, to make the wary adventurer walk round and round it . . . not being somehow what one thought of as a "frank" subject, after the fashion of some, with its elements well in view and its whole character in its face. It stood there with secrets and compartments, with possible treacheries and traps; it might have a great deal to give, but would probably ask for equal services in return, and would collect this debt to the last shilling. (*AN*, 288–89)

Though James's Prefaces typically summarize the technical problems he faced in executing each of his fictions, the Preface to *The Wings of the Dove* is unique in its persistent focus on what James perceives as a whole array of compositional faults and structural failures. Rereading *The Ambassadors*, James feels "the old intentions bloom and flower again" (*AN*, 319); the more chastening lesson drawn from revisiting *The Wings of the Dove* is that "one's plan, alas, is one thing and one's result another" (*AN*, 296) – a lesson that Kate Croy and Merton Densher will learn as well. The profound differences in tone, temper and judgment that distinguish the two Prefaces are perhaps best exemplified in their disparate conclusions. While the Preface to the earlier novel ends with a triumphant assertion that "the Novel remains still, under the right persuasion, the most independent, most elastic, most prodigious of literary forms" (*AN*, 326), James's discussion of the later work peters out in confusion and inconclusiveness – as if the problems he grappled with in writing the novel still elude a satisfactory resolution: "I become conscious of overstepping my space without having brought the full quantity to light. The failure leaves me with a burden of residuary comment of which I yet boldly hope elsewhere to discharge myself" (*AN*, 306).

The Preface's "failure" as criticism reflects the novelist's deep-seated feeling that the work itself was unsuccessful. James speaks of *The Wings of the Dove* as "a tangled web" that "bristles with 'dodges' " of a sort that the critic is "committed to recognize and denounce" (*AN*, 302). The novel, James admits with a "scarce more than half-dissimulated despair" (*AN*, 302), possesses "too big a head for its body" (*L*, 4:247), a "makeshift middle," and a latter half that is "false and deformed" (*AN*, 302). Most damagingly, however, the book counts among its defects a whole series of failures – of "lapsed importances" (*AN*, 298) – in its characterizations. The finished work thus strikes James as most marked "by the happy features that *were*, under my first and most blest illusion, to have contributed to it"; rereading Milly Theale's story, James repeatedly finds himself mourning what might have been – "the absent values, the palpable voids, the missing links, the mocking shadows" (*AN*, 296–97) that measure his failure to realize his subject's full potential.

Yet James, despite his unflinching and perhaps somewhat overzealous recognition of the novel's manifold structural and technical flaws, was nevertheless willing to rank *The Wings of the Dove* among those works most crucial to unfolding "the figure in the carpet" of his long career. This mixed assessment is both odd and intriguing. By some obscure algebra that he can only half-articulate, the novel's difficulties and failures, James seems to sense, signal the presence of something essential in its subject and theme. James once wrote that "we are never so curious about successes as about interesting failures" (*LC*, 2:97) – an observation that describes his own troubled fascination with *The Wings of the Dove*; and in the Preface he alludes to "the degree in which the artist's energy fairly depends on his fallibility" (*AN*, 297). More significantly, James asserts that "as every novelist knows, it is difficulty that inspires," although – and the qualification is of paramount importance – for the artist to achieve "perfection of charm, it must have been difficulty inherent and congenital, and not difficulty 'caught' by the wrong frequentations" (*AN*, 302). James makes it quite clear that the problems he encountered in writing *The Wings of the Dove* were a case of "difficulty inherent and congenital": from the first, Milly Theale's story "stood there . . . with possible treacheries and traps" sufficient "to make the wary adventurer walk round and round it" (*AN*, 288–89). Thus the resistance offered by this particular project to the artist's transforming power may suggest that it harbours a potential richness and resonance – something more "in touch and in relation" (*LC*, 2:329) – superior to anything tendered by a more easily treated subject like that of *The Ambassadors*. Just as the "strange difficulties" attached to Milly Theale's fate reveal to her "still stranger opportunities" (*AN*, 301), so the inherent thorniness of the novel's subject matter indicates to James that "it might have a great deal to give" (*AN*, 289).

The potential for failure is greater in *The Wings of the Dove* because more is at stake. We are not asked here, as we are in *The Ambassadors*, to participate in casuistical speculations about the "virtuous attachments" of others, or to share in half-conscious evasions of "the point" where a purely metaphorical death "comes in"; rather, the novel's form urges us to immerse ourselves in the hearts and minds of people who know the attractions of material wealth, who feel and acknowledge the pressures of sexual desire, who love and are loved, and who – at least in the case of Milly Theale – confront directly the terrible and irreversible fact of death. The issues are more fundamental, our experience of them more direct. No longer confined to the perspective of an observer, we now inhabit the consciousnesses of characters engaged in active choices that entail significant consequences. James's selection of protagonists – his focus, for the first time in many years, on mature young adults who are not "excused" from the simple humanity of sexual longing by virtue of their age (Strether, Maisie) or their questionable mental state (the governess in *The Turn of the Screw*, or even the possibly "crazy" narrator of *The Sacred Fount*) – further contributes to our sense that more is being risked in *The Wings of the Dove*.[4] Indeed, in Merton Densher James created his first sexually potent male protagonist since Nick Dormer of *The Tragic Muse* – a novel completed more than ten years earlier.[5] The inescapable implication is that James returns, in *The Wings of the Dove*, to crucial issues he had long ignored and suppressed.

There is, of course, another more obvious sense in which the book's subject is critically important to the novelist. Minny Temple had been dead for more than thirty years when James, as he writes movingly in *Notes of a Son and Brother*, sought "to lay [her] ghost by wrapping it . . . in the beauty and dignity of art" (*NSB*, 515); and in turning to this profoundly personal memory for the subject of *The Wings of the Dove*, James chose to confront his own psychic and emotional scars with a directness unparalleled elsewhere in his fiction. He begins his Preface to the novel by admitting just how deeply Milly Theale's story is rooted in his consciousness and his experience:

"The Wings of the Dove" . . . represents to my memory a very old − if I shouldn't perhaps say a very young − motive; I can scarce remember the time when the situation on which this long-drawn fiction mainly rests was not vividly present to me. (*AN*, 288)

For many years − and there is ample evidence in the *Notebooks* to confirm James's characterization of the subject as one he had long brooded over[6] − the story of a dying young girl had incubated in the novelist's imagination, at once compelling and threatening, attractive, yet potentially dangerous. "Long had I turned it over," he confesses, "standing off from it, yet coming back to it; convinced of what might be done with it, yet seeing the theme as formidable" (*AN*, 288).

James's decision to confront and explore his memories of Minny Temple − a decision apparently reached after many years of hesitation − implies a new willingness on his part to reexamine a period of critical, determining choices in his own life. At the end of *Notes of a Son and Brother*, James remarks that Minny Temple's death signaled, both for himself and for his brother William, a key turning point: "we felt it together as the end of our youth" (*NSB*, 515). The years between 1865 and 1870, during which James watched his cousin's agonizing struggle against a death which, "at the last, was dreadful to her" (*NSB*, 515) were also the years when he was deciding to devote his life to his art. This decision, for James, involved other choices − to abandon America for Europe, to remain unmarried − which would irrevocably shape his experience. In a general sense, *The Wings of the Dove* may be said to evoke this decisive period in James's personal history, for it is a novel about choices and their irredeemable consequences, about the dangers of failing to take responsibility for the choices we have made. More particularly, the dishonesty of Merton Densher's relationship to Milly Theale reflects the inhibited, evasive nature of James's own bond with Minny Temple. In a letter to William written after Minny's death, James exclaims − "almost," as Leon Edel puts it, "in a tone of triumph" (*The Untried Years*, 331) − that "she has gone where there is neither marrying nor giving in marriage!" Yet in the same letter, after noting "the gradual change and reversal of our relations" − "I slowly crawling from weakness and inaction and suffering into strength and health and hope: she sinking out of brightness and youth into decline and death" − James goes on to regret what might have been: "I always looked forward with a certain eagerness to the day when I should have regained my natural lead, and our friendship on my part, at least, might have become more active and masculine" (*L*, 1:224–26). This mingling of relief and regret typifies the unconscious sophistry of James's feelings about Minny Temple. Whatever the sources of his ambivalence, however, the fact remains that James, in his young manhood, chose to turn aside from the possibility of love – a choice which is central to the tragedy enacted in *The Wings of the Dove* as well.[7]

James's sense that *The Wings of the Dove* constituted a case of "difficulty inherent and congenital" will now seem less obscure: nearing the age of sixty and the end of a brilliant career, he has found the courage to confront and relive his failure, many years before, to love. And in turning to this long-brooded-over, intensely personal memory – to what he called, at the time of Minny's death, "an affection as deep as the foundations of my being" (*L*, 1:221) – for the subject of his novel, James was generating his fictional world in a manner strikingly at odds with his own theory and with his typical practice in the novels immediately preceding *The Wings of the Dove*. In the Preface to *The Spoils of Poynton*, James describes the process by which his fictions originated in "a single small seed . . . minute and windblown . . . a mere floating particle in the stream of talk" (*AN*, 119). We recall that James believed the "virus of suggestion" could best be communicated by "the stray suggestion, the wandering word, the vague echo" (*AN*, 119), rather than by a subject already furnished with its own context and continuity. Like most of the late 1890s experimental novels, *The Ambassadors* found its "germ" in just such a "tiny particle in the stream of talk." In the *Notebook* entry of October 1895 in which James recorded Jonathan Sturges's anecdote concerning W. D. Howell's advice to him to "live all you can," the novelist observes that although "it was only ten words . . . I seemed, as usual, to catch a glimpse of a *sujet de nouvelle* in it" (*N*, 225). Later, in a letter to Howells written shortly after he completed *The Ambassadors*, James explains that it wasn't until "years afterwards (that is three or four) [that] the subject sprang at me, one day, out of my notebook." James goes on to assure Howells that his words to Sturges provided only "the faint vague germ, the mere point of a start, of a subject," and that "in the very act of striking me as a germ," the subject had "got away from you or from anything like you! had become impersonal and independent" (*L*, 4:199).

James here provides a précis of his standard generative method.

In order for the original germ to retain its intransitive freedom and potential infinitude, it must be ripped from its surrounding circumstances and be made discontinuous with the temporal continuity from which it is drawn – must be rescued from the inevitably "stupid work" of "clumsy Life" (*AN*, 121): hence the superiority of "the merest grain, the speck of truth" (*AN*, 119) as a point of departure. The degree to which James abandoned this method in engendering *The Wings of the Dove* is arresting. The novel's subject did not spring at him, one day, from the pages of his notebook; rather, it emerged through a process of extensive, "long-drawn," one might even say obsessive contemplation. And far from finding its beginning in a tiny germ liberated from its temporal and circumstantial contexts and freely expanded, the novel originated for James in a large, profoundly personal reality, one which, by its very nature, insists on being confronted whole, in all its terrible completeness.

In changing his way of beginning, James is also calling into question a central tenet of the desiring mode. The desiring consciousness always locates the best starting points in the smallest, finest fragments of perception and experience, for it is things small and fine that can most readily be made independent of their real and limiting contexts, and that are therefore most susceptible to the figurative transformations of desire. But such "independence" carries a hidden cost. For just as Strether's vision small and fine allows and even requires him to avoid or postpone knowledge of important facts – about himself and about his situation – so James finds "the merest grain, the speck . . . of reality" attractive as a beginning subject because it licenses a kind of writing that is "impersonal" as well as "independent." By generating his novels from small and superficial germs, James in fact abdicates his responsibility – he once called *The Turn of the Screw* a "perfectly independent and irresponsible little fiction" (*AN*, 169) – to confront directly the larger truths of his personal experience. Desire, and the process of writing that embodies desire, harbor a barely concealed impulse to escape, from "poor Life" and especially from the reality of the self. The new generative method of *The Wings of the Dove* – James's willingness to begin with a large, inescapably significant personal reality – signals a movement away from the aesthetic of escape towards a more difficult art of self-examination and acceptance.

James's testimony that the subject for *The Wings of the Dove* represented "a very old . . . motive" finds confirmation in the fact that he had already, in *The Portrait of a Lady*, made a first attempt at transforming Minny's suffering – "so of the essence of tragedy" – into the "beauty and dignity of art" (*NSB*, 515). But a comparison of the two novels exposes a revealing point of contrast. For in *The Portrait of a Lady*, James approaches Minny Temple's story in a manner essentially compatible with the mode of desire. By giving her the chance to live that "poor Life" had denied her, James grants Minny the status of an intransitive beginning: he ignores her fate in favor of her possibilities. James's remarks in a letter to Grace Norton are instructive:

Poor Minny was essentially *incomplete* and I have attempted to make my young woman [Isabel Archer] more rounded, more finished. In truth everyone in life, is incomplete, and it is in the work of art that in reproducing them one feels the desire to fill them out, to justify them, as it were. (*L*, 2:324)

We remember that James found "strange enough the 'aesthetic' of artists who could desire but literally to reproduce" (*SBO*, 113). For as he complains in the Preface to *The Spoils of Poynton*, life "persistently blunders and deviates, loses herself in the sand," submits to "the fatal futility of Fact"; the novelist's task and privilege is therefore to ensure that the original "seed" – in this case the spirit of Minny Temple – is "transplanted to richer soil" (*AN*, 120–22). Thus James's intention in transforming Minny Temple into Isabel Archer is to free her from the real and binding context of her fate in irreversible time, to allow her "might have been" to flower and expand in the alternative world of art.

The language of James's letter to Grace Norton is misleading, even, in all probability, self-deceiving. For when he asserts that "everyone in life is incomplete," James means that everyone is mortal; and his desire to make Isabel Archer "more finished" really constitutes a wish to grant her a potential infinitude, an array of possibilities that escapes the limited reality of Minny Temple's short and restricted life. Minny's incompleteness is in fact her end, the completion, terrible and irrevocable, imposed on her by the finality of death. And it is this end, which James chose to suppress in *The Portrait of a Lady*, that functions as the determining center of *The Wings of the Dove*. For despite the complex tissue of lies and evasions that permeates the novel, there is ultimately – for author, reader, and characters alike – no escape from the presence of this fact: a beautiful young girl, "conscious of a great capacity for life," is "condemned to die under short respite" (*AN*, 288). Within a very few pages of our introduction to this "potential heiress of all ages" (*19*, 109), possessed, James tells us, of a "boundless freedom, the freedom of the wind in the desert" (*19*, 110), we learn that she is "unmistakably reserved for some more complicated passage" (*19*, 125). "Talk of early dying" (*19*, 134) surrounds James's heroine from the first; and the famous scene in Regent's Park where Milly confronts and accepts her doom – "that of a poor girl . . . with her rent to pay" (*19*, 253) – takes place with two-thirds of the novel still remaining. Thus James, persistently engaged in "driving portents home" (*AN*, 305), never allows us to forget the end towards which we are moving; he creates for his readers a perspective that forces us to read every event in the light of the novel's conclusion.

As we have seen in *The Ambassadors*, the idea of ending – of making or choosing an end – is fundamentally at odds not only with Strether's desiring mode but also with James's own activity of *writing*. The *writer* – that part of the novelist's dual nature which adumbrates the desiring mode by wanting only to go on writing *ad infinitum* – habitually indulges Strether's dilatory expansions of every object and moment; though the *author* eventually imposes his authoritative knowledge of each detail's restricted function in the novel's overall scheme, the *writer* submits to that authority with profound reluctance and regret, and in the interim writes *as if* he doesn't know, thus mirroring his protagonist's strategy of deliberate forgetting. In *The Sacred Fount*, James's most *written* work and his purest embodiment of the desiring mode, this *as if* becomes an actuality. James seems literally not to have known, when he began writing this novel, where or how it might end. As a result, he cannot conclude the book, in the sense of bringing the issues it raises to any resolution, or even in the sense of deciding – he cannot decide *because he does not know* – whether the narrator's elaborate speculations have any basis in fact. We are left only with the narrator's rejection of Mrs. Brissenden's "last word" – "My poor dear, you *are* crazy, and I bid you good-night!" – as "too unacceptable not to prescribe that prompt test of escape to other air . . ." (*318–19*).

The Sacred Fount is a novel without an author. And in comparison, *The Ambassadors* may be seen as already effecting a retreat from this *ne plus ultra* of the desiring mode. James may in fact have had *The Sacred Fount* in mind when he argued, in the Preface to *The Ambassadors*, against "the romantic privilege of the 'first person,' " which leads, "when enjoyed on the grand scale," to "the darkest abyss of romance" (*AN*, 320). But judging from a wider perspective, I think it is fair to say that we experience *The Ambassadors* predominantly as written rather than authored. For the writer, predication, the completion of a syntax or a story, is merely the negation of writing, a fall into fixed meaning and silence that must be delayed for as long as possible. And so in *The Ambassadors*, James asks his readers, not to think about where and how Strether will end, but to participate in the proliferating, intransitive "process of vision" generated by his endless desire. The reader's task in *The Wings of the Dove* is clearly of a different nature. For even in its germinating phase, the novel embodied the deep structure of an unmistakably transitive syntax. The subject's completion in Milly Theale's death constitutes an inescapable part of what we might call, following Edward Said, the novel's "beginning intention" (*Beginnings*, 79). To be sure, the work is replete with the evasions and postponements so characteristic of desire: whatever their disparate motives, its characters (including Milly Theale herself) agree on one operative principle – that Milly's impending death must never, not even for a moment, be publicly acknowledged. And like his characters, James himself spends a great deal of time and prose in talking *around* the central fact of Milly's fate; indeed, the novel is famous for James's deliberate refusal to represent directly its most crucial scenes, including the heroine's death. But the characters' evasions here are fully conscious lies in a way Strether's rarely are. And though James may insist, as he does in the Preface, that "the poet essentially *can't* be concerned with the act of dying," though he may claim that the novel is really about "the unsurpassable activity of passionate, of inspired resistance" that comprises "the act of living" (*AN*, 289), he also knows and admits that the underlying structure of *The Wings of the Dove* rests in the "portrayal . . . of a catastrophe determined in spite of oppositions" – a formula that captures "the soul of drama" (*AN*, 290), and that provides a concise definition of tragedy.

The Wings of the Dove thus alters the balance of power between writer and author that had prevailed in *The Ambassadors* and in the experimental fiction of the 1890s. Writing is now contained by authoring; the expansive, desiring imagination of the writer must work within the limited space willed and bound by the author's foreknowledge of the end. The wish to delay is now yoked to a will to conclude, a mixture of impulses that Foucault sees as the basis of all literature: "men . . . speak toward death and against it" ("Language to Infinity," 55).[8]

By thus subordinating his writerly freedom to his authorial foreknowledge, by embracing the end as well as evading it, James once again signals his retreat from the fiction of desire to a kind of fiction that is closer in spirit to traditional realism. The realistic novel is, in Leo Bersani's words, a literary form implicitly or explicitly "shaped by a prior imagination . . . of ends" (*A Future for Astyanax*, 54).[9] Frank Kermode and others have demonstrated the dependence of classical realism on an authorial perspective that issues from a full knowledge of the end of affairs, and have shown how modernist writers break with the realistic aesthetic in abandoning the end-perspective for a "perspective of the middle" (Hollington, 437) – a change which produces that rhythm of "eternal transition" and "perpetual crisis" (Kermode, 101) we have already seen exemplified in *The Ambassadors*.[10] Julia Kristeva, a partisan of modernism's most radical aspirations, has characterized the classical realistic novel as a type of narrative that "is bounded, born dead" (57), a judgment that recalls James's own belief that "the thing done and dismissed has ever, at the best . . . a trick of looking dead, if not buried. . ." (*AN*, 99). In what could serve as a brief but incisive analysis of *The Wings of the Dove*, Kristeva defines realism as a formal construct in which

we already know how the story will end: the end of the narrative is given before the narrative itself ever begins. All anecdotal interest is thus eliminated: the novel will play itself out by rebuilding the distance between life and death; it will be nothing other than an inscription of *deviations* (surprises) that do not destroy the certainty of the thematic loop (life – death) holding the set together. (42)

The Wings of the Dove, like the classical realistic novel, binds the writer's desire consistently and forcefully within the author's authoritative knowledge of "the thematic loop"; because it possesses a conscious will to end – evidenced in its constant forebodings – the narrative instructs us to read its momentary phenomena in terms of its conclusion: forces us, in other words, to see the "anecdotal interest" of each moment as a merely figurative "deviation" from its basic narrative syntax.

In a 1902 essay on Flaubert, James praises the French novelist for his ability to balance a sympathetic immersion in Emma Bovary's consciousness (in her desire) with an unflinching representation of "the tiny world in which she revolves, the contracted cage in which she flutters" (*LC*, 2:326). Like Emma, Milly Theale enjoys only a "caged freedom" (20, 167). Because she knows she is going to die, Milly understands life as a "practical question" that must be addressed within the constricting "box" or "grim breathing space" of her fate (19, 250): her experience, like the novel's form, is in some sense "born dead," and the novelist shares her consciousness of encagement. The writer, James declares elsewhere, builds for himself "a cage in which he [must] turn round and round, always unwinding his reel, much in the manner of a criminal condemned to hard labour for life" (LC, 2:101). The image of the novel as a confining form helps to explain James's sense of difficulty in telling Milly Theale's story. Where the Preface to The Ambassadors emphasizes the writer's unbounded freedom – James speaks of the "enjoyment for the infatuated artist" and the " 'fun' for the reader" made manifest "as soon as an artistic process begins to enjoy free development" (AN, 324) – the Preface to The Wings of the Dove focuses on the author's sense of constraint: "nowhere," James laments, "had I condemned a luckless theme to complete its revolution . . . in quarters so cramped" (AN, 302).

Every "failure" James perceives in The Wings of the Dove is in fact an instance of writing forcibly compromised with authoring – a compromise enacted, we recall, through the "secret of 'foreshortening' " (AN, 278). The novel, especially in its "false and deformed" second half,

bristles with "dodges" . . . for disguising the reduced scale of the exhibition, for foreshortening at any cost, for imparting to patches the value of presences, for dressing objects in an air as of the dimensions they can't possibly have. (AN, 302)

The "artful compromise . . . of 'foreshortening' " (AN, 278) becomes especially difficult and dissatisfying when the novelist perceives and experiences his adopted form not as "the most independent, most elastic" of literary modes (AN, 326), but as the cramped quarters of an imprisoning cage. James felt the thwarting of his writerly freedom nowhere more acutely than in his efforts, doomed to disappointment, to grant each character in The Wings of the Dove the fullest possible attention and presentation. The failures James points to in this respect are all failures of extent; simply put, the novelist feels he hasn't been able to write enough about each character:

One's main anxiety, for each one's agents, is that the air of each shall be given; but what does the whole thing become, after all, as one goes, but a series of sad places at which the hand of generosity has been cautioned and stayed? The young man's [Densher's] situation, personal, professional, social, was to have been so decanted for us that we should get all the taste; we were to have been penetrated with Mrs. Lowder, by the same token, saturated with her presence, her "personality," and felt all her weight in the scale. We were to have revelled in Mrs. Stringham . . . just as the strength and sense of the situation in Venice, for our gathered friends, was to have come to us in deeper draught out of a larger cup, and just as the pattern of Densher's final position and fullest consciousness there was to have been marked in fine stitches, all silk and gold, all pink and silver, that have had to remain, alas, but entwined upon the reel. (*AN*, 298–99)

James's remorse at having left so much unsaid about his "agents" – his regret that so many "fine stitches" of characterization "remain . . . entwined upon the reel" – stems, I think, not only from his general conception of the novel as an encaging form, but also from his specific decision here to employ a narrative strategy involving multiple centers of consciousness. It might seem initially that a novel like *The Ambassadors*, which immerses both writer and reader completely in the consciousness of a single character, entails greater constraints than a book like *The Wings of the Dove*, with its multiple reflectors; where the earlier work confines us to the presence and perspective of a single observer – only those events witnessed by Strether are represented – the later novel, by plunging us successively into the varying perspectives of several major figures, offers a wider and more diversified experience of the world. But in truth, the special kind of "freedom" the writer embraces finds a more congenial vehicle in the single-consciousness narrative, especially when the consciousness in question is, like Strether's, radically imaginative in cast. Writing is a manifestation of desire; and the realm which desire wishes to be free to create and expand and explore, without limits, in every object and instant, is inherently a product of the individual imagination. James can indulge Strether's desire to the extent he does precisely because there is no world presented in the novel outside of the one Strether himself has imagined. But in *The Wings of the Dove*, James sets for himself *as writer* a more difficult and more frustrating task. The problem is only partly that James must limit the extent of his writing about Milly because he is obligated to write about Kate and Densher as well. More importantly, he cannot participate wholeheartedly in Milly's process of vision when he must also partake of Kate's and of Densher's. Milly's desire is hemmed in, qualified, and often negated by the desire of the other characters, just as Densher's and Kate's "free" imaginings are contextualized – bounded and "molested" – by Milly's own vision.

I have borrowed the term "molestation" from Edward Said, who uses it in *Beginnings* to describe and define what he perceives as one of the basic characteristics of the realistic novel:

Molestation . . . is a consciousness of one's duplicity, one's confinement to a fictive, scriptive realm, whether one is a character or a novelist. And molestation occurs when novelists remind themselves of how the novel is always subject to a comparison with reality and thereby found to be illusion. Or again, molestation is central to a character's experience of disillusionment during the course of a novel. (84)

Said goes on to clarify his last point by linking it to that awareness of ends which evokes such mixed responses from James:

The demystification, the decreation or education, of illusions, which is the novel's central theme . . . is thus an enactment of the character's increasing molestation by a truer process pushing him to an ending that resembles his beginning in the midst of negation. (94)

The Ambassadors – and in this respect we acknowledge once again the distance James had travelled from traditional realism – does not incorporate in its form (or, I believe, in its deepest intentions) an enactment of that "truer process" through which the figurations of desire are "molested" by a knowledge of reality. For the novel, while it boasts a large cast of characters, possesses but a single *subject*. The "reality" of *The Ambassadors* is Strether's desire, and the other characters exist only as objects of that desire, objects that can be loaded with all the infinitude of what he wants them to be. And because James has chosen to suppress the presence of the author, who alone knows the truth and foresees the end, the writer is freed to participate uncritically in Strether's efforts to liberate the others from Woollett's deadening vision (or might we say, from the conditions of reality itself?). Thus Strether, and with him both writer and reader, can discover in Chad Newsome a burgeoning "implication of possibilities" (*21*, 198), can find and unfold in Madame de Vionnet the variety of "fifty women" (*21*, 265). The amplitude they are granted is the vastness of their limitless potential transformed into presence in the expansive rhythms of Strether's desire and James's prose.

But what would become of Chad's "possibilities" if we were suddenly removed from Strether's purview and immersed in the vision of

Madame de Vionnet? Could Madame de Vionnet's infinite variety survive a shift in perspective from Strether's desiring consciousness to the
mind of Chad Newsome, a man who is bound to her in the intimacy
of love? The form of *The Ambassadors* does not encourage us – indeed,
it seeks to forbid us – to ask such questions. We do ask them – even
Strether himself begins to wonder whether he inhabits "a false world,
a world that had grown simply to suit him," and to suspect that he has
been "fantastic and away from the truth" (*22*, 80–81); but in asking
them we violate our contract with the novel's form and oppose James's
most fundamental intentions for the work. James's clearest advice to
the reader of *The Ambassadors* is unequivocal: "*don't break the thread*"
(*L*, 4:302)[11] – by which I take him to mean that fine thread of desire
uninterruptedly spun from Strether's expansive imagination.

The Wings of the Dove comprises several threads, and its form
repeatedly forces us to break one that we might pick up another. By
virtue of its multiple centers of consciousness, the novel *does* permit us
to witness a greater range of events, and thus in one sense achieves a
fuller amplitude. For example, because Milly Theale's presence is not
always required – as Strether's was – for a scene to be represented,
we can observe Kate and Densher alone together, can attest and explore their intimacy, as we never could that of Chad and Madame de
Vionnet. Kate and Densher possess an unmistakable reality – the
reality of subjects – apart from their figurative existence as the objects
of Milly Theale's desiring imagination. And when we watch as Kate
and Densher confirm and acknowledge to each other their plot against
Milly – when they "pronounce the words" (*20*, 225), as James puts
it – we are witnessing a kind of scene which the form of *The Ambassadors* cannot accommodate. By employing multiple centers of consciousness, the novelist thus gains, for himself and for his readers, a
greater mobility and latitude, and hence a larger world. But this expanded range of representation, this ability to see more *of* the world,
paradoxically constrains the writer's freedom to see more *in* the world
– in each object and moment and especially in each of its human
agents. With the full force of her desire – a force no less powerful than
that of Strether's imagination – Milly Theale can envelop Merton
Densher in a rich, potentially infinite penumbra of possibilities; as the
object of her desire, he is capable of being transformed into the image
of everything she has ever wanted. But the novel's multiple-
consciousness form prevents both writer and reader from immersing

themselves unquestionably in Milly's vision of Densher; we see him, after all, through Kate's eyes as well, and know him through our own plunges into *his* heart and mind. We do participate in Milly's desire – no omniscient narrator intrudes – but only in cramped quarters; for our identification with the expansive movements of her imagination is unavoidably surrounded and molested by our participation in Kate's process of vision and in Densher's. Similarly, because we know Milly as a subject, we cannot unreservedly accept the other characters' figurations of her: Kate's "dove," Densher's "American girl," or Susan Stringham's "princess." Indeed, these images in and of themselves contradict, modify and negate each other.

Virtually all of James's longer fictions from *The Spoils of Poynton* through *The Ambassadors* manifest their creator's preference for the single center of consciousness form, a form which had, after all, constituted the main line of his development since *Roderick Hudson*. James's decision to employ a multiple-consciousness structure in *The Wings of the Dove* – a choice he reiterated in *The Golden Bowl* and in his unfinished novel, *The Ivory Tower* – involves a fundamental recasting of the conditions in which he embeds the act of writing. Yet not surprisingly, given the widespread acceptance of a "major phase" which includes *The Ambassadors*, this change has gone largely unnoticed in critical discussions of James's later work.[12] One exception to this general critical reticence is J. A. Ward's extended study of James's fictional structures. Ward sees the shift to a multiple-consciousness structure in *The Wings of the Dove* as indicative of a more fundamental change in James's governing aesthetic – a change which he summarizes as a movement from "the novel of character" to "the novel of relations" (*The Search for Form*, 174). In the novel of character, Ward asserts, character relations are "means rather than ends"; they exist mainly to reveal character, and to provide the "raw materials of intelligence: the stuff of experience that only the superior mind can comprehend" (175). The single-consciousness narrative format is particularly appropriate to the novel of character in that it focuses, as we have seen in *The Ambassadors*, less on relations themselves than on the imaginative inner "experience" constructed by and in the central reflector's transforming vision of them. The novel of relations, where "relations among characters actually constitute the subject" – and here Ward specifically cites *The Wings of the Dove* – "logically requires the technique of multiple points of view; the technique not only supports the subject, it is the subject" (175).

Ward's central distinction is both persuasive and suggestive. For in labeling *The Wings of the Dove* a "novel of relations" as opposed to a "novel of character", he is acknowledging that this fiction stresses the actuality of human relations with a consistency almost as determined as that with which *The Ambassadors* evades it. By structurally immersing us in a single mind, *The Ambassadors* subordinates the dramatic representation of enacted relations to a free exploration of the rich potentiality invested in those relations by Strether's desiring consciousness. What is actually going on between Chad and Madame de Vionnet – the truth about their "virtuous attachment" – doesn't matter, since the novel's "reality" coincides with Strether's imagination of events, not with the events themselves. Thus the single-consciousness narrative form is a structural manifestation of the desiring mode: it necessarily directs our attention away from the basic syntax of what is actually happening towards the supplemental figures – the excessive might-have-been and might-still-be – added to that syntax by the combined force of Strether's desire and James's expansive style.

But this priority is reversed by the multiple-consciousness structure. Because our commitment to each character's interior process of vision is interrupted and limited by the form's repeated shifts to other points of view, we are increasingly invited to create for ourselves an alternative perspective which transcends and contextualizes our participation in whatever individual viewpoint the novel is momentarily embodying. This exterior, more objective viewpoint – the reader's substitute for the authorial omniscience James withholds – combines with that foreknowledge of ends we have already discerned in *The Wings of the Dove* to produce a focus that turns persistently from possibilities to actualities, from beautiful imaginings to poor facts, and from relations as they are figured by desire to relations as they are enacted in reality. Pulling us from our immersion in the characters' wanting, the novel's form urges us to judge them by what they say and do.

Indeed, what matters in *The Wings of the Dove* is what happens, a statement that might seem ridiculous were it not for the fact that it cannot be applied with any accuracy to a fiction like *The Ambassadors*. A fruitful revision of Ward's categories would suggest that if *The Ambassadors* is a novel of character (of character as it is conceived by James in the desiring mode), then *The Wings of the Dove* is essentially a novel of plot, a story in which the inescapable syntax of events – the truth of what happens to the characters and of what they make happen –

dominates the characters' freedom to figure alternative possibilities, and in which, moreover, the dramatic representation of actions ultimately counts for more than the beautiful elaborations of style. As we have already seen, James from the first envisioned *The Wings of the Dove* as a transitive dramatic structure. Milly's fate, the plot which includes her end as well as her beginning, was an integral part of James's original intention for the novel, and he never imagined her, as he did Isabel Archer, apart from her situation, or in independence from that "catastrophe determined in spite of oppositions" which he calls "the soul of drama." But the Preface to *The Wings of the Dove* makes it equally clear that James never conceived Milly apart from the interactions of her entangling relations with Kate and Densher. The novel's germ had from the outset included all the complexity of its realized plot:

> I had noted that there could be no full presentation of Milly Theale as *engaged* with elements amid which she was to draw her breath in such pain, should not the elements have been, with all solicitude, duly prefigured. . . one had seen that her stricken state was but half her case, the correlative half being the state of others as affected by her (they too should have a 'case,' bless them, quite as much as she!). (*AN*, 214)

James's initial *Notebook* entry on *The Wings of the Dove* confirms his conception of the novel from the first as a plot. These germinal musings of 1894 already encompass not only "the situation of some young creature" who "is suddenly condemned to death," but also "the idea of a young man who meets her," who represents for the dying girl "the chance to love and be loved," but who is already "entangled with another woman, committed, pledged, 'engaged' to one." In the space of a few pages, James sketches the full structure of the novel's relations, including the lovers' betrayal of Milly; and just four days later – seven years before he actually began to write the novel – James jotted down "the idea of the man's *agreeing with his fiancée that he shall marry the poor girl in order to come into her money and in the certitude that she will die and leave the money to him* – on which basis . . . they themselves will at last be able to marry" (*N*, 169–71). These first thoughts on *The Wings of the Dove*, with their detailed specificity of action and interaction, stand in stark contrast to James's early ruminations on *The Ambassadors*, where, as Matthiessen and Murdock suggest in their commentary on the *Notebook* entry, "in contrast with both *The Wings of the Dove* and *The Golden Bowl*, James started, not with the outlines of a situation, but with the emotional center of his novel" (*N*, 228–29).

That center – Strether's character and temperament as embodied in his declaration for life (modelled after Howells's outburst to Jonathan Sturges) – is sketched with surprising completeness; it is

the little idea of the figure of an elderly man who hasn't 'lived,' hasn't at all, in the sense of sensations, passions, impulses, pleasures – and to whom, in the presence of some great spectacle, some great organization for the Immediate, the Agreeable, for curiosity, and experiment and perception, for Enjoyment, in a word, becomes, *sur la fin*, or toward it, sorrowfully aware. (*N*, 226)

The essence of the novel is Strether's desire, his wanting (in both senses of the word). The "great human spectacle," which might unfold in London or Paris or Italy , and which is, after all, necessary to a depiction of Strether's character, is very much a secondary consideration:

what I seem to see is the possibility of some little illustrative action. The idea of the tale being the revolution that takes place in the poor man, the impression made on him by the particular experience, the incident in which this revolution and this impression embody themselves, is the point *à trouver*. (*N*, 227)

The "little illustrative action" – the plot – remains to be found. And the *Notebook* entry, the only one predating the composition of the novel, is in fact entirely vague about the details of "the incident" James would eventually represent in *The Ambassadors*: there is a hint of Chad, but nothing of Madame de Vionnet, and nothing of Strether's intervention and entanglement in their relationship. Plot is thus an auxiliary element, added to illustrate Strether's special kind of "awareness"; and the supplemental status of plot is confirmed by the single-consciousness narrative form, which causes plot to function primarily as a vehicle for the figurative "living" of Strether's desire and James's writing. The point of Strether's outburst in Gloriani's garden "is that he now at all events *sees*; so that the business of my tale and the march of my action, not to say the precious moral of everything, is just my demonstration of this process of vision" (*AN*, 308). What Strether "sees" – the alternative world projected by his desire – exists prior to the novel's plot; the "march of . . . action" merely provides a convenient "demonstration of this process of vision."

Robert Langbaum has argued that "it is largely the victory of character over action that distinguishes the high literature of modern times" (*Poetry of Experience*, 210); and in this respect, as in so many others, *The Ambassadors* anticipates or perhaps inaugurates the paradigms of modernism. The priority of character over plot in the novel also constitutes another part of that body of evidence linking *The Ambassadors* with the novels which precede it rather than those which follow it. As early as 1883, in an article on Trollope, James had indicated that in respect to "the droll, bemuddled opposition between novels of character and novels of plot," he preferred "the former class, inasmuch as character in itself is plot, while plot is by no means character." "We care what happens to people," James asserts, "only in proportion as we know what people are" (*LC*, 1:1336). In the Preface to *The Portrait of a Lady*, James traces his sense of plot as a subsidiary element to the influence of Turgenev, a novelist whom he had admired and emulated even before his first meeting with him in 1875. The "fictive picture," James writes, originated for Turgenev

almost always with the vision of some person or persons, who hovered before him, soliciting him, as the active or passive figure, interesting him and appealing to him just as they were and by what they were. He saw them, in that fashion, as *disponibles*, saw them subject to the chances, the complications of existence, and saw them vividly, but then had to find for them the right relations, those that would most bring them out; to imagine, to invent and select and piece together the situations most useful and favourable to the sense of the creatures themselves, the complications they would be most likely to produce and to feel.

Thus for Turgenev, as for James in *The Ambassadors*, the plot remains "*à trouver*." The extent to which James followed Turgenev in granting character precedence over plot is clearly evidenced in his recounting of the genesis of *The Portrait of a Lady*:

Trying to recover here, for recognition, the germ of my idea, I see that it must have consisted not at all in any conceit of a "plot," nefarious name, in any flash, upon the fancy, of a set of relations, or in any one of those situations that, by a logic of their own, immediately fall, for the fabulist, into movement, into a march or a rush, a patter of quick steps; but altogether in the sense of a single character, the character and aspect of a particular engaging young woman, to which all the usual elements of a "subject," certainly of a setting, were to need to be super-added. (*AN*, 42)

We are on familiar ground here, for we encounter once again James's typical method of generating his fictions, a method which detaches the original germ – in this case Isabel's "character" – from "any of those situations that, by a logic of their own, immediately fall . . . into movement, into a march or a rush": detaches it, in other words, from the pre-conceived and end-oriented continuity of even the least "nefarious" plot. And we recall as well James's decision to liberate Isabel Archer from the confining, deadly plot which had defined Minny Temple's brief existence – a decision he would significantly reverse in the case of Milly Theale.

But if James's career prior to *The Wings of the Dove* and *The Golden Bowl* can be said to demonstrate the modernist "victory of character over action," the notion of character implied by this victory requires further clarification. If character is not a function of what the individual actually does and suffers, then how are we to define it? To what is James referring when he speaks of "the intensity of suggestion that may reside in the stray figure, the unattached character, the image *en disponibilité*" (*AN*, 44)? In this last formulation, we catch a verbal echo of James's commitment, expressed in *Notes of a Son and Brother*, to nurturing and unfolding "the force of action, unless I call it passion, that may reside in a single pulse of time" (*NSB*, 256). And the resemblance in fact suggests an important link between James's conception of character as "unattached" and "*disponible*" and the desiring mode's emphatically ahistorical time sense. The desiring consciousness, we recall, wants always to be at the beginning, at that instant of intransitive potential when everything is possible and nothing is certain, before choices have been made and consequences incurred. Time – as history or as plot – is desire's greatest enemy, for as soon as the moment is swallowed up into the historical continuity which surrounds it, it loses its radical intransitivity and takes on a narrower predicative function: becomes, in effect, a specifically determining step in an actual sequence of events. Now just as desire seeks to protect the varied possibilities inherent in the moment by detaching each "pulse of time" from history, so it wishes to preserve the infinite potential of character by granting character an existence – *a being* – prior to and independent of the particular *becoming* determined for character by plot. And in the fiction of desire, character is defined by the individual's potentiality, not by his actuality: by what he *might* be, not by what he does. Character is thus identical with free imagination, with desire itself; it is the absence of wanting rather than the presence of action. When character is understood in this sense, plot can only be seen as a betrayal of character; for plot necessarily converts intransitive potentiality into transitive action, and in so doing it chooses to *realize* only a handful of character's infinite possibilities, thus obliterating the remainder. This is why, in novels like *The Portrait of a Lady* and *The Ambassadors*, plot is something belatedly (and, one senses, reluctantly) "super-added":

James instinctively knows that the development of a plot *in time* can only result in a specific deployment of desire, and therefore in the destruction of desire's unlimited beginning potentiality – of Isabel's vision of "freedom," of Strether's wish "to live," and of James's own dream of an infinite writing.

A rejection of this ahistorical approach to character lies at the heart of Georg Lukács's attack, in *The Meaning of Contemporary Realism*, on what he calls "the ideology of modernism" (17). Lukács draws a key distinction – one that is especially relevant to the present discussion – between "abstract and concrete potentiality" as they are manifested in life and, more particularly, in the literature of "contemporary realism." "Potentiality – seen abstractly or subjectively – is richer than actual life. Innumerable possibilities for man's development are imaginable, only a small percentage of which will be realized." What Lukács finds most disturbing about "modern subjectivism" – and here he is referring to high modernist fiction – is its habit of "taking these imagined possibilities for [the] actual complexity of life." "How far," he asks,

> were those possibilities even concrete or 'real'? Plainly, they existed only in the imagination of the subject, as dreams or day-dreams. . . The possibilities in a man's mind, the particular pattern, intensity and suggestiveness they assume, will of course be characteristic of that individual. In practice, their number will border on the infinite, even with the most unimaginative individual. It is thus a hopeless undertaking to define the contours of individuality, let alone to come to grips with a man's actual fate, by means of potentiality. The *abstract* character of potentiality is clear from the fact that it cannot determine development – subjective mental states, however permanent or profound, cannot here be decisive. (21–22)

"Imagined possibilities" are certainly "characteristic," but it is absurd to identify them with character itself. Yet it is precisely this "hopeless undertaking," this attempt to define character by means of an "abstract potentiality" divorced from "man's actual fate" and detached from the determining facts of his "development," that informs the Jamesian mode of desire, and that is abetted by the single-consciousness narrative form of a novel like *The Ambassadors*.

Lukács, however, directs our attention toward another category of potentiality:

> in life potentiality can, of course, become reality. Situations arise in which a man is confronted with a choice; and in the act of choice a man's character may

reveal itself in a light that surprises even himself. In literature – and particularly in dramatic literature – the denouement often consists in the realization of just such a potentiality, which circumstances have kept from coming to the fore. These potentialities are, then, 'real' or concrete potentialities. The fate of the character depends upon the potentiality in question, even if it should condemn him to a tragic end.

In advance, Lukács insists, while it is

> still a subjective potentiality in the character's mind, there is no way of distinguishing it from the innumerable abstract potentialities in his mind. . . The concrete potentiality cannot be isolated from the myriad abstract potentialities. Only actual decision reveals the distinction. (22–23)

Lukács believes that any successful "literature of realism, aiming at a truthful reflection of reality, must demonstrate both the concrete and abstract potentialities of human beings," and must therefore be able to discriminate between them. Such discrimination depends upon the presence of a "dialectic between the individual's subjectivity and objective reality." But the very "ontology on which the image of man in modern literature is based" – its identification of the individual's subjectivity with reality itself – prohibits this dialectic; the single-consciousness form of a novel like *The Ambassadors* thus prevents the emergence of concrete potentialities from the welter of "imagined possibilities" that exist abstractly. The Jamesian mode of desire, moreover, by implicating writer, reader and character in an effort to avoid or at least delay the denouement foredoomed by plot, engages in an active resistance to the realization of concrete potentiality, a resistance based on a recognition that, as Lukács puts it, "a character's concrete potentiality once revealed, his abstract potentialities" – what we have called his desire – "will appear essentially inauthentic" (23). Isabel and Strether evade the responsibility of "actual decision," and James countenances their evasions, because all three know that the act of choice, in revealing the distinction between abstract and concrete potentiality, will destroy the free, infinite and finally illusory "reality" of what they had imagined. Desire wants only to go on wanting, to preserve itself as desire (as abstract potentiality), and therefore resists the realization (the fulfillment) of any particular desire. But in *The Wings of the Dove*, the alternative, external perspective which the novel's multiple-consciousness form offers invites us – perhaps even requires us – to distinguish between imagined possibilities and limited, concrete realities. James's new emphasis on plot, on a dramatic structuring of events that unfolds and develops in time, focuses our attention with ever-greater insistence on the choices enacted by the novel's human agents.

Lukács recognizes a link between the kind of realism he is advocating and the aesthetic of dramatic literature. And *The Wings of the Dove*, by subordinating character to plot, brings James closer than at any previous point in his career to an Aristotelian conception of literary art. When he speaks in the Preface to *The Wings of the Dove* of "the soul of drama . . . which is the portrayal, as we know, of a catastrophe determined in spite of oppositions" (*AN*, 290), James is in all probability echoing Aristotle's dictum that "the Plot . . . is the first principle, and, as it were, the soul of a tragedy: Character holds the second place" (*Poetics*, 63). Indeed, the Aristotelian definition of tragedy is far from inapplicable to this, the most tragic in spirit of all James's longer fictions:

> But most important of all is the structure of the incidents. For Tragedy is an imitation, not of men but of an action and of life, and life consists in action, and its end is a mode of action, not a quality. Now character determines men's qualities, but it is by their actions that they are happy or the reverse. Dramatic action, therefore, is not with a view to the representation of character: character comes in as subsidiary to the actions. Hence the incidents and the plot are the end of a tragedy; and the end is the chief thing of all. (62–63)

If *The Ambassadors* portrays character in the modernist mode, which Langbaum sees as resolutely anti-Aristotelian and where, in his words, "we mean by character just the element in excess of plot requirements, the element we call *individual* because it eludes and defies classification" (*Poetry of Experience*, 223), *The Wings of the Dove* follows Aristotle in its tendency "to reduce Character to a quantity, a weight on the moral scales, and to exclude from judgment . . . all those personal idiosyncrasies which do not lend themselves to moral measurement" (Langbaum, 213). We judge Strether by his desire, but measure Kate and Milly and Densher by their actions.

Whether or not *The Wings of the Dove* can be said to adhere to any strict definition of tragic form, James's critics have been, I think, essentially correct in perceiving this novel as *the* tragedy in the Jamesian canon.[13] For in reverting to the Aristotelian priority of plot over character, James here embraces what Northrop Frye has called "the basis of the tragic vision":

being in time, the sense of the one-directional quality of life, where everything happens once and for all, where every act brings unavoidable and fateful consequences, and where all experience vanishes, not simply into the past, but into nothingness, annihilation. (3)

The Ambassadors transpires in that infinite, timeless space opened up by desire, where past and future, what is remembered and what is imagined, what might have been and what might still be, exist simultaneously in a present that has been effectively removed from the determining flow of history: the space of the "enacted and recovered moment," into which desire can read "the whole content of memory and affection" (*SBO*, 3). The desiring mode aspires to a being outside of time; when Strether, at the very end of *The Ambassadors*, addresses to Maria Gostrey the familiar refrain – "Then there we are!" (*22*, 327) – the "there" he refers to is the space of endless wanting he has always inhabited, and from which he has made no real effort to escape. Strether's envoi invites comparison with Kate Croy's decisive last words to Densher in *The Wings of the Dove*: "she turned to the door, and her headshake was now the end. 'We shall never be again as we were' " (*20*, 405)! Strether's statement describes a state of mind or of being that is (ironically, considering his hatred of anything fixed) permanent; but Kate's pronouncement tells a story, a story of unalterable change and irrecoverable loss, of a being that is really a becoming in irreversible time. Events as apprehended through the filter of desiring consciousness are, in terms of their potentiality, infinite; but lived events, as they are directly experienced and dramatically represented, are finite links in a limited chain of acts and consequences.

In *The Wings of the Dove*, it is, of course, not only Kate and Densher's love, but life itself, that "vanishes . . . into nothingness, annihilation." James makes us feel the terrible pressures that time brings to bear on the lovers' relationship: we witness their constant watching of the clock, and know their dependence on "snatched moments" (*20*, 47) and "the scrap of time" (*20*, 316). But it is Milly Theale's impending death, and the novel's consequent formal emphasis on its own approaching end, that determine the reader's consciousness of an experience bound by time, and that make us feel, with Milly, that we are inhabiting a world in which "short intervals . . . stood now for great differences" (*20*, 137). Death circumscribes life as a finite being in time. "In the tragic vision," Frye tells us,

death is, not an incident in life, not even the inevitable end of life, but the essential event that gives shape and form to life. Death is what defines the individual, and marks him off from the continuity of life that flows indefinitely between the past and the future. (3)

Death grants the individual a distinct identity, "marks him off" from the possibilities for life which surround him; only in realizing this most concrete of all potentialities can he remove himself from the infinite realm of abstract potentiality into the limited, defined "shape" of individuality − a process in which he loses the "freedom" of his desire, but in which he also finds a compensatory solidity of self. Indeed, what he gains is the power to make himself. For within the framework death provides, the act of choosing becomes paramount. Once the individual recognizes and accepts his own duration as finite, each moment becomes crucial, not for what he can, in the desiring mode, read into the moment, but for what he decides to do with it. The indefinite world of desire's endless possibilities gives way to a time-bound existence where he must, through repeated acts of "actual decision," choose among those possibilities.

In *The Wings of the Dove*, Milly Theale's strength and wisdom lie precisely in her recognition and acceptance of her own impending doom; for whatever possibilities it will take from her, death has also given Milly the basis of an identity. Her new sense of her own finitude invests her life with a definite shape and solidity − a change she begins to grasp following her initial consultation with Sir Luke Strett:

> She struck herself as aware, aware as she had never been, of really not having had from the beginning anything firm. It would be strange for the firmness to come, after all, from her learning . . . that she was in some way doomed; but above all it would prove how little she had hitherto had to hold her up. If she was now to be held up by the mere process − since that was perhaps on the cards − of being let down, this would only testify in turn to her queer little history. *That* sense of loosely rattling had been no process at all; and it was ridiculously true that her thus sitting there to see her life put into the scales represented her first approach to the taste of orderly living. (*19*, 236)

Milly's life, once "put into the scales," takes on the orderly, concrete and individuating shape of a "history." And her growing awareness that her danger has endowed her existence with a new significance − with a form and value that are uniquely hers − is reinforced by her second interview with the famous surgeon. Though Sir Luke offers no direct prognosis, Milly leaves his office under sentence of death. The visit has

made a mixture of her consciousness − a strange mixture that tasted at one and the same time of what she had lost and what had been given her. It was wonderful to her . . . that these quantities felt so equal: she had been treated – hadn't she? – as if it were in her power to live; and yet one wasn't treated so – was one? – unless it had come up, quite as much, that one might die. The beauty of the bloom had gone from the small old sense of safety – that was distinct: she had left it behind her there for ever. But the beauty of the idea of a great adventure, a big dim experiment or struggle in which she might more responsibly than ever before take a hand, had been offered her instead. It was as if she had had to pluck off her breast, to throw away, some friendly ornament, a familiar flower, a little old jewel, that was part of her daily dress; and to take up and shoulder as a substitute some queer defensive weapon, a musket, a spear, a battle-axe – conducive possibly in a higher degree to a striking appearance, but demanding all the effort of the military posture.

She felt this instrument, for that matter, already on her back, so that she proceeded now in very truth after the fashion of a soldier on the march – proceeded as if, for her initiation, the first charge had been sounded. (*19*, 248–49)

In the reality of her own finitude Milly discerns a call to arms. Indeed, James's military simile – a species of metaphor he employs with surprising frequency in both *The Wings of the Dove* and *The Golden Bowl* – tempts one to recall Sarpedon's address to Glaukos in Book XII of *The Iliad*:

> Man, supposing you and I, escaping this battle,
> would be able to live on forever, ageless, immortal,
> so neither would I myself go on fighting in the foremost
> nor would I urge you into the fighting where men win glory
> But now, seeing that the spirits of death stand close
> >about us
> in their thousands, no man can turn aside nor escape them,
> let us go on and win glory for ourselves, or yield it
> >to others. (12:322–28)

What Sarpedon expresses and what Milly Theale embraces is the existential truth embedded at the core of the tragic vision: the truth that only the certitude of our dying gives value to our decisions and our actions. If we could "live on forever, ageless, immortal," our choices would become meaningless; nothing would be irrevocable, and there would always be time, as Eliot's delayer Prufrock puts it, "for a hundred indecisions,/And for a hundred visions and revisions." But in the face of death, our actions, for good or for evil, for success or for failure, take on a gravity and significance they could not otherwise possess, for they are performed in irreversible time, and cannot be undone.

Milly adopts her "military posture" not, of course, to battle for glory, but to fight for what James in the *Notebooks* calls her "chance to love and be loved" (*N*, 169). And in the pages that follow, I will argue that Milly, by grounding her existence in a full acceptance of her fate, develops a capacity for love that bears scant resemblance to the "imagination of loving – as distinguished from that of being loved" (*3*, 54) – embodied in the desiring mode. Love, as Plato tells us, knows that "on one and the same day he will live and flourish . . . and also meet his death" (82); but desire carries the conviction of its own immortality, and refuses to imagine or accept its own death – hence its fear of ends, even when the end is the fulfillment of desire. Though Strether believes he is working to liberate reality from Woollett's rigid, utilitarian authority, the subtext of his embassy throughout is an obsessive avoidance of "the point where the death comes in" (*22*, 317). Such evasiveness towards death seems psychologically appropriate to a man of Strether's years, especially to one who feels, as Strether does, that he hasn't yet "lived." But the terrible irony of *The Ambassadors*, which James himself did not, I think, fully grasp at the time of the novel's composition, lies in the fact that Strether's mode of *wanting* to live, with its refusal to believe in death, effectively precludes any real act of *living*. Thus the exclusion of death from the purview of life carries in its train other exclusions and renunciations, foremost among them the renunciation of fulfilled and requited love. Strether *is* a Prufrock, a Hamlet who has yet to learn the chastening lesson of the graveyard: fearful of losing the freedom of his desire, he cannot perform the act of love. But love, unlike desire, can only exist as a concrete potentiality, and therefore must be performed: it is realized through action rather than through imagination (and so involves a masculine power and aggression that run counter to the femininity of desire); it necessitates the choice of a particular object (and therefore the abandonment of desire's infinite abstract potentiality); and it requires an acceptance of the death of desire in the discharge of consummation.

Milly Theale understands and embraces these conditions, and in the brief time remaining to her, seeks to create for herself a history – however "queer" and "little" – that includes the enactment of love. Milly's capacity for love introduces into James's fiction a potentiality heretofore absent, a new impulse that has been largely ignored by his critics, who have, I believe, been far too eager to see in Milly's story only another example of Jamesian renunciation. When Milly stands at "the dizzy edge" of an Alpine promontory, "looking down on the kingdoms of the earth," it is not, as Susan Stringham recognizes, "with a view of renouncing them"; indeed, the only real question here – "was she choosing among them, or did she want them all?" (*19*, 123–24) – is quickly answered when Milly announces just a few hours later that she wants "to go straight to London" (*19*, 133). Milly doesn't renounce, she chooses, chooses among her infinite possibilities – chooses London, chooses Merton Densher. And having made her choice, she pursues her "chance to love and be loved" with an aggressiveness – at one point boldly inviting herself to Densher's rooms – critics have been reluctant to acknowledge. As for her final decision to bestow her fortune on Densher, even though she now knows of his engagement to Kate Croy, it is both more and less than the dovelike, even Christ-like renunciation so many commentators have made it out to be. In truth, Milly's legacy constitutes a purposeful act, in some senses cruel and certainly not free from a trace of jealousy, aimed at achieving what she has wanted all along: that Densher should love her as she loves him.

Though her act enjoys a perverse sort of success – Densher ends by falling in love with her memory – Milly obviously fails to realize the fulfilled, reciprocated love for which she has struggled. She dies, yielding the field and the glory to others. But in failing, Milly lives more fully and more authentically than a character like Strether could ever hope to; *her* actions have altered reality – things can never again be as they were – while Strether, imprisoned in his desire, can change nothing, can only go on wanting. Just as James's own self-adjudged "failures" in composing *The Wings of the Dove* suggest a new willingness on his part to confront long-suppressed issues of fundamental personal importance, so Milly's failure to realize her dream of loving and being loved indicates her commitment to a kind of living that plays for the highest stakes, and her courage in facing whatever risks are involved. The reverse side of the novel's "medal" (*AN*, 294), the unravelling of Kate and Densher's relationship, is also a story of failed love, a different kind of failure, the result, as we shall see, of the lovers' evasion of the realities of time and death, of Kate's refusal to choose between love and fortune, and of Densher's delay in acknowledging what he instinctively knows to be true – that love must be enacted if it is to survive. But here too the potential for love is (or at least was) real; we recognize it as such because the novel's fundamentally dramatic art insists that we see the disintegration of Kate and Densher's love as a product of their own decisions, as a fate they have chosen, as something that did not have to be. Not until his next novel, *The Golden*

Bowl, would James fully attain what had so long eluded him: the authority to represent an achieved, mutually requited passion, the courage to speak the sentence of love. But *The Wings of the Dove* just as emphatically asserts the reality of love, its concrete potentiality; and by so doing, the novel constitutes for James a decisive step away from the beautiful but ultimately sterile and solipsistic freedom of desire's figurations.

5 *The Wings of the Dove* (II): Choosing, acting, and the chance for love

> 'Tis of the essence of life here,
>   Though we choose greatly, still to lack
> The lasting memory at all clear,
>   That life has for us on the wrack
> Nothing but what we somehow chose;
>   Thus are we wholly stripped of pride
> In the pain that has but one close,
>   Bearing it crushed and mystified.
>
> Robert Frost, "The Trial By Existence"

> Words can be *hard* to say: such, for example, as
> are used to effect, or to confess a weakness.
> (: Words are also deeds :)
>
> Ludwig Wittgenstein, *Philosophical Investigations*

When Milly Theale announces her decision to "go straight to London," she makes a decision – takes an "actual fine stride" – that Susan Stringham "was afterwards to recall as a piece of that very 'exposition' dear to the dramatist" (*19*, 133). With her "big freedom" (*19*, 137) and her growing sense of her own doom, Milly chooses to descend into society in quest of what James calls "the human" (*19*, 135); she is prepared to immerse herself totally in the fluctuating and entangling complexity of human relations, and to "tak[e] full in the face the whole assault of life" (*19*, 125). The drama Milly chooses to enact finds its first fully realized scene in the dinner party Maud Lowder gives to introduce the young American heiress. But during this scene of initiation, the drama is momentarily interrupted when Milly, reacting to Lord Mark's casual prediction that she is destined for a brilliant social success ("You'll see everything," he tells her; "you *can*, you know – everything you dream of"), embarks on one of those inordinately extended flights of consciousness so characteristic of the desiring mode. Feeling "as if he were showing her visions as he spoke," Milly begins to imagine what might be contained in Mark's "everything," begins, in fact, with James's writerly indulgence, to infuse his superficial remark with a proliferating array of significances far beyond anything he has intended. In the prolonged moment of her interior voyage – an instance, James tells us, of "the short run and the consciousness proportionately crowded" – she unfolds the potentially infinite implications of the "success" augured for her, and explores as well the manifold alternatives her future might portend: for the duration of this expanded interval, so reminiscent of Lambert Strether's process of vision, she recaptures something of her Alpine perspective, possessing in imagination all the kingdoms (and possibilities) of the earth, and delaying for a time her resumption of the drama at hand.

In a self-conscious gesture familiar to us from *The Ambassadors*, James both acknowledges and defends the excessiveness of Milly's response: "these were immense excursions for the spirit of a young person at Mrs. Lowder's mere dinner-party," he admits; "but what was so significant . . . as the fact of their being possible? What could they have been but just a part, already, of the crowded consciousness?" The passage, however, soon takes a turn toward a kind of resolution unlike anything we have encountered in *The Ambassadors*:

and it was just a part likewise that while plates were changed and dishes presented and periods in the banquet marked; while appearances insisted and phenomena multiplied, and words reached her from here and there like plashes of a slow thick tide . . . : it was just a part that while this process went forward our young lady alighted, came back, taking up her destiny again as if she had been able by a wave or two of her wings to place herself briefly in sight of an alternative to it. Whatever it was it had showed in this brief interval as better than the alternative; and it now presented itself altogether . . . in the place in which she had left it. (*19*, 158–60)

What has happened is simply this: the myriad abstract possibilities conjured up by Milly's desiring consciousness have resolved themselves into a choice between "two courses" – to leave London immediately or "to do nothing at all" (to remain) – and ultimately into a conscious decision to stay. Indeed, Milly "had the strangest sense, on the spot, of so deciding," and recognizes that "she had turned a corner before she went on again with Lord Mark" (*19*, 158).

Throughout *The Wings of the Dove*, in London and even more elaborately in Venice, Milly will demonstrate her capacity, as pronounced as Strether's, for imagining alternatives to the actual; this is, after all, a story of "the unsurpassable activity of passionate, of inspired resistance" (*AN*, 289) to the reductive power of death. But just as markedly and insistently, and quite unlike Strether, she will manifest again and again her determination to return to reality from the seductively "free" realm of abstract possibilities, to "come back" and embrace the fate she is making for herself, and which she here senses is also, in some obscure way, being made *for* her – by Lord Mark, Maud Lowder and "the handsome girl" (*19*, 159), Kate Croy. By willfully "taking up her destiny again," Milly in a single stroke transforms abstract into concrete potentiality, desire into decision, vision into action. The dove, after ascending "by a wave or two of her wings" to gaze at the infinite alternatives, alights to accept and to make a specific, limited reality. To be sure, Milly will experience moments of wishing "not to go down – never, never to go down!" (*20*, 147). But she always descends, and in so doing determines the final issue of her desiring flights, rather than merely suffering, as Strether inevitably does, the annihilation of imagination's riches in the resurgence of inescapably poor facts. Where Strether's intensities of reaction produce perpetual crises that are never resolved, only terminated, Milly's ability and willingness to choose create an organic subsidence of crisis, a resolving integration of desire back into the dramatically "real" events from which it originally took flight.

The arc travelled by Milly's consciousness in this scene traces a shape and adumbrates a rhythm that are profoundly characteristic of *The Wings of the Dove*. Bound within the molesting dramatic structure of the text, desire's expansive, dilatory impulses consistently give way before a contractive, resolving urgency that forcibly subordinates imagined possibilities to the concrete actualities of plot. Indeed, if *The Ambassadors* can be described as a single, sustained embodiment of James's "expansive principle," then Milly Theale's story can only be imaged as an inexorable contraction of desire's beginning infinitude into the solitary fact of her dying. I have already suggested that the feelings of constriction and claustrophobia we experience while reading *The Wings of the Dove* – so distinct from the playfulness and irresponsible freedom offered by *The Ambassadors* – stem from our inescapable foreknowledge of Milly's fate. The young American girl's pain – "the facts of her condition" – can and will be disguised in "a kind of expensive vagueness, made up of smiles and silences and beautiful fictions and priceless arrangements, all strained to breaking." But this "general conscious fool's paradise, from which the specified had been chased like a dangerous animal" – a tribute, as Merton Densher recognizes, to "the mere aesthetic instinct of mankind" – cannot be sustained: as Milly herself realizes from the first, there will come a terrible moment of knowing that "the specified, standing all the while at the gate, had now crossed the threshold" (*20*, 298–99). And if this collapse of "beautiful fictions" into "the specified" describes the overall shape of the novel, it also characterizes the more localized experience offered by the work from scene to scene. Our often oppressive sense of confinement as we move through *The Wings of the Dove* reflects not only our knowledge of the plot as a whole, but also, and I think more directly, our awareness of a repeatedly applied pressure, integral to James's design and enforced by his formal structures, that compels recurrent resolutions of multiple possibilities in specific actions and limiting choices.

Through the excessive figurative activity of his own writing, James allows and even encourages us to join Strether in seeking an "experience" free from the necessity of choice. But in *The Wings of the Dove*, at every step of the story's development, the exigencies of plot confront the characters, and through them the reader, with coercive either/or situations that demand resolution through decisive responses. The novel begins with Kate Croy facing Aunt Maud's requirement that she decide – "she wants me to choose," Kate tells her father (*19*, 21) – between her family-feeling and the promise of Lancaster Gate; it ends with Densher confronting Kate – "You must choose," he insists (*20*, 404) – with the alternatives of marriage without fortune or fortune without marriage. The experience of these characters is consistently defined by and structured around moments involving critical choices, choices which they impose on each other, and which are imposed on them by the sheer progress of events.

In *The Wings of the Dove*, as elsewhere in James's *oeuvre*, events take for the most part the form of talk. And the contractive, resolving rhythm that distinguishes the novel on every level is nowhere more evident than in James's depiction of the characters' verbal intercourse. Conversation in *The Ambassadors*, we recall, provides Strether with a means of opening up and exploring a proliferating array of possible significances. By prying individual words and phrases loose from their syntactical contexts, and by using them as points of departure for speculative flights, Strether and Maria Gostrey transform talk into a vehicle for the free play of imagination's expansive tendencies. But where in *The Ambassadors* do we encounter a represented conversation remotely like the exchange in which Kate and Densher acknowledge and confirm the trap they are setting for Milly? The passage at first bears a superficial resemblance to Strether's conversational mode, with Densher probing and exploring the possible implications of Kate's rather cryptic statements about the "line" he should take with Mrs. Stringham:

"You can tell her anything you like, anything whatever."

"Mrs. Stringham? I *have* nothing to tell her."

"You can tell her about *us*. I mean," she wonderfully pursued, "that you do still like me."

It was indeed so wonderful that it amused him. "Only not that you still like me."

She let his amusement pass. "I'm absolutely certain that she wouldn't repeat it."

"I see. To Aunt Maud."

"You don't quite see. Neither to Aunt Maud nor to any one else." Kate then, he saw, was always seeing Milly much more, after all, than he was; and she showed it again as she went on. "*There*, accordingly, is your time."

She did at last make him think, and it was fairly as if light broke, though not quite all at once. "You must let me say that I *do* see. Time for some thing in particular that I understand you regard as possible. Time too that, I further understand, is time for you as well."

"Time indeed for me as well." And encouraged visibly by his glow of concentration, she looked at him as through the air she had painfully made clear. Yet she was still on her guard. "Don't think, however, I'll do *all* the work for you. If you want things named you must name them."

He had quite, within the minute, been turning names over; and there was only one, which at last stared at him there dreadful, that properly fitted. "Since she's to die I'm to marry her?"

It struck him even at the moment as fine in her that she met it with no wincing nor mincing. She might for the grace of silence, for favour to their conditions, have only answered with her eyes. But her lips bravely moved. "To marry her."

"So that when her death has taken place I shall in the natural course have money?"

It was before him enough now, and he had nothing more to ask; he had only to turn, on the spot, considerably cold with the thought that all along − to his stupidity, his timidity − it had been, it had been only, what she meant. Now that he was in possession moreover she couldn't forbear, strangely enough, to pronounce the words she hadn't pronounced: they broke through her controlled and colourless voice as if she should be ashamed, to the very end, to have flinched. "You'll in the natural course have money. We shall in the natural course be free."

"Oh, oh, oh!" Densher softly murmured.

"Yes, yes, yes." (20, 224–25)

"If you want things named you must name them": like the novel as a whole, the lovers' talk shrinks steadily toward an unflinching confrontation with "the specified." The almost liturgical repetitions in which their conversation culminates enact and ratify a definite, determinant choice. Far from employing language in a playful or "poetic" sense – as a means of freeing abstractly possible significances from the specific and limiting meaning contingent upon syntactical closure – Kate and Densher together pronounce and repronounce the names of things, the defining, predicative terms which complete their "statement" and confirm the concrete reality of the particular scheme they have chosen to carry out. In *The Ambassadors*, conversation usually helps Strether in his efforts to evade the truth, or at least to delay the necessity of facing facts; but here, as at other critical points in *The Wings of the Dove* – most notably in the scene where Densher succeeds in forcing Kate to agree to come to his rooms, and again in the novel's final pages, where each of the lovers makes and affirms a final, irrevocable decision – talk resolves itself into a drama of conscious commitment, into a solemn ceremony, a pledge or an oath-taking, that signals the characters' assumption of responsibility for what they are doing.

There are, of course, other kinds of conversation in *The Wings of the Dove*, episodes, especially between Kate and Milly, where talk "seems more to cover than to free their sense" (20, 139–40). Though Densher wishes "to keep her where their communications would be straight" (20, 19), his relationship with Milly is marked by frequent crises that find him terrified of speaking, for fear that the wrong word "might prove for him somehow a pledge or a committal" (20, 295). And I do not mean to suggest that the characters in *The Wings of the Dove* are uniformly and consistently poised for naming names, for forthright action, or that they never seek to evade or postpone decisions. The exchange in which Kate and Densher confirm their plot against Milly emerges from a long and "cryptic" (20, 223) conversation, and the decision they acknowledge therein is one for which they have long evaded responsibility. Milly's readiness to face alternatives is exemplary precisely because it distinguishes her from the others. Kate's refusal to recognize any incompatibility between her love for Densher and her dream of material ease – "I shall sacrifice nobody and nothing, and that's just my situation, that I want and that I shall try for everything" (*19*, 73) – and Densher's casuistical attempt simultaneously to deceive Milly and to assure himself that he is doing nothing of the kind, constitute clear instances of the failure to confront the specified and to choose, and demonstrate the tragic consequences contingent upon such failure. What makes these evasions so different from Strether's self-blinding, dilatory tactics is James's manifest recognition – a recognition which the novel's insistently dramatic texture invites us to share – that they *do* entail consequences, whether or not the characters acknowledge them: in *The Wings of the Dove*, the avoidance of choice is itself a form of choosing, and doing nothing – as Milly perceives at Aunt Maud's party – is a definitive act.

In a brilliantly executed scene that marks a crucial station in his developing relationship with Milly, Merton Densher, a passive, wavering Jamesian hero who resembles Strether in a number of respects, begins himself to understand that every moment involves defining choices. Much to his own discomfort, Densher finds himself choosing where his intention has been to avoid all decision, acting where he has sought only to do nothing at all. Following Kate's suggestion, he has come to call on Milly "in the name of compassion," full of pity for the little American girl who may be seriously ill; but

it was the very possibility of his betraying a concern for her as one of the afflicted that she had within the first minute conjured away. She was never, never – did he understand? – to be one of the afflicted for him; and the manner in which he understood it, something of the answering pleasure that he couldn't help knowing he showed, constituted, he was very soon after to acknowledge, something like a start for intimacy. When things like that could pass people had in truth to be equally conscious of a relation. It soon made one, at all events, when it didn't find one made. (*20*, 73–74)

In an instant, the comfortably polite and distanced stance of charity Densher has envisioned for himself is exploded and replaced by a real and deepening involvement. Milly acts, as she always does, deliberately and aggressively, by setting the terms for their intercourse. But Densher, though he lacks her forceful intention and volition, is also acting; he chooses to act by acknowledging, accepting and admiring her terms, and is henceforth conscious of his own engagement with Milly in the making of a relation.

Densher's nervousness at finding himself caught up in actions and choices redoubles when Milly turns the tables, displaying her own compassion for the young man whose love for Kate Croy is, she believes, unrequited:

he began to see that if his pity hadn't had to yield to still other things it would have had to yield quite definitely to her own. That was the way the case had turned round: he had made his visit to be sorry for her, but he would repeat it — if he did repeat it — in order that she might be sorry for him. His situation made him, she judged — when once one liked him — a subject for that degree of tenderness: he felt this judgment in her, and felt it as something he should really, in decency, in dignity, in common honesty, have very soon to reckon with.

Indeed, the reckoning is not long in coming; moments later, Densher realizes that Milly's "beautiful delusion" and "wasted charity" are "preparing for him as pretty a case of conscience as he could have desired, and one at the prospect of which he was already wincing":

since it was false that he wasn't loved, so his right was quite quenched to figure on that ground as important; and if he didn't look out he should find himself appreciating in a way quite at odds with straightness the good faith of Milly's benevolence. *There* was the place for scruples; there the need absolutely to mind what he was about. If it wasn't proper for him to enjoy consideration on a perfectly false footing, where was the guarantee that, if he kept on, he mightn't soon himself pretend to the grievance in order not to miss the sweet? Consideration — from a charming girl — was soothing on whatever theory; and it didn't take him far to remember that he had himself as yet done nothing deceptive. It was Kate's description, his defeated state, it was none of his own; his responsibility would begin, as he might say, only with acting it out. The sharp point was, however, in the difference between acting and not acting: this difference in fact it was that made the case of conscience. He saw it with a certain alarm rise before him that everything was acting that was not speaking the particular word. "If you like me because you think *she* doesn't, it isn't a bit true: she *does* like me awfully!" — that would have been the particular word; which there were at the same time but too palpably such difficulties about his uttering. (*20*, 75–77)

The knowledge that he *is* now acting — not only in the sense of pretending but also in the more literal sense of making and implementing decisions — closes in around Densher like an ever-tightening net. Each attempt to evade brings a deeper involvement; the slightest gesture takes on the terrifying gravity of an "act . . . never to be recalled or recovered" (*20*, 391), and propels him toward still further choices and actions and involvements. And in particular, every word and every silence begins to carry with it the "responsibility" of choosing. Thus when Densher, in a stumbling effort to direct the conversation away from its unsettling focus on the nature of his relationship with Kate, remarks to Milly, "I don't feel as if I knew her − really to call know," Milly's response − "Well, if you come to that, I don't either!" − brings him up sharply.

The words gave him, as soon as they were uttered, a sense of responsibility for his own; though during a silence that ensued for a minute he had time to recognize that his own contained after all no element of falsity... And before he spoke, and before Milly did, he took time . . . for feeling how just here it was that he must break off short if his mind was really made up not to go further. It was as if he had been at a corner − and fairly put there by his last speech; so that it depended on him whether or no to turn it. The silence, if prolonged but an instant, might even have given him a sense of her waiting to see what he would do. (*20*, 86)

The responsibilities inherent in the act of speech are most obviously apparent in those crisis situations where the need for acknowledging the specified, naming the names, or pronouncing the particular word is unavoidable. But in an atmosphere where doing nothing is itself a determinant act, even the most casual words become deeds, replete with consequences for which the speaker is wholly accountable. When Susan Stringham, having discovered Milly gazing "into gulfs of air" from the edge of an Alpine precipice, stands "as motionless as if a sound, a syllable, must have produced the start that would be fatal" (*19*, 124), her terror at the possibility speech might realize provides a literal analogue for a situation that arises repeatedly throughout the novel. Whether it be Milly's reluctance to admit to Mrs. Stringham that she "likes" Merton Densher − "the speech," James tells us, "that was to figure for her . . . as the one she had ever uttered that cost her most" (*19*, 226) − or Kate and Densher's growing fear of honest intercourse with each other, "as if there were almost danger, which the wrong word might start" (*20*, 382), or Densher's virtually paralyzing awareness that a careless remark to Milly might shatter her fragile equilibrium, James consistently imbues his characters with an acute sense of the ominous power they wield by speaking.

The source of that power lies in the simple fact that words, in *The*

Wings of the Dove, are never spoken in a vacuum; because the novel's multiple-consciousness form recognizes and validates the reality of *other* subjectivities, speaking is stripped of the playful, irresponsible, often solipsistic qualities that characterize its practice in *The Ambassadors*. With Milly there "waiting to see what he would do" (or more precisely, what he would *say*), it is impossible for Densher to blind himself to the consequences his words entail, or to postpone indefinitely the need "to go further" by once again breaking the silence. Thus when Milly invites him to accompany her in her carriage, Densher hesitates once more before responding, feeling, "with a vengeance, that he must do either one thing or the other." But after "waiting for some moments, which probably seemed to him longer than they were . . . because he was anxiously watching himself wait," he realizes that "he couldn't keep that up for ever; and since one thing or the other was what he must do, it was for the other that he presently became conscious of having decided": "I'll go with you," he tells Milly, "with pleasure. It's a charming idea." By the time Milly retires to dress for the excursion, "he was quite round it, his corner" (*20*, 88–89).

In its nearly compulsive propensity for resolving the abstract multiplicity of consciousness into the concrete singleness of enacted choice, the scene adumbrates the novel's essential rhythm; James's treatment of Milly and Densher's intercourse demonstrates clearly the extent to which the balance and relationship between the inner process of consciousness and the surface reality of events has shifted, as compared to *The Ambassadors*, towards an emphasis on events. In *The Ambassadors*, actual events matter mainly insofar as they provide successive points of departure for Strether's imaginative expansions and transformations. But *The Wings of the Dove* stresses the manifest appearances of the events themselves, the unadorned actuality of what the characters say and do; imagination's inner "world of thought" (*19*, 79) is now important primarily to the extent that it feeds those events and issues in action. In this context, ideas and motives and intentions which exist only as desire, which fail to emerge from the abstract being of consciousness into the concrete becoming of action, have a tendency to vanish into insubstantiality; whereas what is enacted, what is spoken, even when it is a pretense, takes on the full power of a reality. Densher is perhaps already sensing this when he winces at the responsibility implied by his remark that he doesn't really know Kate.

Because his words have observable effects on Milly and evoke in her consequent responses, they wield the force of a truth – speaking the words *makes* them, in an almost insidious way, true.

The only reality – as Densher will belatedly come to understand – is an action. When he arrives for the visit with Milly which we have been examining, Densher is "really" motivated by his love for Kate: he has come out of loyalty to her and her "design,"[⁴] determined "not to give away the woman [he] loved, but to back her up in her mistakes" (*20*, 77). It is in fact this secret motive that encourages him in his repeated attempts to deny to himself his own accountability for what he is doing there on the spot. Thus when Milly leaves to dress and Kate unexpectedly comes to call, Densher is hypocritically insistent: "It's not *I* who am responsible for [Milly]," he tells Kate. "It seems to me it's you" (*20*, 91). But much later, in Venice, long after he has repeated his visit to Milly, and knowing now how one visit spawns another and still another, Densher reassesses these first hours with the American girl, and realizes how little Kate had mattered to what was happening between Milly and himself:

He had more than once recalled how he had said to himself even at that moment, at some point in the drive, that he was not *there*, not just as he was in so doing it, through Kate and Kate's idea, but through Milly and Milly's own, and through himself and *his* own, unmistakeably. (*20*, 186)

By the operation of what he felt at the time as "a force absolutely resident in their situation" (*20*, 80), Densher and Milly have enacted a relation, a reality – have made a difference. At this juncture, Densher is still deeply in love with Kate. But Kate willfully absents herself – she departs abruptly before Milly finishes dressing, and thus leaves the field of action to Milly and Densher. And what is absent cannot be engaged in acts of love, can only be imagined as the object of desire. Love is always an action, and action is a mode of presence. And so when "Milly, three minutes after Kate had gone, returned in her array – her big black hat [and] her fine black garments" (*20*, 95) – the intimacy which she and Densher are engaged in creating, through their words, their awkward silences, the myriad choices involved in their simply being there together, is already on the way to becoming a reality in which Kate Croy has no place. The scene has resolved itself into the present actuality of what is happening between them, an actuality which comes perilously close to realizing Kate's cautionary words to

Densher, uttered – as she leaves Milly's room – in response to his demand that she swear she loves him: "Here? There's nothing between us here" (20, 94). As if to prove her words false, Densher moves to embrace Kate; but she checks his advance, and "by the time he had dropped her hands he had again taken hold, as it were, of Milly's. It was not, at any rate, with Milly he had broken" (20, 95).

Densher is frightened and paralyzed by the thought that his actions and words can invest his pretended interest in Milly Theale with the power of reality. By going through the motions of falling in love with Milly, he *is*, he fears, doing just that – a phenomena he finds as appalling as Hamlet finds "monstrous" the palpably *real* grief of the player who, in acting out Hecuba's lament for Priam, "but in a fiction, in a dream of passion," can "force his soul . . . to his own conceit," while he himself, with the goad of "a dear father murdered," remains passive and silent (*Hamlet*, 2.2.560–69). What Densher fears is what Strether hates and, with all the intensity of his desire, rejects: the sheer, often brutal power of action, even when it is utterly divorced from the beautiful ideals of consciousness, to determine reality. Milly Theale also knows that power; for she is engaged in acting out, despite the urgency of her desire to live, the terrible reality of her own dying. But as we have seen, Milly accepts and even wills her own fate; and she is determined to fulfill what Freud identifies as the essential wish of every living organism – "to die only in its own fashion" (18:39). Possessed of a fully tragic vision, Milly is thus in a position to recognize the productive potentiality of action, and to see that its power can be used to realize what the desiring consciousness can only imagine. If Densher resembles Hamlet, then Milly may be said to evoke young Fortinbras, the existential hero whom Hamlet ultimately comes to admire and emulate, the

> delicate and tender prince
> Whose spirit, with divine ambition puffed,
> Makes mouths at the invisible event,
> Exposing what is mortal and unsure
> To all that fortune, death, and danger dare,
> Even for an eggshell. (4.4.48–53)

Milly, of course, fights not for a patch of ground but for Merton Densher. But though she loads this rather unworthy vessel with all the vastness of her desire to live, she also sees – with a clarity no previous Jamesian character comes close to matching – that she can fulfill her desire only if she succeeds in engaging this man, not as he might be but *as he is*, in the conjoined acts of loving and accepting love.

Milly's greatest weapon in her heroic struggle to win Densher is her knowledge that even the slightest action possesses the power to alter reality and make a difference. From the beginning of her strange courtship of Densher, she is aware of his secret motive, recognizes that he loves Kate Croy; but in terms of what she is about, that motive matters little. Although Milly at one point becomes caught up in an extended interior exploration of the multiplicitous possibilities comprised by the "question" of Densher's feelings for Kate, she soon realizes how irrelevant this "world of thought" is to her chosen course: "it was at this point that she saw the smash of her great question complete, saw that all she had to do with was the sense of being there with him" (*19*, 300). It should be noted here, however, that Milly is not, in this or in any other instance, implicated in the type of deliberate self-blinding to facts so marked in Strether. She does not shrink from acknowledging that Densher loves Kate. And she is not guilty – as some critics have tried to paint her – of deceiving herself about Kate's love for Densher.[1] Rather, and more straightforwardly, she has been tricked, as James himself insists in what must be considered, by virtue of its unadorned directness, one of the most significantly uncharacteristic sentences he ever composed: "So Milly Theale was successfully deceived" (*20*, 69). Milly's basic tactic is then, simply, a matter of "being there with him." The essence of her strategy is to seek Densher's love by involving and implicating him in what she at one point calls "her reality" (*20*, 158), and to demonstrate her love for him by entering into *his* reality, by "doing – that is [by] being – what he liked in order perhaps only to judge where it would take them" (*20*, 255). Milly thus sets out to realize her desire – to make it love – through decisive actions of every magnitude, from the most trivial conversational responses to the elaborate performances required for her Venetian grand manner. Strether, like the *writer* who predominates in *The Ambassadors*, sees every moment as significant for the possibilities that might be read into it. But Milly shares the plot-oriented perspective of the *author* of *The Wings of the Dove*; she is aware of herself at every instant as implementing choices, whether she is merely reacting with disproportionate enthusiasm to Densher's embarrassed small talk about "the scenery in the Rockies" (*19*, 301), or is, in a bolder stroke, aggressively pressing him to invite her to his rooms. These acts, and a thousand others like them, become Milly's life-line. And when, dressed all in white and acting under the influence of "some supreme idea" (*20*, 214), she descends the grand staircase of the Palazzo Leporelli, "comes down" to join her friends in the resplendent reality she has imagined and created – it is her last appearance in public, and her fullest expression both of her desire to live and of the unique fashion in which she has chosen to die – Milly is essentially attempting, and not without success, to overwhelm Densher with the "embodied poetry" (*20*, 217) of her magnificent style.

Once Kate and Mrs. Lowder have departed Venice, leaving him to remain alone with Milly, Densher becomes painfully, inescapably aware of the sheer reality-making power exerted by Milly's slightest actions. He now knows without equivocation that

> it was neither Kate nor he who made his strange relation to Milly. . . Milly herself did everything – so far at least as he was concerned – Milly herself, and Milly's house, and Milly's hospitality, and Milly's manner, and Milly's character, and perhaps still more than anything else, Milly's imagination. . . Something incalculable wrought for them – for him and Kate; something outside, beyond, above themselves, and doubtless ever so much better than they. (*20*, 239)

Day by day, through the progressive accumulation of actions and their consequences, Milly's insistent "doing" has invested her relation with Densher with more and more of the reality she had imagined possible. Densher's initial pity for Milly and his amused appreciation for her quaint American qualities have changed into respect and admiration for her quiet courage, and that admiration in its turn has given way to a kind of adoration that already verges on love. Now "he was mixed up in her fate, or her fate, if that should be better, was mixed up in *him*" (*20*, 252). And paradoxically, by acting, by drawing him into her fate and entering into his, Milly begins to restore to Densher what he has been so ruefully aware of lacking in his relation with Kate: a sense of *his* own power. His life mixed up with Milly's in the dailiness of intercourse and interaction, his consciousness acutely attuned to "her deep dependence on him," Densher finally sees that "her pass was now . . . just completely his own . . . Anything he should or shouldn't do would have close reference to her life, which was thus absolutely in his hands. . . It was on the cards for him that he might kill her" (*20*, 252–53). He can kill Milly – can also help her to live; but for Kate, whose absence is now complete, he can do nothing.

Milly's last and most powerful act – an act so forceful that it reaches from beyond the grave to determine the lovers' doom – leads Densher to a full and responsible acceptance of the fateful power resident in his own acts and choices. By leaving him her fortune, even though she now knows the truth of his engagement to Kate, Milly is once again seeking to win Densher's love by demonstrating her own passion and generosity. But if she succeeds – though too late – in making Densher love her, it is, I think, primarily because she has given back to him a sense of his own power and manhood. Densher has all along been conscious of his entrapment within "a circle of petticoats," has from the beginning felt ashamed at the emasculated role he has consented to play; at one especially humiliating juncture he expresses his relief that "there were no male witnesses": "he shouldn't have liked a man to see him" (20, 209). Milly's gift both enables and forces Densher to choose and enact the course he has always guessed to be the only honest and productive and manly one: to force Kate, in her turn, to decide between her love for him, as he is, and her dream of fortune.

We might say that Milly's act – confirmed in the direct speech of her Christmas letter to Densher – embodies a kind of grace through which he learns that he can, like her, will his own fate. And Densher himself ultimately feels that he has been somehow redeemed – "forgiven, dedicated, blessed" (20, 343) – through the agency of that grace. But those critics who see in Milly's final choice evidence of a "divine" or "supernatural" power, who read her bequest as "the smile of Beatrice," as a Christ-like work of forgiveness or an expression of some transcendent moral authority, succeed only in robbing her act of its remarkable existential power and its entirely human courage.[2] Milly's faith is all in herself, and the only thing she believes in is the inevitability of her own death. In leaving her fortune to the man who has betrayed her, Milly does – heroically, and with her last breath – what she has always done: uses the finite interval of her life to seek the fulfillment of her desire, the realization of her vision of loving and being loved. Milly, to put it simply, acts from her desire; indeed, she forges a reality-altering alliance between desire and action. And in creating her, James has taken a decisive step away from his obsessive fascination with the kind of excessive, powerless imagination he portrays in the novels leading up to and including *The Ambassadors*. What Strether "sees" – the proliferating realm of possibilities he imagines – maintains no effective commerce with the real; the figures projected by his desire remain unnecessary to the basic syntax of what is happening. But Milly integrates desire and reality, figure and syntax, through repeated, predicative acts of choice. And though she does not fully realize her dream, she succeeds in restoring to life and to James's fictional universe the sense that desire *can* attain concrete fulfillment, that it can become love: her efforts, as Laurence Holland so eloquently puts it, have "render[ed] the world not redeemed but redeemable" (327). *The Wings of the Dove* thus manifests a new willingness and ability on James's own part to fashion a productive link between imagination and reality, to mediate between the inner life of consciousness and the facts of the objective world. But this renewed commerce between the heretofore sundered realms of desire and actuality brings in its wake not only a concrete potential for fulfillment, but also a real potential for irretrievable loss. Strether, we know, protects himself against loss by adopting a mode of "living" that refuses to risk anything; he preserves intact the beauty and infinitude of his abstract potentiality precisely because he never tries to realize any particular possibility. In a world where what is imagined can be made real, however, the opposite process is equally valid: what is real can, if it is not acted upon, be unmade, can wither into a merely figurative kind of existence.

The latter transformation is the one Kate and Densher choose, albeit unconsciously, to enact. Their mutual love, which James is at great pains to substantiate as vibrant and passionate in the opening chapters of the novel, vanishes into the might-have-been of desire, into the archetypal Jamesian reality of the missed chance. All the time that Densher and Milly are together making a relation he and Kate are, apart, unmaking their own. Densher instinctively grasps what is happening, and with "an exasperation, a resentment, begotten truly by the very impatience of desire" (*20*, 175), he repeatedly challenges Kate to abandon her impossible and indecisive vision of having "everything" – "everything's nothing," he tells her at one point (*19*, 68) – and to join him in enacting the love which is, he fears, unravelling with every passing moment. When Kate first intimates her intention to sacrifice neither Densher nor Aunt Maud's money, he responds by asking her to "settle it by our being married tomorrow – as we can, with perfect ease" (*19*, 72). Later, in reaction to Kate's suggestion that he "go to see Milly," he bursts out imploringly, "Why won't you come to *me*?" (*20*, 29). At a still later point, in Venice, sensing himself at a corner which, once turned, will make an irreparable difference in his relationships with both women, he literally begs Kate to join him in decisive action: " 'Why not have done with it all and face the music as we are?' It broke from him in perfect sincerity. 'Good God, if you'd only take me!' " (20, 198). The explicitly sexual urgency which informs these outbursts – an urgency rarely approached in James's earlier fiction – should give pause to those critics who have judged him incapable of representing physical desire. For sexual passion is an important (if subliminal) component of Milly's desire to live; and in Densher we encounter the thwarted sexuality of a man who feels "in fact a kind of rage at what he wasn't having" (20, 175). As Kenneth Graham has written, "there is no book by James more sexually *aware* than this one, in the continual ache of specific desire and disturbance that fills Densher's broodings" (177).

Brooding, however, even brooding as intense as Densher's, is not action. Again and again he allows Kate to evade his pressure, while he acquiesces in *her* strategy of patience and postponement. And when he finally does succeed in forcing Kate to come to him in his rooms – she capitulates when he threatens to leave Venice and abandon her design – the resulting consummation is less an act of love than a desperate attempt to create a token or a symbol of a relationship that has already been drained of its reality. Though his "idea" has been converted "from a luminous conception into a historic truth," that truth has little to do with the daily, mutually-willed intercourse and interaction of love. Rather, what Densher has purchased, and at great cost, is a hollow image of a desire that is now – with Kate returned to London – wholly divorced from any possibility of concrete satisfaction. Instead of filling his want he has intensified it still further: "what had come to pass within his walls lingered there as an obsession." A helpless captive of his own desire, Densher begins to infuse his abode with the hermetic, timeless, venerative atmosphere of a museum dedicated to the memory of something that is, like the Bronzino portrait Milly views at Matcham, "dead, dead, dead" (19, 221). The recollection of his union with Kate – "it was just once" – thus

played for him . . . the part of a treasure kept at home in safety and sanctity, something he was sure of finding in its place when, with each return, he worked his heavy old key in the lock. The door had but to open for him to be with it again and for it all to be there; so intensely there that, as we say, no other act was possible to him than the renewed act, almost the hallucination, of intimacy. Wherever he looked or sat or stood . . . it was in view as nothing of the moment, nothing begotten of time or chance could be, or ever would;

it was in view as, when the curtain has risen, the play on the stage is in view, night after night, for the fiddlers. He remained thus, in his own theatre, in his single person, perpetual orchestra to the ordered drama, the confirmed "run" . . . No other visitor was to come to him. (20, 235–37)

In the aestheticizing impulse at work here, in Densher's effort to remove the present from its historical context and to transform it into the timeless space of memory and desire, we discern a pattern familiar to us from *The Ambassadors*. Indeed, Densher here seems to be on the verge of losing himself in the labyrinth of desire's perpetual wanting. For like Strether, Densher at this moment is prevented from acting in any real sense by the intensity of his own remembering and imagining; he cannot make love, can only fantasize or "hallucinate" intimacy. But significantly, the illusory, abstract "presence" projected by his desiring consciousness collapses abruptly when it is confronted with Milly Theale's real presence. Milly, in stark contrast to Kate, asks Densher if she can visit him, once again demonstrating her willingness to enter into his reality. And though he at first tries to put her off, fearing that the incursion into his sanctuary of a "third person" will break "the spell of what he conceived himself – in the absence of anything 'to show' – to be inwardly doing" (20, 237), it takes only a few minutes of conversational engagement with Milly before "his great scruple suddenly broke, giving way to something inordinately strange, something of a nature to become clear to him only when he had left her. 'You can come,' he said, 'when you like.' " What Densher has experienced is "the drop, almost with violence, of everything but a sense of her own reality" (20, 246–47). Milly's small but real act of love penetrates and destroys Densher's private theater of desire; and "to destroy it was to destroy everything, to destroy probably Kate herself . . . " (20, 242).

Densher's inability to blot out those things "begotten of time" with a timeless image adumbrates the fundamental problem inherent in the design which Kate proposes and to which Densher reluctantly adheres. At the heart of the lovers' strategy lies a wishful belief that they and their love can remain immune from what James calls "the workings of time" (20, 346); they assume – at least Kate does – that they can, even after so much intervening experience, end where they began, and still be as they were. What they fail to recognize is the very nature of love, so beautifully expressed by Shakespeare in *Hamlet*, when Claudius responds to Laertes' umbrage at the suggestion that his filial grief may be only "the painting of a sorrow,/A face without a heart." It is not, Claudius insists,

> that I think you did not love your father,
> But that I know love is begun by time,
> And that I see, in passages of proof,
> Time qualifies the spark and fire of it.
> There lives within the very flame of love
> A kind of wick or snuff that will abate it,
> And nothing is at a like goodness still
>
> That we would do
> We should do when we would, for this "would" changes,
> And hath abatements and delays as many
> As there are tongues, are hands, are accidents,
> And then this "should" is like a spendthrift sigh,
> That hurts by easing. (4.7.108–23)

By postponing the enactment of their love, by failing to do what they "would" *when* they would, Kate and Densher have sacrificed the passion which motivated in the first place their flawed strategy of secrecy and delay. Real love, moreover – and for James this represents a crucial recognition – must consist in repeated acts of sexual, moral and spiritual intercourse; it cannot be contained in an isolated, symbolic consummation, just as it cannot – as we will discover – be put in a "golden bowl." For love is a becoming *in time*, a process of ebb and flow, of living and dying, in which every encounter between two lovers alters both the individuals and their relationship, thus necessitating further efforts to rediscover and reaffirm the changing reality of the other.

At first glance Kate's awesome consistency, her determination to stick to her plan, might appear to suggest a most un-Strether-like resemblance to Mrs. Newsome's masculine power and unwavering conviction, or even an affinity with Maud Lowder herself, the "very essence" of whom, as Kate explains to Densher, "is that, when she adopts a view, she – well, to her own sense, really brings the thing about, fairly terrorizes, with her view, any other, any opposite view, and those with it who represent it" (*20*, 188). But *The Wings of the Dove* is not, like *The Ambassadors*, a novel of neat, perhaps all too easy contrarieties. And mixed in with Kate's aggressive determination to pursue and gain what she wants is a fatal inability, very much akin to

Strether's, to believe that the "everything" she desires is subject to the changes wrought by time and by her own actions in time. Kate's refusal to accept the workings of time is linked to her unwillingness to confront the reality of death. Unlike Milly, Kate shrinks from every intimation of mortality; the possibility that the American girl might die is, Kate tells Densher, "a matter in which I don't want knowledge." Rather, she prefers to focus with Densher on "the selfish gladness of their young immunities. It was all they had together, but they had it at least without a flaw – each had the beauty, the physical felicity, the personal virtue, love and desire of the other" (20, 54–55). Kate blinds herself to Milly's death and dying because she does not believe in her own vulnerability, and because she will not acknowledge that love is bound by time. Thus for James, as Dorothea Krook has perceived, "a final incapacity for love is intimately linked with a final incapacity to confront the fact of death" (213).

But Kate and Densher's love is not immune from "the hunger of time" (20, 395) and the coming of death. Their unwillingness to accept what Milly knows as "the rift within the lute" (19, 175) – to acknowledge "the great smudge of mortality across the picture" (20, 298–99) – is itself the fatal "flaw" that undermines and consumes their love. And when they are at last reunited in London, after months of separation, their meeting is dominated from the first by an inescapable sense of the extent to which they and everything connected with them has changed:

It was in seeing her that [Densher] felt what their interruption had been, and that they met across it even as persons whose adventures, on either side, in time and space, of the nature of perils and exiles, had had a peculiar strangeness. He wondered if he were as different for her as she herself had immediately appeared.

Because they have chosen to act separately, they have become strangers. Kate's "difference" – part of which, significantly, is "her striking him as older in a degree for which no mere couple of months could account" – confirms for Densher "the reality of what had happened – of what, in fact, for the spirit of each, was still happening": "if she was different," he now understands, "it was because they had chosen together that she should be" (20, 313–14). And as the scene unfolds, James invokes once again the contractive, resolving movement which informs the novel throughout, and which is oppressively tangible in these closing chapters. The lovers' conversation, slowly but persistently, leads them back not only to an unflinching acknowledgment of the specified, brutal facts – from which even Kate can no longer keep away – of Milly's "so consciously and so helplessly dying" (*20*, 317), but also to a sense of their own "responsibilities" (*20*, 322) and profound involvement in the dying girl's reality, and to a chilling awareness of the chasm that has opened up between them.

For Densher has "come to tell her everything" – "to the last syllable" (*20*, 314). He has come to speak the particular word. And as he recites the naked facts of what has happened in Venice – Lord Mark has revealed their secret to Milly, she has "turned her face to the wall" (*20*, 323) and then, in a final act of courage, has summoned her betrayer for one last encounter – the lovers' difference erupts through the fragile surface of their talk with violence. Upon learning that Milly had received Densher at the last, Kate speculates aloud whether it wouldn't

"have been possible then to deny the truth of the information? I mean of Lord Marks's."

Densher wondered. "Possible for whom?"

"Why for you."

"To tell her he lied?"

"To tell her he's mistaken."

Densher stared – he was stupefied; the 'possible' thus glanced at by Kate being exactly the alternative he had had to face in Venice and to put utterly away from him. Nothing was stranger than their difference in their view of it. "And to lie myself, you mean, to do it? We *are*, my dear child," he said, "I suppose still engaged." (*20*, 322–23)

When Kate presses her point, Densher responds with what might at first glance appear to be a hypocritically belated moralism:

"If I had denied you moreover," Densher said with his eyes on her, "I'd have stuck to it."

She took for a moment the intention of his face. "You mean that to convince her you'd have insisted or somehow proved – ?"

"I mean that to convince *you* I'd have insisted or somehow proved – !"

Kate looked for her moment at a loss. "To convince 'me'?"

"I wouldn't have made my denial, in such conditions, only to take it back afterwards."

With this quickly light came to her, and with it also her colour flamed. "Oh you'd have broken with me to make your denial a truth? You'd have 'chucked' me" – she embraced it perfectly – "to save your conscience?"

"I couldn't have done anything else," said Merton Densher. "So you see how right I was not to commit myself, and how little I could dream of it. If it ever again appears to you that I *might* have done so, remember what I say." (*20*, 325–26)

That Kate and Densher should find the sharpest point of their difference in their divided sense of what it means to speak seems to me entirely appropriate. For though Densher still loves Kate – in the next chapter he will once again press her to marry him immediately, "to *do* it and announce it as done" (*20*, 348) – he has now consciously and fully adopted the mode of action which Milly has revealed to him. His change is in fact demonstrated by his insistence on the need for a public confirmation of love through the direct speech of an announcement. For what he had begun to sense so many months earlier when he flinched at the responsibilities involved in talking to Milly has become inescapably clear: that the act of speaking to another necessitates a commitment to the truth of the words we utter, and that speech possesses the power to determine the real, whatever the secret motives that lie behind our words might be. Speaking the particular word, naming the names, is morally imperative, even – perhaps especially – when those names bring us face to face with ugliness and mortality and vulgarity, "as throughout, in love," James tells us, "the names of things, the verbal terms of intercourse," are "vulgar" (*20*, 7). But James intends no simplistic equation between lying and wrong-doing. Indeed, *The Wings of the Dove* is a veritable web of lies – lies told by Milly and Sir Luke and Mrs. Stringham as well as by Kate and Densher, and in which James himself is deeply implicated. James's more subtle point is that the only kind of lie worth telling is one we are prepared to will into truth through determined action – the kind of lie Milly Theale embraces when she tells herself and the world that she can live if she wants to.

Densher's new sense of speaking as choosing and acting – a leitmotif sounded again in a minor key when, having lied to Mrs. Lowder that he is on his way to church, he is suddenly moved to fulfill his lie out of a desire "not to have wasted his word" (*20*, 361) – reflects, I believe, something crucial in James's attitude toward the act of speech he himself has performed in writing *The Wings of the Dove*. For James speaks here in order to make and complete a reality, not merely – as is so often the case in the experimental novels of the nineties – to imagine unrealizable alternatives to a reality he only wishes to resist and evade and postpone. In so doing, he invests his tragedy with a conception of language and of literary style that contrasts suggestively with the parallel conception embodied in *The Ambassadors*. James speaks in the earlier novel almost exclusively as a *writer*, consistently suppressing the *author*'s end-oriented authority and responsibility in favor of the *writer's* desiring, irresponsible freedom. Language, as it is employed in *The Ambassadors*, becomes a mode of intransitive figuration that is less interested in grasping and confirming the real presence of events than in granting an imagined presence to the absence of desire that lies at the novel's core. The result is a style that is ultimately only an excess. For despite its elaborate beauty and amplitude and its magnificent reach towards an endlessly proliferative infinitude – indeed, precisely because of these qualities – James's web of words in *The Ambassadors* is in some sense as insubstantial and inessential as the illusory world Strether builds in his imagination. And by using his stylistic talents to participate uncritically in the evasions and irresolutions of Strether's desire, James not only allows his character to escape the responsibilities of choosing, but also turns aside from his own duty to confirm and judge the concrete choices by which Strether commits himself to living in and by his desire. In Lukács's terms, James fails to distinguish between Strether's abstract and concrete potentiality.

Desire *is* a mode of living; but it is not life itself. In *The Ambassadors*, however, James – deliberately or unconsciously? – blurs the distinction, for reasons that bring us back to our beginning sense that the novel, in contrast to *The Wings of the Dove*, presented James with all too easy a task. *The Ambassadors* may indeed constitute "the best, 'all round,' of [his] productions." But its very roundness and perfection, not to mention its ease of composition and facility of style, suggest that James had not yet achieved the authority needed for a fully honest and responsible approach to a character whose decisions in life so closely resemble his own. *The Wings of the Dove* is neither round nor perfect, and it was, by James's own testimony, one of the most difficult works he ever brought to fruition. The novel is centered around the presence of a plot, not the absence of desire, and its clotted, hesitant contractive style presses always towards the resolution of that plot, towards a naming of names and a grasp of the specified that makes it one of James's least pleasurable fictions, but also one of his most compelling. I am tempted to suggest that James was thinking of his own experience with *The Wings of the Dove* when, in an essay on Flaubert written simultaneously with the novel, he described the inherent ugliness and "bristling" qualities which characterize "our modern tongues," and which make of the stylist's "desired surface a texture pricked through, from beneath, even to destruction, as by innumerable thorns" (*LC*, 2:340).

The essay on Flaubert, in fact, to the extent that it reflects James's thinking about the nature and function of style as he worked on *The Wings of the Dove*, is an intriguing document. With great subtlety and obvious sympathy, James summarizes Flaubert's belief

that beauty comes with expression . . . and that we move in literature through a world of different values and relations, a blest world in which we know nothing except by style, but in which also everything is saved by it, and in which the image is thus always superior to the thing itself.

The passage describes an artistic creed that most critics would unhesitatingly conflate with James's own, and that accurately reflects, in my judgment, the aesthetic of desire and *writing* which informs *The Ambassadors*. But James goes on to voice a crucial reservation about Flaubert's unquestioning faith in style:

style itself moreover, with all respect to Flaubert, never *totally* beguiles; since even when we are so queerly constituted as to be ninety-nine parts literary we are still a hundredth part something else. This hundredth part may, once we possess the book – or the book possesses us – make us imperfect as readers, and yet without it should we want or get the book at all? (*LC*, 2:340)

The "hundredth part something else" is, simply stated, our need to engage with reality, to connect with life itself. And any work of art which attempts, as *The Ambassadors* does, to "save" us from life by means of style is, James seems to suggest, both fundamentally flawed and profoundly suspect.

The thorny surfaces that distinguish the style of *The Wings of the Dove*, like the difficulties and failures that for James marked the novel as a whole, provide a measure of his new willingness to accept and explore his own "hundredth part," to confront the facts of life, even the terrible fact of death and the vulgar facts of love, even, moreover, the personal facts of his own experience. With its dramatic form and contractive stylistic rhythms, the novel moves towards an embrace of reality rather than seeking to evade it; James speaks here less as *writer* than as *author*, not so much against death as towards it. His style can no more save the work from its own finitude – nothing, in fact, could be further from James's intention – than the "pervasive mystery of Style" (*20*, 203) Milly creates and elaborates in Venice can save *her* from the inexorable approach of death. The achievement of *The Wings of the Dove*, what can only be called its courageous success, lies elsewhere; it is perhaps nowhere more in evidence than in James's responsible use of his authorial power to represent and confirm the concluding series of choices through which Merton Densher determines his own complex fate.

I have already suggested that in telling Densher's story James is consciously returning to that period in his youth when, for a variety of reasons including his failed relationship with Minny Temple and best summarized by his public assertion, in *Notes of a Son and Brother*, that he had during these critical years suffered a "horrid even if an obscure hurt" (*NSB*, 298), he chose to withdraw from life into his art. Now Densher enacts a similar withdrawal: faced in the end with the alternatives of marrying Kate on Milly's money or living on in solitary communion with the dead girl's spirit, he deliberately chooses to disappear into the absence of his "love" for Milly's memory, to retreat into a private theater of memory and desire not unlike the one imaged by his rooms in Venice, but where thoughts of Milly rather than of Kate occupy center stage. His consciousness of Milly is now

all his own, and [Kate] was the last person he might have shared it with. He kept it back like a favourite pang; left it behind him, so to say, when he went out, but came home again the sooner for the certainty of finding it there. Then he took it out of its sacred corner and its soft wrappings; he undid them one by one, handling them, handling *it*, as a father, baffled and tender, might handle a maimed child. But so it was before him – in his dread of who else might see it.

With Milly no longer present to save him from himself, and Kate incapable of entering into what is now, for all intents and purposes, his "reality," Densher's "inward doing" becomes an obsession. And in particular, his consciousness hovers over the letter – destroyed unopened by Kate – in which Milly has presumably announced the legacy that represents her final act of love:

then he took to himself at such hours, in other words, that he should never, never know what had been in Milly's letter. The intention announced in it he should but too probably know; only that would have been, but for the depths of his spirit, the least part of it. The part of it missed for ever was the turn she would have given her act. This turn had possibilities that, somehow, by wondering about them, his imagination had extraordinarily filled out and refined. It had made of them a revelation the loss of which was like the sight of a priceless pearl cast before his eyes – his pledge given not to save it – into the fathomless sea, or rather even it was like the sacrifice of something sentient and throbbing, something that, for the spiritual ear, might have been audible as a faint far wail. This was the sound he cherished when alone in the stillness of his rooms. He sought and guarded the stillness, so that it might prevail there till the inevitable sounds of life, once more, comparatively coarse and harsh, should smother and deaden it – doubtless by the same process with which they would officiously heal the ache in his soul that was somehow one with it. (*20*, 395–96)

With its focus on an absence – the never-to-be-known "turn" Milly *might* have given her gift – its figurative filling out of "possibilities," and its acute sense of imagination's helpless vulnerability in the face of life's "coarse" and "inevitable sounds," the passage shows Densher sinking into something very much like Strether's desiring mode. Indeed, the paradox of the novel's closing movement is that Densher, possessed at last of Milly's belief in the power of action, and keenly aware of the finitude of "the time, whatever it might be, long or short, in store for him" (*20*, 390), in effect chooses to become Lambert Strether. Densher ends where Strether begins *and* ends – imprisoned in the might-have-been of a wasted youth, lost in the labyrinthine memory of an unfulfilled desire that will, we feel, continue to dominate his consciousness, and that will determine for him a life of endless wanting. We might even say that in willing and witnessing Densher's drama, James is filling in and fleshing out the history – so evasively presented in *The Ambassadors* – of "the far-away years" (*21*, 52) when Strether suffered *his* obscure hurt and made his own fateful decisions. James intimates that Strether's sense of having failed to live and the consequent intensity of his desiring consciousness are the result of the events – the death of his wife and son – of his lost youth, and of his determinant responses to those events, especially his unwitting "sacrifice" of his "little dull boy" (*21*, 84) to his obsessive grief for his wife. But this story – the story of how Strether came to live in and by his desire – is barely touched on in *The Ambassadors*; the details of Strether's past are accorded far more attention in James's *Notebook* entries and in his preliminary sketch for the novel than in the finished work itself – a sign perhaps that James here deliberately suppressed material which too closely mirrored his own losses and failures and choices.

We thus return once more to our sense that James risked and

therefore gained little in writing *The Ambassadors*, that the novel was for him all too easy a success. By failing to hold Strether responsible for the choices and actions through which he has made his sterile, solipsistic fate, James demonstrates his own unwillingness to grapple with the difficult personal truths that inform his novelistic "lie," and evades his own responsibility – both authorial and human – to confront and affirm the sources of his "beautiful fictions" in the "harsh" and "coarse" realities of his experience. *The Wings of the Dove*, in contrast, evokes the mood of Yeats's "The Circus Animals' Desertion," where the poet in old age returns to old themes, tracing the roots of his "masterful images" to their origins in "the foul rag-and-bone shop" of his own heart and life, and acknowledging what he has given up by assuming the power to create them. For if Densher is the young Strether, he is also the young James. Like the novelist, Densher misses his chance for love. And in his final veneration for the memory of the woman he failed to love in life, Densher clearly echoes James's own strange satisfaction, so many years before, at seeing Minny Temple "translated from this changing realm of fact to the steady realm of thought" (*L*, 1:226).

But it is the way in which James chooses to tell Densher's story that really defines the novel's difference from *The Ambassadors* and from all the desiring fictions of the preceding years. For while we do participate in Densher's evasions, we also stand outside them, and see them for the decisive, determinant actions they are. Through our experience of the novel's insistently dramatic form, we come to understand that Densher's fate is the product of his own choices. We know moreover that his final response to life's pain and ugliness and fatal futility – his withdrawal into the sterile safety of desire – is uniquely his own: that it is *the* potentiality *he* has chosen to realize. For James offers us Milly's example as well as Densher's; in the midst of the novel's tragic waste of passion stands the heroic figure of a young woman who in the face of a hurt that is anything but obscure can still summon the courage to perform the act of love. By dramatizing both Milly's way *and* Densher's, James affirms the possibility of love as an alternative to the mode of desire. And though he eschews the simplifications of a rigid, Woollett-like moral scheme, he does invite us to compare and judge these alternatives, and to measure the capacity of each for achieving the human happiness which is the end of all action. If we ultimately judge Milly's mode of living to be superior, it is not because she is better than

Kate or Densher, but because she succeeds in investing life with the fullest value it can possess – the purely human and existential value of having been chosen. It is precisely such value that James grants the lives of his characters through his formal and thematic insistence on the reality of their choices, and that he restores to his own life by his decision to tell, at last and to the end, the long-brooded-over story of *The Wings of the Dove*. For James achieves "the rout of evasion" (*20*, 20) that Densher seeks but fails to attain. Through the courageous speech-act embodied in this most difficult of his fictions, the "master" discovers within himself the authority and humility to accept responsibility for the life-determining choices he made in his youth, and to affirm the fate he has chosen.

6 *The Golden Bowl* (I): The resumption of authority

> Let it not your wonder move,
> Lesse your laughter; that I love.
> Though I now write fiftie yeares,
> I have had, and have my Peeres;
> Poets, though divine are men:
> Some have lov'd as old agen.
>
> Ben Jonson, "A Celebration of Charis"

All of which amounts doubtless but to saying that as the whole conduct of life consists of things done, which do other things in their turn, just so our behaviour and its fruits are essentially one and continuous and persistent and unquenchable, so the act has its way of abiding and showing and testifying, and so, among our innumerable acts, are no arbitrary, no senseless separations. The more we are capable of acting the less gropingly we plead such differences; whereby, with any capability, we recognize betimes that to "put" things is very exactly and responsibly and interminably to do them. Our expression of them, and the terms on which we understand that, belong as nearly to our conduct and our life as every other feature of our freedom.

> Henry James, The Preface to *The Golden Bowl*

James's last completed novel is also his first to end in the achievement of love. With the renewal of Maggie Verver's marriage – an action completed and emblematized in the embrace of husband and wife which brings *The Golden Bowl* to a close – James attains at last what Stephen Spender has eloquently described as the discourse "of a person who, profoundly with his whole being, after overcoming great inhibition, has accepted the idea of people loving" (194). Yet this extraordinary, belated affirmation of love has consistently troubled James's critics. Held fast in her Prince's arms, "his whole act enclosing her,"

Maggie may know "at last really why – and how she had been inspired and guided, how she had been persistently able, how to her soul all the while it had been for the sake of this end" (*24*, 367–68). But James's commentators have rarely shared her conviction. Indeed, faced with an end which seems to overturn the basic assumptions of James's long career, some of his most sympathetic readers have been driven to dismiss *The Golden Bowl* as "decadent" if not "morally absurd," and to judge the work a failure (Matthiessen, *The Major Phase*, 102; Sears, 222).[1] In novel after novel, James had denied his characters the experience of fulfilled passion; how then are we to account for Maggie Verver's attainment of love, or to explain James's arrival – at the age of sixty – at a stage where he could represent and celebrate such an outcome?

Critics have generally agreed that *The Golden Bowl* is the biggest problem child in James's novelistic nursery – a consensus inextricably linked to an equally pervasive belief that the novel is, in some undeniable sense, his summa. Critical response to the novel, though varied, reflects a persistent dilemma. On the one hand, few readers would be quick to quarrel with Dorothea Krook when she remarks that "the experience of *The Golden Bowl* . . . presupposes all that has gone before in James's poetic experience, and [that] all that went before implies what is unfolded here" (233). Indeed, in the novel's repeated echoes of familiar Jamesian themes, and in the self-consciously baroque rhythms of its prose, many have heard a deliberate valedictory note, not unlike that sounded by Shakespeare in *The Tempest*. Yet on the other hand, admiration for *The Golden Bowl* has often been grudging, precisely because the resolution the novel offers to James's career has in fact struck many critics as wrong, anomalous and therefore unconvincing in light of his previous work. With its unprecedented representation of enacted love, the novel seems disjoined from James's *oeuvre* as a whole; it is as if a career composed almost entirely in a minor key has suddenly come to rest on a resounding major chord. Nearly forty years ago F.O. Matthiessen set the tone for much subsequent opinion about James's last novel when he complained about "the unsatisfactory nature of the positive values" in *The Golden Bowl*. "In both *The Ambassadors* and *The Wings of the Dove*," Matthiessen asserts, "we are moved most deeply by loss and suffering"; *The Golden Bowl*, in contrast, with its transformation of James's habitual renunciatory ending into a consummatory embrace, suffers from the fact that

"James was less convincing in imagining success" (*The Major Phase*, 101).

Not surprisingly, given its final position in the Jamesian canon, *The Golden Bowl* has often invited a kind of attention insufficiently attuned to the uniqueness of its inner dynamic and truth. Philip Weinstein, who shares Matthiessen's doubts about the novel, has displayed an instructive honesty in discussing the problems presented by Maggie and the Prince's final embrace: "it is only candid to say," he admits, "that an unqualified assent to this conclusion . . . would call into question my reading of James" (169). In Weinstein's view – and here again he is close to Matthiessen – "passion and intimacy" are always "imagined, not encountered, by James's heroes" (199). But *The Golden Bowl*, which moves beyond the perpetual yearning of desire to a representation of enacted love, obviously overturns this formula. Weinstein acknowledges that James's last novel "attempts – unlike anything else he wrote – massively to integrate the requirements of the imagination with 'the conditions of life,' to dramatize their fusion," and recognizes that "uniquely, *The Golden Bowl* seems to focus upon the realization, not simply the imagination, of life's possibilities" (166). He senses too that James is trying "once and for all to redress the failure to live . . . that culminates in Milly Theale" (199). But like Matthiessen, Weinstein finds this intention to be at odds with fundamental aspects of the novelist's sensibility and temperament. James, he argues, views the Prince and Maggie's achievement of love with a hopelessly contradictory mixture of "ostensible assent" and "implicit rejection" (194). The result is a novel that is often "confusing," occasionally "grotesque," and finally unsatisfactory (199).

Matthiessen and Weinstein's uneasiness about the conclusion of *The Golden Bowl* appears to be twofold. In part they are puzzled by the "positive" content of the novel's resolution – by the embrace, and by the achieved experience of "passion and intimacy" it represents. This is, as Leon Edel remarks, "James's only novel in which things come out right for his characters" (*The Master*, 191). And in this regard there is little if anything in the novelist's prior work to prepare us for the "success" embodied in *The Golden Bowl*. But Matthiessen and Weinstein are also perplexed by the mode in which the events leading up to and including the novel's conclusion are presented; this is what the latter critic has in mind when he speaks of the narrative's focus "upon the realization, not simply the imagination, of life's possibilities." Now

Weinstein, I submit, is mistaken when he asserts that this focus is manifested "uniquely" in *The Golden Bowl*. For *The Wings of the Dove*, which James completed just six months before he began writing *The Golden Bowl*, is very much concerned with "the realization . . . of life's possibilities," even if the possibilities its characters choose to realize are those of failure and loss and isolation. Indeed, I think the critics would be less skeptical about *The Golden Bowl* if they would only recognize that the crucial changes in James's vision and aesthetic which permit the novel's stunning conclusion had, in large part, already been effected in *The Wings of the Dove*.

The wide differences between *The Ambassadors* and *The Wings of the Dove* — especially in regard to James's attitude towards "life's possibilities" — need to be reemphasized here. In *The Ambassadors* — the novel, significantly, around which Weinstein shapes his entire reading of James — everything is imagined, nothing realized. The repressed reality which surfaces in the end to obliterate the figurative world projected by Strether's desire is in no sense made by him; it is, rather, simply a set of facts which he has determinedly evaded, and which James, through his own formal choices, has helped him to evade. For all his imaginative "freedom," Strether is powerless to determine the outcome of events: he can delay that outcome by envisioning illusory alternatives to it, but cannot contribute to it — cannot in any way create the end he suffers. But if *The Ambassadors* closes with a mere collapse of desire's figurative "presence," *The Wings of the Dove* ends with the resolving force of a tragic denouement. The truth that closes in around Kate and Densher — their recognition that they will never again be as they were — is only partly comprised of previously suppressed facts; more importantly, it represents a reality which is the culminating issue of their own actions and of Milly's, an end which they have made and which they are, at the last, acutely conscious of having made. For unlike Strether, Kate and Milly and Densher are more than their desire; they are actors in a drama of realization, and the decisive participation of each is crucial in determining the particular end which comes to be through the unfolding of the novel's plot.

Thus the tragic resolution of *The Wings of the Dove* bears only a superficial resemblance to the renunciatory collapse which terminates *The Ambassadors*. And when Matthiessen persists in linking these two novels — and what he sees as their moving depiction of "loss and suffering" — in opposition to the "positive values" and "success" represented in *The Golden Bowl*, he is looking only at the surfaces of events, not at the way in which those events are experienced by James, his readers, and his characters. Weinstein makes a similar mistake when he sees in Milly Theale a reprise of Strether's "failure to live." We feel no real sense of loss or failure as Strether's embassy unwinds, for he loses only his illusions – his desiring fantasies of a life and love he never had – and "fails to live" only insofar as he fails even to try. Indeed, *The Ambassadors* "ends" where it began, in the absence – the might-have-been – of what is in truth an endless wanting. But *The Wings of the Dove* concludes, in the strongest sense of that word, on a note of full presence. The novel is, in Aristotle's formula, "an imitation of an action that is complete" (*Poetics*, 65). So while the content of this conclusion is overwhelmingly negative – and here the loss, of life *and* of love, is palpably real – its form is positive, in that it validates the existential choices by which the characters have created the tragedy which destroys them. Seen in this light, the denouement of *The Wings of the Dove* has far more in common with what Ruth Bernard Yeazell has called the act "of literary as well as literal enclosure" (the Prince's embrace of Maggie) that concludes *The Golden Bowl* (100) than it does with the passive irresolution which marks the end of *The Ambassadors*.[2] The collapse of Strether's wholly imaginary adventure is at best a negation. But the closing pages of *The Wings of the Dove* prepare the ground for Maggie Verver's success by embodying, in René Girard's words, "not only a historical but an individual possibility finally and triumphantly actualized" (309). The unexpected affirmation of *The Golden Bowl* issues at least in part from James's enactment, in the preceding novel, of what Girard has defined as the essence of all strong novelistic conclusions: "a successful effort to overcome the inability to conclude" (308).[3]

As we have seen, the strong conclusion of *The Wings of the Dove*, with all of its painfully realized possibilities, is partly a function of our knowledge – a knowledge we share with the novel's characters and with James himself – that Milly Theale is going to die. There can be, in this work, no Strether-like evasions of "the point where the death comes in." And I will return to this theme again in connection with *The Golden Bowl*, for while death is not literally present in the novel, I believe that the success its resolution encompasses is predicated upon Maggie Verver's coming-to-terms with the fact that she and her father must die to and away from each other, and upon James's own mature acceptance of the death which he *as author* must inflict upon himself *as writer*. More immediately, however, we should recall that James's shift in focus from imagined to realized possibilities, from abstract to concrete potentiality, is closely linked to his adoption of a multiple-consciousness narrative structure for *The Wings of the Dove*. By directing our attention away from relations as they are figured by desire toward relations as they are actualized in the world, the novel's rotation of viewpoints allows us to judge Kate and Milly and Densher, to hold them responsible for what they say and don't say, do and don't do, for the choices they make, the actions they complete, and the consequences they effect; it is what authorizes not only the strong conclusion of *The Wings of the Dove*, but also James's tentative but genuine affirmation of Milly Theale's quest for love. For in restoring the individual's power and responsibility to choose his own fate and make his own end, James discovers a vantage from which he can glimpse for the first time the possibility of a kind of love that moves beyond the helpless, solipsistic wanting of desire.

James returns to the multiple-consciousness form in *The Golden Bowl*, and he does so, I believe, with the clear and conscious intention of realizing once and for all the possibility he had discerned amidst the tragic waste of *The Wings of the Dove*. Having found a way to liberate Milly Theale from the prison-house of desire, James can now allow Maggie Verver to consummate her predecessor's dream of loving and being loved. Significantly, *The Golden Bowl* marks the first instance in many years of James's having employed the same narrative structure in two successive novels;[4] after nearly a decade of frantic experimentation, James seems to have found the compositional key for which he had been searching. For what we see transpiring in *The Golden Bowl* is the result of James's mastery, not only of the technical problems implied by the multiple-consciousness form – many critics have contrasted the awkwardness of the point-of-view shifts in *The Wings of the Dove* to the exquisite balance and classical symmetry of this last novel[5] – but also of the ethical and existential consequences, the opportunities as well as the responsibilities, it entails. What had been in the earlier novel a difficult, sometimes clumsy experiment in a new narrative mode becomes in *The Golden Bowl* the triumphant expression of a sure and deliberate artistry. In *The Wings of the Dove* we watch James as he encounters, struggles against, and ultimately comes to terms with the implications of his formal choice; we witness his painful, halting, profoundly reluctant acquiescence in the death of desire's illusory freedom, infinitude and originality. But *The Golden Bowl* is informed throughout by a full understanding and conscious acceptance of those implications; less concerned with regret for the beautiful illusions which have been lost, it focuses rather on the new range of positive representational possibilities opened to James's fiction by the multiple-consciousness form. Revealingly, James's only direct discussion of the multiple-consciousness structure occurs in his Preface to *The Golden Bowl*. There he begins his commentary on the novel by noting in it "the still marked inveteracy of a certain indirect and oblique view of my presented action"; he finds in the book yet another example of what he calls

> my preference for dealing with my subject-matter, for "seeing my story," through the opportunity and the sensibility of some more or less detached, some not strictly involved, though thoroughly interested and intelligent, witness or reporter, some person who contributes to the case mainly a certain amount of criticism and interpretation of it. (*AN*, 327)

One immediately wonders, of course, how James can reconcile his depiction of either the Prince or Maggie with this model of an observer who is "more or less detached" and "not strictly involved." But the novelist quickly goes on to acknowledge that, in *The Golden Bowl*, "there is no other participant . . . than each of the real, the deeply involved and immersed and more or less bleeding participants," and to admit, moreover, that the most revealing aspect of the center-of-consciousness technique in *this* novel is "the manner in which it betrays itself" (*AN*, 328). Elsewhere in the Prefaces, James cites his penchant for approaching his narratives through the mind of some "intense perceiver" as the main source of continuity in his large and diverse *oeuvre* (*AN*, 70). But here he recognizes that by multiplying the number of reflective centers, he has not extended or elaborated the premises of the novel of consciousness, but rather overturned them altogether; he knows that he has "betrayed" the form which most critics still see as virtually synonymous with his achievement, and is prepared, moreover, to acknowledge the benefits of that betrayal. For the new form, as it operates in *The Golden Bowl*, effectively doubles the value and function of James's characters, especially, he insists, of the Prince and Maggie. The former,

> in the first half of the book, virtually sees and knows and makes out, virtually represents to himself everything that concerns us – very nearly (though he doesn't speak in the first person) after the fashion of other reporters and critics of other situations. Having a consciousness highly susceptible of registration,

he thus makes us see the things that may most interest us reflected in it . . . and yet after all never a whit to the prejudice of his being just as consistently a foredoomed, entangled, embarrassed agent in the general imbroglio, actor in the offered play. The function of the Princess, in the remainder, matches exactly with his; the register of her consciousness is as closely kept . . . as his own . . .; the Princess, in fine, in addition to feeling everything she has to, and to playing her part in just that proportion, duplicates, as it were, her value and becomes a compositional resource, and of the finest order, as well as a value intrinsic. (*AN*, 329)

The passage provides a theoretical recapitulation of James's practical experience in writing *The Wings of the Dove*. With considerable pride in what he calls the novel's "handsome wholeness of effect" (*AN*, 329), James accurately traces the process by which the multiple viewpoints of *The Golden Bowl* explode once and for all the myth that his characters are "not strictly involved," and restore to each of them the status of a "value intrinsic" – the reality of being not only a "compositional resource," but also "an actor in the offered play." James is in error, of course, when he ignores the importance of those crucial sections in Book I where we plunge, if only briefly, into the minds of Charlotte Stant, Adam Verver, and the Assinghams. Like the Prince and Maggie, the novel's other characters manifest a concrete dramatic presence that cannot be found in those shadowy figures – Chad and Madame de Vionnet, for example – who live only in someone else's imagination. And even Fanny Assingham, arguably the least involved of the participants, is agonizingly aware that she shares responsibility for the events that unfold. But James's curious and seemingly willful "misreading" of *The Golden Bowl* in this regard – he first asserts that Book I is narrated entirely through the Prince's consciousness, and then, after half-heartedly admitting to a lapse in consistency in the case of Mrs. Assingham, pronounces "this disparity in [his] plan" to be "but superficial" (*AN*, 329–30) – is suggestive; for while the multiple-consciousness structure necessarily entangles Charlotte, Adam and the Assinghams in the "general imbroglio," James clearly wants to emphasize the effect of his formal choice on his presentation of Maggie and the Prince's relationship. The novel, he writes,

abides rigidly by its law of showing Maggie Verver at first through her suitor's and her husband's exhibitory vision of her, and of then showing the Prince, with at least an equal intensity, through his wife's, the advantage thus being that these attributions of experience display the sentient subjects themselves at the same time and by the same stroke with the nearest possible approach to a desirable vividness. It is the Prince who opens the door to half our light upon Maggie, just as it is she who opens it to half our light upon himself; the rest of our impression, in either case, coming straight from the very motion with which that act is performed. (*AN*, 330)

In one important sense, then, our answer to the question of Blake's which James echoes in the novel's title – can love be put in a golden bowl?[6] – must be affirmative. For as a formal construct, *The Golden Bowl is* capable of containing a representation of the enacted reality, the realized possibility, which I have called love. "For one human being to love another: that," Rilke once wrote, "is perhaps the hardest of all our tasks, the ultimate, the last test and proof, the work for which all other work is but preparation." And it is this "more human love" – "the love that consists in this, that two solitudes protect and touch and greet each other" (Rilke, 52–60) – that James has belatedly discovered a means of embodying in his last novel. The real "advantage" of the multiple-consciousness form, its supreme potentiality, first, glimpsed by James in the preparatory work entitled *The Wings of the Dove*, is that it restores to James's fictional universe that "dialectic between the individual's subjectivity and objective reality" which Lukács insists is the necessary ground of any true realism (24), and without which the depiction of actual human intimacy is impossible.

For love requires the full presence of "two solitudes" – of a true self and a true other – neither of which can be realized or represented in the framework of the single-consciousness narrative. If the world of *The Golden Bowl* were coextensive with Maggie Verver's consciousness of that world, she would become, as Strether does, a parodic inversion of Sir Thomas Browne's God – an oddly powerless divinity whose circumference would be everywhere, her center nowhere.[7] Strether can possess no "value intrinsic," no concretely realized dramatic presence; he is only the endless absence of his desire. Freed by the form of *The Ambassadors* from the necessity of reconciling his inner vision with an outer reality – in the single-consciousness narrative, the distinction evaporates – he can never achieve the solid personal and historical identity which Milly Theale assumes when she chooses to embrace her tragically limiting fate. And if James had imposed this kind of structurally-determined solipsism on *The Golden Bowl*, Maggie would be unable to attain the existential "solitude" which Rilke affirms as the basis for love. As for the Prince, seen wholly through Maggie's vision, he could have only the simulacrum of an identity. Like Madame de Vionnet, who "lives" only in Strether's imagination of her, he would exist only as an image of his wife's desire. He too would be an absence, a chimera incapable of solitude. Thus had James chosen to turn his back on the lessons of *The Wings of the Dove*, the conclusion of *The Golden Bowl* would be nothing but a shade embracing a shade. For the single-consciousness form can encompass only that "imagination of loving" which I have called desire. Without the dialectic of subject and object provided by the multiple points of view in *The Golden Bowl*, Maggie could love her Prince only in Stendhal's romantic mode: "every time she meets her lover she [would] enjoy, not the man as he really is, but the wonderful inner vision she has created" (54).

Stendhal's formula in fact offers an accurate description of Maggie's relationship with her husband in the novel's early stages. The Prince understands from the first that Maggie, like most Americans in James, is "almost incredibly romantic" (*23*, 11); and he perceives, with some foreboding, that she values him primarily *as* a prince, as an exotic, romantic image – fed by her vague knowledge "of the history, the doings, the marriages, the crimes, the follies, the boundless *bêtises*" of his ancestors – that is really her own creation. But "there are," he playfully protests to Maggie just a few days before their marriage, "two parts to me." And it is the other part, "very much smaller doubtless, which, such as it is, represents my single self, the unknown, unimportant – unimportant save to *you* – personal quantity. About this," he tells her, "you've found out nothing" (*23*, 9). At this point Maggie's relationship to Amerigo is fundamentally one of desire; she cannot touch his solitude, for she sees in him what Strether sees in Marie de Vionnet – not the reality of another human being, but the imagined embodiment of an aristocratic worldliness, power and style which she herself lacks. But the form of *The Golden Bowl* also permits James to show Maggie engaging her husband – his "other part," his "single self" and "personal quantity" – in an entirely different kind of relationship, even, ultimately, in the reciprocal enactment of love. Because we see both characters through each other's eyes as well as through their own, each possesses the double value of subject *and* object. And as James recognizes in the Preface, the result of this doubling is that even the mere process of seeing the other becomes a vivid encounter with his or her presence, an action – the novelist speaks of "the very motion with which that act is performed" – that reveals the seer's presence in "the same stroke" that it "opens the door" into the other's reality and being. One thinks in this connection of Milly's inviting herself to visit Merton Densher in his rooms – an almost literal attempt to open a door into the loved one's solitude. And we need only recall James's famous image of the "house of fiction," with its "million" apertures, each one the prison from which a detached "pair of eyes" observes the human scene – "they are," James tells us, "but windows at the best, mere holes in a dead wall, disconnected, perched aloft; they are not hinged doors opening straight upon life" (*AN*, 46) – to realize just how radically James is revising the bases of his art.[8]

Thus in its focus upon the realization rather than the imagination of possibilities, James's last novel emerges not as an inexplicable anomaly in his career, but as a natural out-growth of the discoveries he had made in writing *The Wings of the Dove*. Centered, like the earlier novel, in its plot, not in the desiring inner vision of any one "pair of eyes," *The Golden Bowl* possesses the capacity to embody the concretely actualized human potentiality of love. But capacity is one thing, the exercise of capacity another. *The Wings of the Dove* is equally a novel of plot, a novel where the reality of enacted love *could* be represented, and yet it ends in deprivation, isolation, and the failure of love. Having explained the positive mode of the success which culminates *The Golden Bowl*, we are still faced with the positive content of that success – with the bald fact that, as Edel says, "things come out right" for James's characters as they never have before. The obvious answer here is that James selected a comic plot rather than a tragic one for *The Golden Bowl*. But as I hope to show through a more detailed analysis of the shape of that plot, this apparently simple observation – that James in effect *chose* to tell a different kind of story in *The Golden Bowl* – is really an insight with far-reaching implications for our understanding of James's final conception of the art of fiction.

If the structural value which James places on the plot of *The Golden Bowl* finds its only precedent in *The Wings of the Dove*, the pattern of events which forms that plot will strike many readers as much more familiar. Like so many of James's protagonists – one thinks of Isabel Archer and Milly Theale, of Strether and Maisie – Maggie Verver is cruelly betrayed by the very people in whom she has most placed her confidence. And when she discovers the terrible truth of the Prince and Charlotte's adultery – when she sees at last "the horror of the thing hideously *behind*, behind so much trusted, so much pretended, nobleness, cleverness, tenderness" (*24*, 237) – Maggie suffers the same fall into bitter knowledge experienced by Strether when he finally perceives the real nature of Chad and Madame de Vionnet's "virtuous attachment," and by Milly when she learns that Kate and Densher have all along been secretly engaged. In each of these instances, as elsewhere in James, the "innocent" eyes of the central character are opened to the reality of a sexually intimate relationship that has been deliberately concealed. Almost all of James's works are structured around the unveiling of *some* hidden truth, around the revelation, abrupt or gradual, but always devastating, of a secret – whether it be the illicit liaison of Gilbert Osmond and Madame Merle, the lurid skeleton in the Bellegarde family closet, or the mysterious "figure in the carpet" of Hugh Vereker's fictional art.

Tzvetan Todorov has seen in this last example a key to the underlying structure of Jamesian narrative. James, Todorov argues, always posits "the existence of an essential secret, of something not named, of an absent and superpowerful force which sets the whole present machinery of the narrative in motion." And this motion, he points out, is typically "a double and, in appearance, a contradictory one. . . On one hand [James] deploys all his forces to attain the hidden essence, to reveal the secret object; on the other, he constantly postpones, protects the revelation – until the story's end, if not beyond" (175). As we have already seen in *The Ambassadors*, this second motive is often, for James, the dominant one. Neither Strether nor James wants the truth revealed, for its emergence will necessarily mean the collapse of the former's "inward adventure" – of his manifold imaginative possibilities, which the presence of *the* truth will invalidate – and an end to the latter's dream of an infinite *writing*. The Jamesian secret, as Todorov puts it, "is the text's logical origin and reason for being":

the absence of knowledge provokes the presence of the narrative. The appearance of the [hidden] cause halts the narrative; once the mystery is disclosed, there is no longer anything to tell. The presence of the truth is possible, but it is incompatible with the narrative. (147)

Todorov's last assertion is arresting, but far from inaccurate. For as the example of *The Ambassadors* clearly testifies, the text, *insofar as it is conceived as an embodiment of desire*, depends upon the absence of truth for its very existence. Strether is free to envision alternatives to "the poor actual" (*SBO*, 175) only so long as he remains ignorant of the facts; and James can continue to indulge his hero's imaginative flights – as well as his own penchant for textual play – only by postponing, through the expansive, dilatory processes of his *writing*, the revelation of the truth which, as the *author*, he already knows. The novelist guards his secret until the last possible moment in order to protect the fragile and ultimately illusory "presence" of desire's beautiful figures.

But the effect of this deliberate strategy of delayed disclosure is to deprive the revelation – if and when it does come – of any practical value for the protagonist. The truth emerges at last, but always "too late" to be of any use: the narrative is finished, and "there is no longer anything to tell." Intriguingly, however, Todorov's structural model breaks down in this regard when one attempts to apply it to *The Golden Bowl*. For in James's last novel the presence of truth *is* compatible with the presence of narrative. Maggie discovers the adulterers' secret with a full third of the novel still remaining; and her timely accession to what she calls "real knowledge" – her penetration of the secret contained by the golden bowl – becomes the authorizing and empowering basis of her successful effort to remake her marriage (*24*, 201). For all its "decorative grace," the golden bowl, "as a 'document,' somehow, [is] ugly" (*24*, 165). But "seeing herself finally sure, knowing everything, having the fact, in all its abomination, so utterly before her that there was nothing else to add" (*24*, 185), Maggie is delivered from her helpless, obsessive speculations about what *might* be happening between Charlotte and Amerigo. Even before she purchases the golden bowl from the Bloomsbury antiquary, Maggie senses the existence – although not the nature – of its secret. Like "some wonderful beautiful but outlandish pagoda," this secret "had been occupying for months and months the very centre of the garden of her life":

she had walked round and round it – that was what she felt; she had carried on her existence in the space left her for circulation, a space that sometimes seemed ample and sometimes narrow: looking up all the while at the fair structure that spread itself so amply and rose so high, but never quite making out as yet where she might have entered had she wished. She hadn't wished till now – such was the odd case; and what was doubtless equally odd besides was that though her raised eyes seemed to distinguish places that must serve from within, and especially far aloft, as apertures and outlooks, no door appeared to give access from her convenient garden level. The great decorated surface had remained consistently impenetrable and inscrutable.

At this point Maggie already has "ceased merely to circle and scan the elevation, ceased so vaguely, so quite helplessly to stare and wonder"; indeed, "she had caught herself distinctly in the act of pausing, then in that of lingering, and finally in that of stepping unprecedentedly near" (*24*, 3–4). But her helpless circling and staring and wondering – a nightmarish version of Strether's desiring process of vision – can ultimately cease only when she finds a door into the knowledge hidden within the pagoda, when she replaces the absent secret at the "centre . . . of her life" with the presence of the truth. The justly celebrated pagoda image, I might add, suggests once again that the "house of fiction" no longer offers an adequate metaphor for James's multiple-consciousness narrative art. For if Maggie serves as the "pair of eyes" through which we experience this scene, she also stands outside the house looking in, is already, in fact, on the verge of becoming an "actor in the offered play." And as she prepares to force an entry into the "outlandish" structure from which Charlotte and the Prince peer back at her through "apertures and outlooks," as she gathers her strength to break through the "dead wall" which separates her from her husband's solitude, she is also readying her knock at the "hinged door" which opens "straight upon life." Indeed, "she had knocked –

had applied her hand to a cool smooth spot and had waited to see what would happen. Something *had* happened; it was as if a sound, at her touch, after a little, had come back to her from within; a sound sufficiently suggesting that her approach had been noted. (*24*, 4)

Maggie finds her "access" to the truth through her encounter with the golden bowl – through the revelation of the crack concealed beneath *its* "decorated surface." And once she knows the worst, she is in effect released from the prison of her desiring consciousness. She finds herself "beautifully free" (*24*, 193): free not to imagine possibilities in Strether's mode, but to choose among them in Milly Theale's. Strether's "freedom" depends upon his ignorance; but Maggie's is grounded in knowledge, and thus involves not only an assumption of power, but also a recognition of "the responsibility of freedom" (*24*, 186). Face to face with "the horror of the thing hideously *behind*" the Prince and Charlotte's pretended "nobleness" and "tenderness," Maggie feels for herself "that temptation of the horribly possible," and understands that she can "sound out their doom in a single sentence" (*24*, 233). But if her new knowledge brings her the power to destroy, it also gives her the power – and the responsibility – to construct and create. This is the choice which Maggie ponders as she and her husband stand together, gazing in silence at the "shining pieces" of the "precious vessel" which Fanny Assingham has shattered by "dash[ing]" it boldly to the ground" (24, 179-82). The golden bowl is broken – its crack exposed, its secret revealed. And Maggie almost immediately begins to feel

within her the sudden split between conviction and action. They had begun to cease on the spot, surprisingly, to be connected; conviction, that is, budged no inch, only planting its feet the more firmly in the soil – but action began to hover like some lighter and larger but easier form, excited by its very power to keep above ground. It would be free, it would be independent, it would go in – wouldn't it? – for some prodigious and superior adventure of its own. What would condemn it, so to speak, to the responsibility of freedom – this glimmered on Maggie even now – was the possibility, richer with every lapsing moment, that her husband would have on the whole question a new need of her, a need which was in fact being born between them in these very seconds. (24, 186)

With her "conviction" – her sure knowledge of the truth – firmly beneath her feet, Maggie now possesses the freedom and power to choose and to act. And what she is already choosing to enact is the possibility of renewal – just as James is choosing to resume the story of the Prince and Maggie's marriage, to continue rather than to end the narrative which began with their wedding vows. "Something," James insists, "now again became possible for these communicants . . . something that took up that tale and that might have been a redemption of pledges then exchanged" (24, 180). For Maggie has realized that in penetrating the terrible secret of the golden bowl, in finding an entrance into the pagoda, she has also opened the door into her husband's inner being; she has touched for the first time Amerigo's "single self, the unknown . . . personal quantity" about which she has previously "found out nothing." Indeed,

hadn't she fairly got into his labyrinth with him? – wasn't she . . . in the very act of placing herself there for him at its centre and core, whence, on that definite orientation and by an instinct all her own, she might securely guide him out of it? (24, 187)

Having centered herself in the ugly but fully acknowledged truth, Maggie can offer herself as a "definite orientation" for her husband, can begin at last to engage him in the act of love.

Maggie thus acquires her knowledge *in time*, before it is too late, before the narrative is finished. And by giving her the chance to respond, freely and powerfully, to a truth that is no longer a secret, James is radically altering what had always been his basic narrative structure. But if this change is in itself suggestive, the way in which Maggie discovers the truth is even more revealing. The story of "the little Bloomsbury shopman" – who sells Maggie the golden bowl but then, having been taken with "his purchaser's good faith and charming presence" and feeling "a scruple rare enough in vendors of any class," returns to disclose the "flaw in her aquisition," and ultimately the flaw in her marriage (*24*, 222–26) – constitutes one of the most curious and unlikely bits of plotting in all of James's fiction. Maggie buys the bowl as a birthday present for her father; but the shopman, although he has "made a most advantageous bargain," hasn't "liked what he had done." Inspired by a mysterious sympathy for Maggie – "he *told* me," she tells the Prince, "his reason was because he 'liked' me!" – the *antiquario* writes and then visits her, revealing the crack in the bowl, "which would make it verily, as an offering to a loved parent, a thing of sinister meaning and evil effect," and intending to return part of her money. "It was after this that the most extraordinary incident of all, of course, had occurred": the shopman notices, in Portland Place, photographs of Charlotte and the Prince, and recalls that "he had made acquaintance with them, years before, precisely over the same article." Under Maggie's intense questioning, he remembers his impression of "the 'terms' on which his other visitors had appeared to be with each other," and produces his "conviction of the nature and degree of their intimacy under which, in spite of precautions, they hadn't been able to help leaving him. He had observed and judged and not forgotten. . . " Finally, he is able to pinpoint for Maggie the date of their visit, "positively, to a day – by reason of a transaction of importance, recorded in his books, that had occurred but a few hours later" (*24*, 222–25). Maggie thus learns of the Prince and Charlotte's prior relationship – their visit to the Bloomsbury shop predates her marriage – and so confirms her already aroused suspicions.

The whole business is, of course, "extraordinary," if not preposterous; the chain of coincidences which leads Maggie to her "real knowledge" is worthy of the creakiest Victorian melodrama. Maggie herself "had felt her explanation weak, but there were the facts and she could give no other" (*24*, 222); and the Prince, upon first hearing the tale, remarks that "the coincidence is extraordinary – the sort of thing that happens mainly in novels and plays" (*24*, 195). Indeed, throughout his recounting of this "so distinctly remarkable incident,"

James seems to be deliberately calling our attention to its absurdity, and to the clumsiness of his own plotting. He dwells especially on what is obviously the most far-fetched circumstance of all: "the difficulty in respect to the little man," "the question of his motive" (24, 222). The shopkeeper "had known conscientious, he had known superstitious visitings, had given way to a whim all the more remarkable to his own commercial mind, no doubt, from its never having troubled him in other connexions" (24, 223).

James's odd emphasis on the apparent inconsequence of the *antiquario*'s motive will seem less mysterious once we recognize, as Laurence Holland has, that the shopman is unmistakably a figure for James himself (345–46). When Charlotte and Amerigo enter the Bloomsbury shop, ostensibly in search of a wedding gift for Maggie, they encounter a man who is himself "the greatest curiosity they had looked at." Possessed of a "mute, but singularly coercive" manner, the dealer – in a manner which recalls the similarly authoritative and riveting glances of Gloriani and Dickens – immediately "fixe[s] on his visitors an extraordinary pair of eyes," somehow investing "their relation" with "a sort of solemnity." He is "clearly the master and devoted to his business"; and as Charlotte remarks, "He likes his things – he loves them. . . I think he would love to keep them if he could; and he prefers at any rate to sell them to right people." Despite "their due proportion of faint poetry," however, his "things" produce for the couple "no great force of persuasion." Yet as the antiquary offers his "heterogeneous" treasures for his customers' perusal, James suggests a deeper resonance:

Of decent old gold, old silver, old bronze, of old chased and jewelled artistry, were the objects that, successively produced, had ended by numerously dotting the counter where the shopman's slim light fingers, with neat nails, touched them at moments, briefly, nervously, tenderly, as those of a chess-player rest, a few seconds, over the board, on a figure he thinks he may move and then may not.

As Holland notes, James's own artistry is implicated here. For the novelist at this very moment is playing a game of chess, manipulating his characters, making them move or not move in ways that will determine the outcome of the game. More specifically, he is using his authorial power to set up the revelation which will come to Maggie later in the novel: with his "extraordinary pair of eyes," the dealer has "observed and judged," and he will not forget. And when he produces at last "a drinking-vessel larger than a common cup, yet not of exorbitant size, and formed, to appearance, either of old fine gold or of some material once richly gilt," the shopkeeper becomes an embodiment of James's controlling presence in the novel:

he handled it with tenderness, with ceremony, making a place for it on a small satin mat. "My Golden Bowl," he observed – and it sounded on his lips as if it said everything. He left the important object – for as "important" it did somehow present itself – to produce its certain effect. (*23*, 104–12)

In one sense the scene provides an almost literal manifestation of what James sees in his Preface to *The Golden Bowl* as his impulse "to get down into the arena and do my best to live and breathe and rub shoulders and converse with the persons engaged in the struggle" (*AN*, 328). More importantly, however, the shopkeeper's symbolic identity with the novelist helps to explain James's purpose in hinging his entire plot – and ultimately Maggie's achievement of love – on this odd character's unprecedented "scruple" and strange "sympathy" for the young woman: it demystifies what Maggie describes to her husband as "the wonder of my having found such a friend."

"I inspired him with sympathy – there you are! But the miracle is that he should have a sympathy to offer that could be of some use to me. That was really the oddity of my chance," the Princess proceeded – "that I should have been moved, in my ignorance, to go precisely to *him*." (*24*, 196)

Maggie discovers the adulterers' secret because James in effect wills that discovery by selling her his golden bowl. Like the *antiquario*, James has felt "conscientious visitings." And what has "perhaps most moved" both the novelist and his double is "the thought that she should ignorantly have gone in for a thing not good enough for other buyers"; "his having led her to act in ignorance was what he should have been ashamed of." The bowl "wasn't a thing for a present to a person she was fond of." But "if she would pardon, gracious lady as she was, all the liberties he had taken, she might make of the bowl any use in life but that one" (*24*, 224). James *has* taken "liberties" with Maggie, as any novelist must with his characters, no matter how "free" or "*disponible*" he wishes to imagine them: like the Prince and Charlotte, Maggie is a pawn in a game the artist alone controls. But James atones for his tyranny by releasing Maggie from her ignorance, even though his revelation requires an act of authorial intrusion as awkwardly obvious as that embodied in the vendor, "clearly the master," of the bowl. For all its polysemous symbolic value — and the interpretive possibilities it admits of are seemingly endless[9] — the golden bowl also produces its "certain effect": Maggie learns the truth, learns it in time that "she might make of it any use in life" that she chooses. James thus goes out of his way to accentuate the contrived nature of the plot which permits Maggie's triumph. He seems to be deliberately emphasizing the fictionality and artificiality of the experience represented in *The Golden Bowl* — an intention that is equally manifest in the ornate, rococo complexities of James's now fully-elaborated "later manner," in the fancifulness, sometimes bordering on absurdity, of the extended metaphors which permeate the text, and perhaps even in the novel's apparently conventional conclusion, which, "with its marriages reaffirmed and its couples neatly paired off," resembles, as Yeazell points out, "the closed structure of comedy" (125). But in calling our attention to his fiction's status as artifice, James is also proclaiming his own role as artificer. He is both wielding and self-consciously acknowledging his power *as the author* to shape and manipulate the fictional world he has created — is in fact celebrating his possession of an authority which he had previously tried to disguise or even to disavow.

Twenty years before he wrote *The Golden Bowl*, James published an essay in which he attacked Trollope for his "deliberately inartistic" and "pernicious trick of reminding the reader that the story he was telling was only, after all, a make-believe," and for his habit "of letting the reader know that [he] could direct the course of events according to his pleasure" (*LC*, 1:1343). Now James is not really denying the author's power to "direct the course of events" here so much as he is advocating an ostensibly realist aesthetic, one which requires a certain kind of novelistic reticence. Like Flaubert, James feels that "the artist must be in his work as God is in creation, invisible yet all-powerful" (quoted in Allott, 271).[10] But Jamesian realism — where reality is defined not by any given set of events, but by someone's consciousness of those events — shades imperceptibly into an aesthetic of desire. And if James's tendency to suppress the signs of his own authorial presence and power stems in part from his determination to create an effective illusion of reality, it also reflects another motive, more radical and, I think, more fundamental: an attempt less to disguise the author, than to eliminate him altogether. As I have argued elsewhere, James in his most extreme fictions of desire had dreamed of banishing the *author*, and all his authoritative knowledge and power, from the *writer*'s paradise of an infinite text. A book like *The Ambassadors* comes close to realizing Roland

Barthes's ideal of an endless, self-generating *écriture*, where the author is present only "as a 'guest,' " and where his "signature is no longer privileged and paternal, the locus of genuine truth, but rather, ludic" ("From Work to Text," 78). Indeed, by the time he embarked on his "major phase" novels, James had arrived at a style in which sentences, seemingly possessed of a will of their own, show less interest in conveying the author's intended meaning than in playfully exploring the connotative possibilities generated by their own surfaces; at a narrative syntax which mirrors that style by perpetually postponing predication – in effect staving off any conclusion – in order to protect the plot's abstractly infinite potential; and at a fictional art of desire which believes, or pretends to believe, that a narrative can unfold and develop in all freedom from any "paternal" or *a priori* purpose on the part of the author.

In the desiring text, the presence of the *author*, like the presence of the truth, is "incompatible with the narrative." It is precisely the *author*'s truths – his inescapable knowledge of the ends towards which sentences and stories and works of art are proceeding – which the *writer* attempts to evade with his strategy of "deliberate forgetting." But like the Bloomsbury shopman who figures his presence in the novel, that *author* of *The Golden Bowl* does not forget; at the critical moment, and with a fullness of intention made "all the more remarkable" by "its never having troubled him in other connexions," James ceremoniously exercises his authority, intervenes to disclose the empowering truth. As surely, if perhaps more subtly, than Trollope, James in *The Golden Bowl* reasserts his control over the make-believe world he has fashioned.[11] And I think the significance of James's striking resumption of authority – of his deliberate exercise of that authority to reveal the truth to Maggie in time that it might be of some use to her – can only be fully grasped if we recognize that in most of his earlier works he had just as deliberately allowed his characters to "act in ignorance" until it was "too late," all the while evading his own responsibility for the "liberties" he was taking with them, and disclaiming his power to "direct the course of events according to his pleasure." Maggie's chance to live and love undoubtedly comes to her through an "unrealistic" chain of circumstance and coincidence that strains the limits of our credulity. But as several critics have noticed, James's plots had always been improbable and prone to melodramatic excess; the "geometry of destruction" – the phrase is Sallie Sears's (56) – in which James usually enmeshes his characters is as much "the sort of thing that happens mainly in novels" as the more generous plot which permits Maggie's success.[12] Sears in fact argues that

James's habitually destructive and life-denying plots embody a negative version of what the novelist himself, in the Preface to *The American*, defined as "the art of the romancer." For as surely and as "insidiously" as the fictions of any fabulist who ever wrote "of caravans, or of tigers," of "ghosts, or of forgers" or of "pistols and knives," James's unremittingly negative imaginations "cut the cable" which ties "the balloon of experience . . . to the earth," and to "the conditions which we usually attach to it" (*AN*, 32–34). Sears quite correctly sees James as "the most unsentimental of our great romanticists" in that "the unusual severity of the conditions that in fact attend the lives and possibilities of his characters . . . is itself a romantic phenomenon . . . not so much improbable as extraordinary and uncontrolled," as James says, "by our general sense of 'the way things happen.' " Sears thus finds in the excessively severe and "unusually restricted" conditions faced by James's characters the contours of a fictional design as deliberately ordered and artificially contrived as the most elaborately benign plots of any romancer. And indeed, James repeatedly places his fictional men and women in extremely limiting situations – he in fact surrounds them with a staggering and finally unrealistic array of barriers and obstacles and dead walls – which seem expressly designed to prevent them from realizing their desires, from loving or even from living. For all the breadth and intensity and beauty of his characters' imaginings, James never – or at least not until he feels his unprecedented "scruple" in regard to Maggie Verver – gives them a chance.

Intriguingly, when Sears characterizes James's fatalistic and obsessively "negative imagination" as romantic, she is following the novelist's own lead; though she does not pursue its implications, her reference to the Preface to *The American* is far from accidental. For James's famous attempt to locate "the dividing-line between the romantic and the real" (*AN*, 37) is occasioned by his own belated recognition that the plot of *The American*, especially insofar as it embodies the thwarting of Christopher Newman's chance for love by the Bellegardes, offers precisely that "disconnected and uncontrolled experience – uncontrolled by our general sense of 'the way things happen' – which romance alone more or less successfully palms off on us." Rereading *The American* some thirty years after he wrote it, James finds himself forced to admit that

the way things happen is frankly not the way in which they are represented as having happened, in Paris, to my hero. . . The great house of Bellegarde, in a word, would, I now feel, given the circumstances, given the whole of the ground, have comported itself in a manner as different as possible from the manner to which my narrative commits it; of which truth, moreover, I am by no means sure that . . . I had not all the while an uneasy suspicion. (*AN*, 34–35)

In retrospect, James recognizes that the Bellegardes' rejection of Newman, measured by almost any standard of "realism," is preposterous: their "preferred course, a thousand times preferred" (*AN*, 36), would naturally have been made to marry Claire to the American millionaire without a moment's hesitation.

When James tries to explain his curious blindness, as he wrote the novel, to what he now perceives as a blatant distortion of "the way things happen," he discerns a suggestively double motive. In the first place, he conjectures that his attention and energy, at the time of composition, must have been focused primarily on other aspects of his novelistic art:

it is difficult for me to-day to believe that I had not, as my work went on, *some* shade of the rueful sense of my affront to verisimilitude; yet I catch the memory at least of no great sharpness, no true critical anguish, of remorse: an anomaly the reason of which in fact now glimmers interestingly out. My concern, as I saw it, was to make and to keep Newman consistent; the picture of his consistency was all my undertaking, and the memory of *that* infatuation perfectly abides with me. He was to be the lighted figure, the others . . . were to be the obscured; by which I should largely get the very effect most to be invoked, that of a generous nature engaged with forces, with difficulties and dangers, that it but half understands. If Newman was attaching enough, I must have argued, his tangle would be sensible enough; for the interest of everything is all that it is *his* vision, *his* conception, *his* interpretation: at the window of his wide, quite sufficiently wide, consciousness we are seated, from that admirable position we "assist." He therefore supremely matters; all the rest matters only as he feels it, treats it, meets it. (*AN*, 37)

The passage clearly echoes James's discussion of the genesis of *The Portrait of a Lady*, the "germ" of which, we recall, consisted according to the novelist "not at all in any conceit of a 'plot,' " but "altogether in the sense of a single character, the character and aspect of a particular engaging young woman, to which all the usual elements of a 'subject,' certainly of a setting, were to need to be super-added" (*AN*, 42). But here James acknowledges that his focus on Newman's inner process of vision at the expense of "his tangle," his valuation of character over plot and setting, led him first to commit and then to ignore the serious "affront to verisimilitude" which mars his presentation of the Bellegardes. What is especially striking in this analysis is James's almost explicit admission that the novel's lapses in realism resulted from his "infatuation" with the center of consciousness narrative technique. Preoccupied with his scheme of seeing "everything" through the single "window" of Newman's desiring imagination, James failed, as he himself retroactively recognizes, to pay sufficient attention to the actual web of events and relationships which his protagonist's consciousness "feels" and "treats" and "meets." In keeping Newman "consistent," he had "exclude[d] the outer air"; the novel, in consequence, now seems to him an "aching void," albeit one in which he finds himself "on re-perusal . . . able to breathe at last." One wonders if James is not passing judgment on the single-consciousness technique, and perhaps on his entire *oeuvre*, when he concludes that

here then, at any rate, is the romantic *tout craché* – the fine flower of Newman's experience blooming in a medium "cut off" and shut up to itself. . . I was perhaps wrong in thinking that Newman by himself, and for any occasional extra inch or so I might smuggle into his measurements, would see me through my wood. (*AN*, 39)

Revealingly, however, James offers an alternative explanation for the romantic excesses of *The American*, one which actually contradicts his assertion that the novel's plot must have seemed to him, in 1877, of scant importance. And I think James is probing his own youthful motives with considerable acuity when he remarks that "the very effect most to be invoked" in this early novel was "that of a generous nature engaged with forces, with difficulties and dangers, that it but half understands." James senses, in other words, that he had deliberately kept Newman – as he would keep Isabel and Maisie and Strether – in ignorance of the very truths which determine the shape of his experience, and which might help him to succeed. And if the novelist claims in the Preface that the thwarting circumstances which surround Newman were of little concern to him as he wrote the book, he also acknowledges just how purposefully – and in the face of any reasonable sense of "the way things happen" – he had arranged the course of events in *The American* in order to achieve "the very effect most to be invoked," the effect of defeat and disaster. The Bellegardes' preferred course,

a thousand times preferred, would have been to haul [Newman] and his fortune into their boat . . . and there accommodate him with the very safest and most comfortable seat. Given Newman, given the fact that the thing constitutes itself organically as *his* adventure, that too might very well be a situation and a subject: only it wouldn't have been the theme of "The American" as the book stands, the theme to which I was from so early pledged. . . I had wanted a "wrong." (*AN*, 36–37)

James now sees that he might easily have written a more realistic novel in which Christopher Newman would have succeeded in fulfilling his desire, and in consummating his love; and he reiterates his belated grasp of the strangely negative romanticism which animates *The American* in another passage from his Preface, one that begins with an especially resonant sentence:

I had dug in my path, alas, a hole into which I was destined to fall. I was so possessed of my idea that Newman should be ill-used – which was the essence of my subject – that I attached too scant an importance to its fashion of coming about. Almost any fashion would serve, I appear to have assumed, that would give me my main chance for him; a matter depending not so much on the particular trick played him as on the interesting face presented by him to *any* damnable trick. (*AN*, 34–35)

Might we not say that "the essence of [James's] subject" in nearly all of his fictions – with the crucial exception of *The Golden Bowl* – resides precisely in the "idea" that his protagonist, in one way or another, "should be ill-used?" James seems always to have "wanted a 'wrong.'" And in his remarkable critique of *The American* James comes very close to acknowledging that his lifelong fascination with the desiring process of consciousness was somehow inextricably intertwined with a destructive, life-denying, ultimately unrealistic fantasy, the implications of which he largely succeeded in concealing even from himself. For if James demonstrates a kind of perverse romantic ingenuity in shaping plots and circumstances which leave his characters utterly thwarted and defeated, he nevertheless clearly believes – and wants us to believe – that life is like this, that the disasters which overwhelm his fictional men and women are really quite ordinary instances of "clumsy Life again at her stupid work" (*AN*, 121). Writing the Preface to *The American* in 1907, James can recognize the romantic tenor, not just of this novel, but of all his work.[13] But in 1877, and throughout most of his career, James unmistakably thought of himself as a realist, and of his "geometry of destruction" as a faithful representation of a "ferocious and sinister" reality, as a picture of "life *without* rearrangement" (*LC*, 1:58). The design which James believes and means us to believe in consistently takes the form of a disastrous and inexorable fatality, mitigated only by the illusory figurations of desire.

For James, then, "reality" is almost inevitably a "catastrophe announced by the associated Fates, powers conspiring to a sinister end and, with their command of means, finally achieving it" (*AN*, 290).

And one need only glance at James's memoirs to discover the source of those "unusually restricted" situations he so persistently imagines for his characters. In *A Small Boy and Others*, we recall, the novelist speaks of himself as a helpless victim of "nature and fortune," condemned to "a foreseen and foredoomed detachment" from life (*SBO*, 10); even as a child, he claims, he was "all acutely and yet resignedly, even quite fatalistically, aware" that "the only form of riot or revel ever known to [him] would be that of the visiting mind" (*SBO*, 25). But the extent to which James's discourse is permeated by the language of fate is nowhere more apparent than in his narration, in *Notes of a Son and Brother*, of the incident in which he suffered his notoriously "obscure hurt." The novelist's emotional and intellectual appropriation of this episode in his life offers what must be considered the most central and disturbing instance of his self-created fatalistic myth. The facts concerning the back injury which James incurred while fighting a fire in Newport in 1861 – he was eighteen at the time – can be found in Professor Edel's biography (*The Untried Years*, 173–83).[14] But as Edel himself makes abundantly clear, the facts in this case are far less important than the ways in which James disguised and transformed them. Just how successful he was in obscuring the reality of this incident is manifest in the perennial suspicions of James's critics that the novelist had sustained a sexually-incapacitating genital wound.[15] The critics' mistake in this regard is hardly surprising, for James quite obviously invites such speculation; indeed, it is apparent from James's recounting of the event that he wanted to convince *himself* that this "vast visitation" of "fortune's hand" (*NSB*, 296–97) had made it impossible for him to participate actively and directly in life.

"I had done myself," he writes, "a horrid even if an obscure hurt; and what was interesting from the first was my not doubting in the least its duration" (*NSB*, 298). Edel sees in this "intuition" an "attempt at prophecy" that constitutes "in effect a wish that the hurt might endure" – an analysis that seems to me unarguably correct, and that points to a strong masochistic element in James's psychological dynamic (*The Untried Years*, 180).[16] But when he tries to explain this self-destructive wish in terms of James's unconscious need to identify with his father – the senior Henry James had in his own youth lost a leg in fighting a stable fire – Edel is overlooking a more obvious and, I think, more helpful interpretation (*The Untried Years*, 180–81). James clearly wanted the hurt to endure because it provided him with a cornerstone for the myth he would spend much of his life constructing – the myth that he was a powerless victim of a pre-determined fate – and relieved him of responsibility for the life-choices he had made and was still engaged in making. James's injury thus became for him an excuse for his chosen indirect and introverted mode of living – a rationalization for his decision not to fight in the Civil War, and most importantly, a justification for his failure to pursue his romantic interest in Minny Temple. Even at a distance of some fifty years, the novelist is intent on discovering in the episode the signature of an all-controlling destiny: "the twenty minutes had sufficed," he insists, "to establish a relation – a relation to everything occurring round me not only for the next four years [the duration of the war] but for long afterward – that was at once extraordinarily intimate and quite awkwardly irrelevant" (*NSB*, 297).

James's fatalistic vision of human experience – and in this regard his affinity with the naturalist currents of his era invites further study[17] – finds a particularly extreme expression, ironically, in Lambert Strether's famous exhortation to little Bilham to "live all you can." For this apparent affirmation of individual freedom harbors at its core a bleak estimate of man's powerlessness in the face of a universe that is, as Sears notes, as "overdetermined" as Hardy's (56). Strether himself, of course, "hasn't lived, hasn't at all" (*N*, 226); and when he charges the younger man not to make the same mistake, he seems for a moment almost to believe that he *could* have averted his own losses and failures. "It's as if the train fairly waited at the station for me," he admits, "without my having had the gumption to know it was there." But Strether immediately invalidates the advice he has so passionately given – and also absolves himself of all responsibility for his failure to live – by retreating into a radical fatalism which the whole tenor of the novel unmistakably, if regretfully, endorses:

"the affair – I mean the affair of life – couldn't, no doubt, have been different for me; for it's at the best a tin mould, either fluted and embossed, with ornamental excrescences, or else smooth and dreadfully plain, into which, a helpless jelly, one's consciousness is poured – so that one 'takes' the form, as the great cook says, and is more or less compactly held by it: one lives in fine as one can." (*21*, 217–18)

In one sense, Strether's sense of powerlessness is justified. For a character in a novel cannot determine the particular "tin mould" – the plot – into which his consciousness, with all the intensity and originality of its desire, will be "poured": that privilege belongs to "the great cook," to the novelist himself. But Strether's fatalism is only a pale reflection of his creator's; and James is capable of arguing that the artist "never really chooses" his

general range of vision – the experience from which ideas and themes and suggestions spring: this proves ever what it has *had* to be, this is one with the very turn one's life has taken; so that whatever it "gives," whatever it makes us feel and think of, we regard very much as imposed and inevitable. (*AN*, 201)

James thus believes – somehow needs to believe – that his stories of relentless waste and destruction and disaster are the only ones he can tell: they constitute, he insists, "my appointed thematic doom" (*AN*, 277). And just as Strether, deprived as he is of any real power to choose or change his destiny, must settle for the compensatory "illusion of freedom" (*21*, 218) that consists in imagining rather than realizing life's possibilities, so James, consigned to his own unalterable authorial fate, can turn for solace only to the vain "freedom" of writing:

the range of choice as to treatment, by which I mean as to my pressing the clear liquor of amusement and refreshment from the golden apple of composition, *that* blest freedom, with its infinite power of renewal, was still my resource. (*AN*, 277)

The artist's negative and narrow "range of vision" is "imposed and inevitable," is "ever what it has *had* to be"; but within the confines of this "thematic doom," his "range of choice as to treatment" – his opportunity to *see* the painfully "poor actual" (*SBO*, 175) in as many lights and from as many angles as he can imagine – remains open and "infinite." Understood in these restricted terms, artistic expression can seem little more than a futile exercise in escapism, an ineffectual protest against the "ferocious and sinister" forces of life. But in James's deterministic universe, where even the author resides "in the cage," the only freedom remaining is the freedom to figure manifold, beautiful, but finally unrealizable alternatives to "the fatal futility of Fact" (*AN*, 122): the freedom, in other words, to desire.

It is impossible to quarrel with James's assertion that an artist's themes spring from his personal experience, that his "range of vision" is "one with the very turn his life has taken." But the novelist's conviction that he is in some sense the prisoner of an "imposed" and "appointed thematic doom" – a fallacy that James himself exposes, in the Preface to *The American*, when he admits that he had dug in his path "the hole into which [he] was destined to fall" – is another matter entirely. Indeed, it is this disturbing, ultimately masochistic aesthetic fatalism, and its concomitant failure of artistic responsibility, that James emphatically rejects in *The Golden Bowl*. When James alters his habitual plot structure in order to give Maggie a chance, when he breaks with the negative design which had dominated his fictions from the first, he is proclaiming his power to shape his own aesthetic fate. He experiences, we might say, a transforming accession of freedom, not in his range of treatment, but in his range of vision. Thus James's remarkable refashioning of his "thematic doom" – his sudden expansion of his visionary range to embrace human possibilities, including the possibility of love, heretofore excluded – represents the final fruition of the assumption of freedom and responsibility enacted in *The Wings of the Dove*.

As I have argued, James embodies his own recognition of Milly Theale's tragic knowledge – that we can and must choose our own fate – in his presentation of Merton Densher in the final pages of *The Wings of the Dove*. When James insists that Densher could have loved Milly if he had so chosen, when he shows him deliberately rejecting Kate in order to withdraw into an obsessive, unfulfillable desire for the dead girl's memory, he is assuming responsibility for the determining choices he had made in his own youth, especially for his decision, so many years before, to turn his back on love in order to pursue the solitary path of an artist. By remembering his own past truly, without the self-absolving, fatalistic myth of an "obscure hurt," James restores to his personal experience the value of its having been freely chosen.

Surprisingly, this liberating re-vision of the past is echoed in the very pages from *Notes of a Son and Brother* where James seeks to establish the inevitability of his "hurt." The novelist's treatment of the accident in his memoirs offers a complex admixture of – to borrow Paul de Man's phrase – "blindness and insight." On the one hand, James obviously still feels the need to surround the incident in what he once called "the positive saving virtue of vagueness" (*NSB*, 292), and to assign responsibility for his injury to a powerful and impersonal fate. Yet as he looks back on this crucial juncture of his life, James is also willing to admit, however belatedly, that his response to the accident at the time of its occurrence in effect constituted a series of "steps by which I came to think of my relation to my injury as a *modus vivendi* workable for the time" (*NSB*, 299). After confessing that his physician had assured him that there was "nothing to speak of the matter with me," James goes on to acknowledge that the graceful course, on the whole ground again . . . was to behave accordingly, in good set terms, as if the assurance were true; since the time [the outbreak of the war] left no margin at all for one's gainsaying with the right confidence so high an authority. There were a hundred ways to behave – in the general sense so freely suggested, I mean; and I think of the second half of that summer of '62 as my attempt at selection of the best. The best still remained, under close comparisons, very much what it had at first seemed, and there was in fact this charm in it that to prepare for an ordeal essentially intellectual, as I surmised, might justly involve, in the public eye, a season of some retirement. The beauty was – I can fairly see it now, through the haze of time, even as beauty! – that studious retirement and preparatory hours did after all supply the supine attitude, did invest the ruefulness, did deck out the cynicism of lying down book in hand with a certain fine plausibility. This was at least a negative of combat, an organized, not a loose and empty one, something definitely and firmly parallel to action in the tented field. (*NSB*, 300–01)

The startling mixture of obfuscating prose and penetrating insight evident in this passage defines a tension which I take to be fundamental to James's entire "later manner." For if the evasive tendencies of the Jamesian style are undeniably apparent here, it is equally clear that the novelist is struggling towards an honest self-assessment. As an old man he can see that the doctor's "comparative pooh-pooh" (*NSB*, 300) necessitated his appeal to the higher authority of fate, and can recognize that his injury conveniently justified – in "the public eye" and thus in his own – his withdrawn and "supine" mode of living. He can at last acknowledge the truth behind the myth of his foredoomed wounding: that all the while he was really engaged in the "selection," from a "hundred ways to behave," of an individual "*modus vivendi*," in choosing and making for himself the "essentially intellectual," strangely narrow and isolated life of the artist. By the time the Civil War was over, James would have achieved his initial victories in his own chosen and parallel field of combat by publishing his first stories and reviews. And many years later, he would look back upon the months immediately following his accident, and see in them the turning point of his life: "I must then . . . have stood at the parting of my ways, recognized the false steps, even though few enough, already taken, and consciously committed myself to my particular divergence" (quoted in Edel, *The Untried Years*, 201).

However encumbered and compromised it may be by the persistence of the very myth it exposes, James's recognition of the true nature of his "relation to [his] injury" is nevertheless crucial. For it confirms the movement we have already observed in *The Wings of the Dove*: the novelist's growing need, as he approaches the end of his career, to reassess his life, and to redeem his past by assuming responsibility for its shape. But in *The Wings of the Dove*, James seems determined to redeem his *artistic* past as well. For if he returns in that novel to a subject – the thwarting of life and love – which seems very much of a piece with his lifelong, self-acknowledged "imagination of disaster" (*Letters to Benson and Monod*, 35), he does so in a fully tragic mode which defines the work, not as the helpless expression of a passively experienced "thematic doom," but as a freely undertaken artistic and human act. Kate and Milly and Densher learn that they have chosen and made the painful end which comes to be through the unfolding of the novel's plot. Yet it is above all James himself who wills and shapes that plot, who speak the novel's tragic and self-revealing sentence through to its bitter end. And in *authoring* this conclusion, instead of merely *writing* against it, James asserts the existential validity of his artistic choices. He assumes responsibility, in other words, for the narrow and negative "range of vision" which he alone had imposed on his fictional art, and so liberates himself to write a different kind of story in *The Golden Bowl*.

In its persistently negative representation of life, James's *oeuvre* prior to *The Golden Bowl* embodies an aesthetic manifestation of that psychic "compulsion to repeat" painful and unpleasurable experiences which ultimately led Freud to posit the existence of some mental force "beyond the pleasure principle" (18: 12–23). Freud first discerned the repetition compulsion in the dream-life of certain types of neurotics, and in the play of children, but he argues that the phenomenon can also be observed in the lives of some normal adults, who usually give the impression "of being pursued by a malignant fate." He is particularly fascinated "by cases where the subject appears to have a *passive* experience, over which he has no influence, but in which he meets with a repetition of the same fatality." Freud illustrates his point with an example from Tasso's *Gerusalemme Liberata*. The hero, Tancred,

unwittingly kills his beloved Clorinda in a duel while she is disguised in the armour of an enemy knight. After her burial he makes his way into a strange magic forest which strikes the crusaders' army with terror. He slashes with his sword at a tall tree; but blood streams from the cut and the voice of Clorinda, whose soul is imprisoned in the tree, is heard complaining that he has wounded his beloved once again.

Here, surely, is something akin to the romantic fatality of James's fictional world, where the truth remains concealed until it is too late, where the presence of the other is always disguised, and where love is doomed to fail and fail again.

Freud takes the view that the "fate" of these subjects "is for the most part arranged by themselves" (18: 21–22). Yet a number of factors convince him that, alongside the obviously neurotic aspect of repetition, there exists a more productive, potentially therapeutic purpose for this "compulsion of destiny" (18: 23). In one sense, obsessive repetition is basically masochistic and self-destructive. In his game of "*fort . . . da*," the child repeats his original experience of pain and loss – the thwarting of his Oedipal fantasies – "as a contemporary experience," instead of "remembering it as something belonging to the past" (18: 18): "no lesson has been learnt from the old experience of [this situation] having led . . . only to unpleasure" (18: 21). This is the pattern enacted by Strether, or by James in his work prior to *The Wings of the Dove*; the individual suffers the collapse of all that he has imagined, only to desire again, in the same mode and with the same futility. But the child's game also implies a more constructive end. By transforming his pain, originally experienced "in a *passive* situation," into play, "by repeating it, unpleasurable though it was, as a game, he [takes] on an *active* part." He "repeats even the unpleasant experiences because through his own activity he gains a far more thorough mastery of the strong impression than was possible by mere passive experience" (18: 18). Thus understood as, in Lionel Trilling's words, an act "of the mind embracing its own pain for some vital purpose" ("Freud and Literature," 56), repetition seems less an endless obsession than an awakening into the possibility of a more productive and fulfilling life. And I think it is in this more positive sense that we must grasp James's deliberate act of repetition in *The Wings of the Dove*: he repeats, we might say, his primal *fictional* scene, in order to transform what had always been the passive experience of a destructive "thematic doom" into an active artistic choice.

In his essay on "Freud and Literature," Trilling notes that "Freud, at this point, can scarcely help being put in mind of tragic drama," and specifically of "the cathartic theory of tragedy" (55–56). And indeed, like the children's games which interest him because of their apparent focus, not on fulfilling wishes, but on repeating unpleasurable experiences, "the artistic play and artistic imitation carried out by adults" intrigue Freud because they "do not spare the spectators (for instance, in tragedy) the most painful experiences and can yet be felt by them as highly enjoyable" (18: 17). But the catharsis effected in *The Wings of the Dove* is crucial not so much for the audience as for the novelist himself. For James's tragedy embodies that long-delayed moment in his development as an artist which René Girard, in *Deceit, Desire, and the Novel,* has identified as the determining crisis in the careers of all major novelists: the moment, when "a romantic writer" becomes "a true novelist" (307). Like the artists of Girard's great tradition, James at last moves beyond "the romantic he was at first and who refuses to die" by achieving "a victory over desire," a "reconciliation between the individual and the world," between the desiring imagination and the unavoidable limits of reality (29, 308). Girard could easily be speaking of *The Wings of the Dove* when he says that "great novels always spring from an obsession that has been transcended" (300). And he pinpoints the nature of James's relationship to Milly Theale when he asserts that "the title of the hero of a novel must be reserved for the character who triumphs over metaphysical desire in a tragic conclusion and thus becomes *capable of writing the novel.*" If Milly, to adapt Girard's brilliant formulation, "succumbs as [she] achieves truth," she also "entrusts [her] creator with the heritage of [her] clairvoyance" (296).

Milly leaves her fortune to Merton Densher; but to her creator she entrusts a legacy of far greater value – the freedom and power she has gained through her courageous acceptance of life's tragic finitude. James's moving and productive response to that heritage is embodied in the remarkable authorial act by which he grants Maggie Verver *her* chance to live and love. And if *The Golden Bowl,* at least in its early stages, is still haunted by the spectre of "associated Fates . . . conspiring to a sinister end," it also shows us the artist conspiring with his heroine to defeat and transform that end. The world depicted in *The Golden Bowl* is the one James had always known: a place of loneliness, of suffering, of treachery and tyranny, unredeemed by any transhuman grace. But the mode and valence of James's response to that world have changed. No longer a prisoner of desire's helpless wanting, he has discovered, as Maggie will, the authority of "the constructive, the creative hand" (*24*, 145); and what he chooses to construct and create with her is the reality of love. For years James had deliberately, almost diabolically thwarted his characters' chances for love, all the while blaming these "imagination[s] of disaster" on an uncontrollable and implacable fate. *The Golden Bowl*, in contrast, stands as a conscious act of free artistic will. It is a story told from the other side of that strange "magic forest" where he had lost his way, and where he had been condemned, not by fate but by his own enchantment, to "wrong" the characters he loved.

7 *The Golden Bowl* (II): For the sake of this end

Or ever the silver cord be loosed, or the golden bowl be broken, or the pitcher be broken at the fountain, or the wheel broken at the cistern.
Then shall the dust return to the earth as it was; and the spirit shall return unto God who gave it.

Ecclesiastes 12, 6–7

"Whatever the reality, it *is* a reality. The door isn't shut. The door is open. . . It's never too late."

Henry James, "The Beast in The Jungle"

Near the end of the first book of *The Golden Bowl*, "the beautiful symmetry of her plan" (*23*, 389) grotesquely shattered by the resumption of the Prince and Charlotte's affair, Fanny Assingham boldly predicts Maggie Verver's ultimate "triumph." "We're in presence," she insists to her ever-skeptical husband, "of something possibly beautiful. Beautiful as it *may* come off" (*23*, 383–84). The positive resolution Fanny forsees is, as she herself emphasizes, contingent rather than inevitable: everything will depend on Maggie. And with characteristic hyperbole, Fanny proceeds to define the conditions that the Princess must meet if she is to succeed in transforming the ugliness which surrounds her into a possible beauty. Maggie, Fanny tells the Colonel,

"was the person in the world to whom a wrong thing could least be communicated. It was as if her imagination had been closed to it, her sense altogether sealed. That therefore," Fanny continued, "is what will now *have* to happen. Her sense will have to open."
"I see." He nodded. "To the wrong. . . To the very, *very* wrong."
But his wife's spirit, after its effort of wing, was able to remain higher. "To what's called Evil – with a very big E: for the first time in her life. To the

175

discovery of it, to knowledge of it, to the crude experience of it." And she gave, for the possibility, the largest measure. "To the harsh bewildering brush, the daily chilling breath of it." (23, 384–85)

When James arranges Maggie's extraordinary encounter with the Bloomsbury shopman and his flawed golden bowl, he in effect gives her a chance to fulfill Fanny's prophecy, to begin her progress towards triumph by opening her sense to the terrible knowledge of evil. But if James liberates Maggie from the fatal ignorance which thwarted his previous protagonists, the "harsh" and "chilling" nature of the knowledge she acquires suggests that the world of *The Golden Bowl* is very much the same "lurid," "abominable," "ugly" place (*24*, 127, 185, 111) James had always seen when he looked out on life through the window of his "house of fiction." In evaluating James's surprising authorial intrusion in *The Golden Bowl*, we must be careful not to inflate or distort its significance: he intervenes not to alter the "conditions of life" which Maggie faces, but to permit her to know them truly; he acts not to save her, but to grant her the opportunity to save herself.

Maggie's achievement of love cannot be attributed to any substitution, on James's part, of a beneficent providential order for the negative myth of fate he had exorcised in *The Wings of the Dove*. Those critics who hunt for signs of a spiritual transformation in the Jamesian universe of *The Golden Bowl* succeed only in undervaluing the novelist's real accomplishment. Several commentators have sensed something miraculous or supernatural behind Maggie's triumphant repossession of her husband; a few have even attempted to read the novel as an explicitly Christian allegory of sin and redemption, with Maggie serving as an agent of the divine will (Anderson, 281–346; Crews' 105–08; Krook, 232–324, *passim*). But I think James was never further from relying on the efficacy of religious faith or heavenly intervention. The world of *The Golden Bowl* – the arena where James's "more or less bleeding participants" (*AN*, 328) struggle for an entirely human happiness – is unredeemed by any hint of a transcendent grace. The novelist himself calls our attention to the irrelevance of such "religious readings" in a scene, late in the novel, where he brings together the members of his "community of dread" – Maggie, Charlotte, Adam, the Prince, and the Assinghams – for a "cool ceremonious semblance of luncheon" at Fawns. The moment's barely concealed tension, with its "marked reserves of reference in many directions," is "relieved only by the fitful experiments of Father

Mitchell," a "good holy hungry man" who has "taken for a week or two the light neighbouring service, local rites flourishing under Maggie's munificence." Maggie, like her husband, is a Roman Catholic. But her sponsorship of Father Mitchell's "rites" clearly represents a social formality, not a spiritual commitment. The only "relief" the priest can offer his companions – the terrified participants in what Sallie Sears describes as a bizarre "*ménage à quatre*, or *à cinq* if one includes Fanny Assingham" (165) – is the distraction of his gossipy, urbane conversation. Recognizing that she has, "from the first of her trouble, really found her way without his guidance," Maggie wonders if Father Mitchell has "suspected how more than subtly, how perversely, she had dispensed with him," and imagines that

some day at some happier season she would confess to him that she hadn't confessed, though taking so much on her conscience; but just now she was carrying in her weak stiffened hand a glass filled to the brim, as to which she had recorded a vow that no drop should overflow. She feared the very breath of a better wisdom, the jostle of the higher light, of heavenly help itself. (24, 297–98)

Maggie – to use a Jamesian expression – is "beyond" Father Mitchell. She knows that her purpose is authorized not by any "better wisdom," but by the intensity of her own desire, and knows too that she must find her way alone in a moral universe where "the right" will more often than not take the "extraordinary form" of her "not by a hair's breadth deflecting into the truth" (24, 250–51). Most of all, she knows that if she is to succeed – or even to survive – she must depend upon her own power to act, her own capacity to create and, if necessary, destroy.

Thus while "Father Mitchell prattle[s]," Maggie feels herself surrounded by "prowling dangers," like some "night-watcher in a beast-haunted land who has no more means for a fire" (24, 299–300). And this image – one of many in the novel which evoke treacherous, primitive, or uncharted landscapes – suggests that the moral milestones of secular civilization are as irrelevant to Maggie's "improvised 'post'" (24, 323) as Father Mitchell's "higher light." Most of James's nineteenth-century predecessors had already detached their fictions from any sure or sustaining faith in a providential, theocentric universe; half a century before James wrote *The Golden Bowl*, Thackeray could describe the characters of his greatest novel as a "set of people living without God in the world" (*Letters*, 309). But *Vanity*

Fair, like the fictions of Austen and Dickens and George Eliot, is still centered in a conception of an ideal society, where the individual's experience can be anchored, defined and made purposeful by his adherence to objective standards of ethical conduct, and by his participation in morally significant communal structures and institutions – the most important of these being the family and marriage.

The marriages that typically conclude Victorian novels complete and reassert a social order that is also a moral order. If the nineteenth-century novelists are no longer primarily concerned with marriage as a religious sacrament, they nevertheless still see in it a powerful and meaningful secular ritual: the marital vows implicitly affirm a larger, transpersonal structure of values and duties as well as a personal commitment. But in James's fiction marriage, like Father Mitchell's "rites," has become an empty form, an increasingly arbitrary gesture that has more to do with manners than with morals, a remnant of a once coherent societal ideal that has utterly collapsed. Only a handful of James's novels culminate in anything even remotely resembling the conventional, resolving marriage of Victorian fiction; and those that do – one thinks of Ransom's union with Verena in *The Bostonians*, or even of Isabel's return to Gilbert Osmond at the conclusion of *The Portrait of a Lady* – depict marriage as destructive and entrapping. James's fictional world is crowded with refugees from bad and broken marriages, with Mrs. Touchetts and Mr. Waymarshs and Madame de Vionnets, with characters like Mrs. Rance, the American lady who, in *The Golden Bowl*, makes romantic overtures to Adam Verver, despite her possession of "a husband in undiminished existence" in "Texas, in Nebraska, in Arizona or somewhere" – a "somewhere" James locates in "the great alkali desert of cheap Divorce" (*23*, 133). For a man of his era, James demonstrates a remarkably unsentimental attitude towards marriage. He can contemplate the frantic round of weddings and divorces of *What Maisie Knew* or the casual adulteries of *The Sacred Fount*, if not with indifference, then with a cool, half-amused detachment from any conventional social morality. And have we not seen already how little James shares Woollett's rigid judgment of Chad and Madame de Vionnet's adulterous liaison in *The Ambassadors*? The ethics of passional and erotic relationship constitute a central preoccupation of James's fiction, especially of his later work; but marriage and the socially-grounded moral structures it symbolizes play an increasingly marginal role in determining James's own moral determinations.

The Golden Bowl begins with two marriages that are the issue of contradictory, perverse and highly dubious motives, and that succeed in bringing the members of James's fictional community to the brink of an unfathomable moral chaos. In this novel, marriage, like religion, is basically an empty form. As the entire episode at Matcham testifies, the Prince and Charlotte's adultery − like that of Lady Castledean and her Mr. Blint − is largely acceptable to society's "complacency" and "wonderful spirit of compromise" (*23*, 354). More importantly, Maggie herself, having learned the truth about her husband and stepmother, decides to abjure "the straight vindictive view" (*24*, 236) and to forego any public rupture with the lovers − a choice which suggests how little a concern for the institutional sanctity of marriage enters into her calculations. If Maggie, like James, judges the Prince and Charlotte harshly, it is not because they have traduced the marriage bond − Maggie, I think, eventually feels a kind of jealous admiration for a passion so strong that it cannot be contained within society's strictures − but because they have personally betrayed both her and her father. Leo Bersani is thus largely justified in claiming that even "the happy marriage which Maggie manages to reconstitute at the end of the story is in fact the experience of a passion to which both marriage and society are irrelevant." Bersani compares the conclusion of *The Golden Bowl* with that of *Mansfield Park*, and argues that "Maggie's marriage, unlike Fanny Price's, is merely a convenient institutional context for desires which have no place at all on any map of social structures" (*A Future for Astyanax*, 82) − a remark which echoes Maggie's own realization that the location of the love she ultimately achieves with Amerigo "would have been sought in vain in the most rudimentary map of the social relations as such. The only geography marking it would be doubtless that of the fundamental passions" (*24*, 324).

Well in advance of his modernist inheritors, James had seen that there could be no retreat to the stable sources of authority − whether transcendent or merely transpersonal − which had anchored the moral vision of earlier novelists; his affirmation of love in *The Golden Bowl* cannot be attributed to any belated adoption of a redeeming religious or social ethos. The world in which Maggie and the Prince fashion their act of love is as spiritually unregenerate and as ethically decentered as any James had ever imagined. And while at least one critic has attempted to explain Maggie's breakthrough as the result of a "mysterious psychic magnetism" working through "circuits of telepathic divination that seem little short of magical" (Sicker, 147–50), there is no magic, here or elsewhere in James, that will allow his characters such a miraculous overleaping of the formidable barriers which separate human beings from one another. "The port from which I set out," James once wrote, "was, I think, that of the essential loneliness of my life" (L, 4:170). And James's characters – the men and women of *The Golden Bowl* included – are all denizens of this "essential loneliness." Throughout her ordeal, Maggie knows herself to be "very much alone" (*24*, 45). When we watch her as she stands beside Charlotte on the terrace at Fawns, gazing through the window at her father and husband – or at Charlotte's husband and lover? – and wondering if reality "could be no more after all than a matter of interpretation, differing always for a different interpreter" (*24*, 244), we are reencountering a nightmare of total isolation that had always haunted James's characters.[1] There can be no doubt that his protagonists want desperately to escape from their isolation, to connect with another human heart and mind. But while they often attempt to do so through a kind of magic – through desire's fantasized short circuit between wish and fulfillment – such magic inevitably fails. Maggie finds her way into her husband's arms not through desire, but through the difficult work of loving.

What we witness in *The Golden Bowl*, according to R.P. Blackmur, "is Maggie learning in the abyss of a London stage drawing room . . . that love in action is a harsh and terrible thing" (136). And as we have seen in our encounter with *The Wings of the Dove*, love – as distinguished from desire's "imagination of loving" – exists only as an enacted relation. Yet in a world that lacks a divine or even a social center, where the individual is cut off from any sure knowledge of the other, personal relations are almost invariably controlled by those – the Madame Merles, the Mrs. Newsomes, the Kate Croys – who are most willing to manipulate and brutalize others, and to see them only in terms of their utility. James's secretary, Theodora Bosanquet, once described her employer's vision of human intercourse with an eloquent if appalling precision:

when he walked out of the refuge of his study into the world and looked about him, [James] saw a place of torment, where creatures of prey perpetually thrust their claws into the quivering flesh of the doomed, defenseless children of light. . . The essential fact is that wherever he looked Henry James saw fineness apparently sacrificed to grossness, beauty to avarice, truth to a bold front. He realized how constantly the tenderness of growing life is at the mercy of personal tyranny and he hated the tyranny of persons over each other. (275–76)

For James, real relations – as opposed to imaginative ones – are essentially struggles for power. He saw the "personal tyranny" he so hated in every kind of human relationship, especially, I think, in marriage and in love. Couldn't it be said, for example, that Maggie's repossession of her husband is also a victory over him, a victory which she achieves by gradually stripping him of his freedom until he must acknowledge to her, "I see nothing but *you*" (*24*, 369)? The conclusion of *The Golden Bowl*, with its couples paired off and its marriages reaffirmed, does partake of the resolving structure of comedy; but the emotions Maggie experiences as she accepts and reciprocates the Prince's embrace are largely the tragic ones of "pity and dread" (*24*, 369). And human relations – including love – as they are depicted in *The Golden Bowl* are very much what they have always been in James's work: a theater of pain and treachery and violence, where a word can call up "the hot blood as a blow across the mouth might have called it" (*24*, 182); a battlefield where the loser will end "thrown over on her back with her neck from the first half-broken and her helpless face staring up" at the victor (*24*, 242).

Such is the reality to which Maggie Verver must "open her sense," such the "conditions of life" within which she will fashion her ambiguous triumph. In the Preface to *What Maisie Knew*, James eloquently expresses his belief that

no themes are so human as those that reflect for us, out of the confusion of life, the close connexion of bliss and bale, of the things that help with the things that hurt, so dangling before us forever that bright hard medal, of so strange an alloy, one face of which is somebody's right and ease and the other somebody's pain and wrong. (*AN*, 143)

But this "strange alloy" – the very substance of which Maggie's act of love and *The Golden Bowl* itself are made – comprises a mixture that James and his desiring protagonists had always had difficulty accepting. In *The Portrait of a Lady*, Henrietta Stackpole defines Isabel's incapacity for seeing what Maggie will ultimately know as "the awful mixture in things" (*24*, 292):

"you think you can lead a romantic life, that you can live by pleasing yourself and pleasing others. You'll find you're mistaken. Whatever life you lead

you must put your soul in it — to make any sort of success of it; and from
the moment you do that it ceases to be romance, I assure you: it becomes grim
reality! And you can't always please yourself; you must sometimes please other
people. That, I admit, you're very ready to do; but there's another thing that's
still more important — you must often *dis*please others. . . That doesn't suit
you at all. . . You think we can escape disagreeable duties by taking romantic
views — that's your great illusion, my dear. But we can't. You must be
prepared on many occasions in life to please no one at all — not even yourself."
(*3*, 310–11)

Maggie's achievement of love — her success in fulfilling Milly
Theale's dream of loving and being loved — is predicated most essentially upon her acceptance of the "grim reality" of "disagreeable
duties." To put it simply, she can only regain her husband by destroying his relationship with Charlotte; she must be prepared not only to
"displease others," but if necessary to make them bleed. Maggie's
"right and ease" are very much Charlotte's "pain and wrong," and no
one, unless it be James himself, is more aware of that other face of the
medal of her "success" than Maggie herself. "It's as if," the Princess
tells her husband in the end, "[Charlotte's] unhappiness has been
necessary to us — as if we needed her, at her own cost, to build us up
and start us" (*24*, 346). And it is through the medium of Maggie's consciousness that we come to understand the full extent of Charlotte's
suffering. It is Maggie, her victory within reach, who sees Charlotte
"removed, transported, doomed" (*24*, 271), who hears in the strained
preciseness of Charlotte's lectures on Mr. Verver's art collection
something like "the shriek of a soul in pain" (*24*, 292). It is Maggie
alone who can envision her adversary "off somewhere all unaided, pale
in her silence and taking in her fate," banished to "the hard glare of
nature . . . virtually at bay, and yet denied the last grace of any protec-
ting truth" (*24*, 303).

Maggie understands, more acutely than Mr. Verver or even the
Prince himself, the reality of Charlotte's pain. But more importantly,
she accepts and acknowledges her large share of responsibility for
Charlotte's pitiable fate. If she has resisted adopting "the straight vindictive view" or indulging "the rights of resentment, the rages of
jealousy, the protests of passion" (*24*, 236) — and Maggie knows that
she possesses the power of making the adulterers "start, stare and turn
pale" by "sounding out their doom in a single sentence" (*24*, 233) —
it is only that she might, in pursuit of her aims, practice what can only

be described as a more insidious, more brutal kind of aggression. If she eschews "the ways usually open to innocence outraged" (24, 237), it is because she knows that love in action cannot remain innocent, and that the time has come to exchange her "blunt and idle tools" and "weapons that [don't] cut" for the "gleam of a bare blade" (24, 9). Maggie wants her husband back; and she understands without evasion the price which she as well as Charlotte must pay:

> our young woman, who had been, from far back, by the habit of her nature, as much on her guard against sacrificing others as if she felt the great trap of life mainly to be set for one's doing so, now found herself attaching her fancy to that side of the situation of the exposed pair which involved . . . the sacrifice of the least fortunate. (24, 227–28)

"The sacrifice of the least fortunate": it would seem that Fanny Assingham's prediction – that Maggie's "sense will have to open" to the "knowledge" and "experience" of evil – is inadequate. For this Princess comes not only to know and experience the evil perpetrated by others, but to discover the possibilities for evil within herself. She has "felt the thing," as James once wrote of Hawthorne, "at its source, deep in the human consciousness" (LC, 2:155).

Thus when Maggie chooses to "possess and use" her companions – "even to the extent of braving, of fairly defying, of directly exploiting, of possibly quite enjoying, under cover of an evil duplicity, the felt element of curiosity with which they regarded her" (24, 49) – we have clearly reached a point where conventional moral standards of any description have become irrelevant. In her quest for the fulfillment of her love, the Princess adopts the very weapons – manipulation, tyranny, the lie of "a bold front" – which her betrayers have used against her and her father. If we are willing to give even a qualified assent to Maggie's achievement of love, then we must also be prepared to see in *The Golden Bowl* the embodiment of a most un-Jamesian proposition: that the end justifies the means. Maggie's aggressive tactics – especially her new willingness to "use" and "exploit" others in pursuit of her aims – in fact indicate that James has broken, not only with conventional moral structures, but more importantly with the morality of desire he had implicitly advocated through his sympathetic portrayal of Lambert Strether in *The Ambassadors*. For unlike Strether, Maggie Verver wants very much, "out of the whole affair, to have got [something] for [her]self" (22, 326). And in acting to fulfill her

desire, she engages in precisely that kind of evil which Strether comes
to hate and resist in Woollett: the evil of human manipulation, of seeing others as means to an end rather than as ends in themselves, of
valuing them according to their utility.

Early in the novel, the Prince thinks of Maggie as existing "in a state of
childlike innocence, the state of our primitive parents before the Fall" (23,
335). When she begins "to doubt, for the first time . . . of her wonderful
little judgement of her wonderful little world" (23, 380), she is embarking
on an experience which James unmistakably wants us to regard as a fortunate fall. But the "Eden" from which Maggie is ultimately both banished
and liberated is more than a state of moral innocence or of childish
immaturity – although it is certainly both of these. Rather, the perniciously
perfect, "wonderful little world" which Maggie inhabits at the beginning
of the novel is essentially a projection of her desire, a dream-like world
where wishes are fulfilled through a kind of hallucination, and where a
knowledge of reality is simply, as the Prince recognizes, not "one of [her]
needs" (23, 334). Maggie begins, in other words, in the kind of world which
Strether sought to create through the expansive, dilatory processes of his
desiring consciousness: a world which magically shapes itself to fit the contours of her imagination.

The Maggie we meet in the opening pages of *The Golden Bowl* is
radically undefined. In Bob Assingham's typically apt appraisal, she is
"very nice . . . but more than anything else, the young woman who
has a million a year" (23, 77). The Colonel's boredom with Maggie's
"improbably good" nature (23, 393) echoes the Prince's more complex
and ominous awareness of his wife's singular dullness. For Amerigo,
Maggie is "a little dancing-girl at rest, ever so light of movement but
most often panting gently, even a shade compunctiously, on a bench";
she seems almost to lack an individual identity in the way she recalls
for him "the transmitted images of rather neutral and negative propriety that made up, in his long line, the average of wifehood and
motherhood." At dinner in Eaton Square, the Prince finds himself
comparing Charlotte's "intenser presence" to the "neutral" image offered by Maggie:

It was not indistinguishable to him, when once they were all stationed, that his
wife too had in perfection her own little character; but he wondered how it
managed so visibly to simplify itself – and this, he knew, in spite of any desire

she entertained – to the essential air of having overmuch on her mind the felicity, and indeed the very conduct and credit, of the feast.

Maggie's "little character" is really nothing more than an appendage to Adam Verver's personality; "the party," after all, "was her father's party, and its greater or smaller success was a question having for her all the importance of *his* importance" (*23*, 321–23). Their "felicity" is what matters most to Maggie and Adam; but as James tells us elsewhere in the novel,

there may have been a kind of helplessness in their felicity. Their rightness, the justification of everything – something they so felt the pulse of – sat there with them; but they might have been asking themselves a little blankly to what further use they could put anything so perfect. They had created and nursed and established it; they had housed it here in dignity and crowned it with comfort; but mightn't the moment possibly count for them – or count at least for us as we watch them with their fate all before them – as the dawn of the discovery that it doesn't always meet *all* contingencies to be right? (*23*, 167)

The specific "contingencies" referred to here are, comically enough, "the hovering forces of which Mrs. Rance was the symbol" (*23*, 167); but the real weakness in Maggie and Adam's magnificently constructed and maintained happiness is something much more serious, a profound failure to engage actively in life. "They didn't," as Fanny Assingham retroactively recognizes, "know *how* to live" (*23*, 389). And it is precisely their efforts to preserve the vast edifice of their felicity that stand in the way of their learning *how* to live. The "littleness" of Maggie's concrete, public identity is in fact inseparable from the monstrous infinitude of the private fantasy-world figured by her desire. Protected from life by her father's love and money, as well as by her own fears, Maggie has never been required to define herself through active choice. She has never, as she tells Adam, "had the least blow," has never known what it means to be "lonely and sore" (*23*, 186). And so, unlike Milly Theale, who learns in the fact of her own dying the necessity of choosing amongst the kingdoms of the earth, Maggie sees no obstacle to wanting and having all of them. She seems, without the slightest effort, to possess the "everything" which Kate Croy sought in vain in *The Wings of the Dove*.

But as Densher tells Kate, "everything's nothing" (*19*, 68). And the most conspicuous flaw in the perfect, golden world Maggie inhabits

is her naive belief that she can marry Amerigo without in any way altering her relationship with her father. When she weds the Prince, Maggie is not conscious of making a choice. She blinds herself to the consequences of her act, and revels in a "sense of a life not only uninter-
rupted but more deeply associated, more largely combined" with her
father's (*23*, 156). Much later, the Princess will assume full responsibility for her part in creating the perverse "arrangement − how
otherwise was it to be named? − by which, so strikingly, she had been
able to marry without breaking, as she liked to put it, with her past"
(*24*, 5). But throughout the first half of the novel, she remains oblivious
to the fact that, in clinging to her childish bond with Adam, she *has*
made a choice − a choice which prevents her from engaging with her
husband in the relationship of love. Indeed, she sees her father's marriage to Charlotte, like her own to Amerigo, as simply another element
in the undifferentiated, seemingly limitless medium of her felicity:

she had surrendered herself to her husband without the shadow of a reserve
or a condition and yet hadn't all the while given up her father by the least little
inch. She had compassed the high felicity of seeing the two men beautifully
take to each other, and nothing in her marriage had marked it as more happy
than this fact of its having practically given the elder, the lonelier, a new friend.
What had moreover all the while enriched the whole aspect of success was that
the latter's marriage had been no more measurably paid for than her own. . .
That it was remarkable that they should have been able at once so to separate
and so to keep together had never for a moment, from however far back, been
equivocal to her. (*24*, 5)

With the combined resources of their enormous wealth and their
extraordinary romantic innocence, the Ververs have thus purchased for
themselves a paradisiacal world, where it is literally possible for them
to have their cake and eat it too. But choice becomes meaningless in
a universe where separating and keeping together are entirely compatible. And this paradise is a dangerous illusion. "Lying like gods
together, all careless of mankind" (*24*, 91), in a realm of "innocent
pleasures, pleasures without penalties" (*23*, 11), Adam and Maggie
are, as Charlotte puts it, "fatally safe" (*23*, 343). If Strether's desiring
imagination seeks always to postpone "the reckoning to come" (*22*,
293), the Ververs have by some strange alchemy fantasized into being
an alternative world where there are no reckonings, where nothing
is ever "paid for." And in this protected, womblike atmosphere −
one thinks here of the maternal component of Strether's desire −

where need and contradiction are unknown, mature, productive relationships are impossible.

Before he loses himself in this all-encompassing felicity, where he comes to believe that he can have Maggie and Charlotte at one and the same time, the Prince demonstrates his awareness of the potential sterility of such perfection. When Amerigo, in a jocular reference to his marriage settlement, tells Maggie, "I cost a lot of money," she responds by insisting, "I haven't the least idea . . . what you cost" (23, 12). And he is increasingly forced to recognize the larger implications of her statement. If Maggie's choice costs her nothing, the Prince soon learns that he too need not pay.

It was as if he had been some old embossed coin, of a purity of gold no longer used, stamped with glorious arms, medieval, wonderful, of which the 'worth' in mere modern change, sovereigns and half-crowns, would be great enough, but as to which, since there were finer ways of using it, such taking to pieces was superfluous. That was the image for the security in which it was open to him to rest; he was to constitute a possession, yet was to escape being reduced to his component parts. What would this mean but that, practically, he was never to be tried or tested? What would it mean but that, if they didn't 'change' him, they really wouldn't know – he wouldn't know himself – how many pounds, shillings and pence he had to give? (23, 23)

As "a rarity, an object of beauty," a "*morceau de musée*" (23, 12) in a human equivalent to the "palace of art" (23, 145) Adam intends to erect in American City, the Prince is to be looked at, not touched, admired, not engaged with in a relationship which might reveal his value. The Ververs' failure to connect with or even acknowledge the Prince's "single self" and "personal quantity" (23, 9) thus embodies a disturbing denial of life, of experience, and – for Maggie – of the possibility of love. Amerigo's assessment of his wife and father-in-law, however bemusedly it is phrased, contains a searing indictment of their refusal to relate to him actively and creatively:

that was what it all came back to again with these people among whom he had married – that one found one used one's imagination mainly for wondering how they contrived so little to appeal to it. He felt at moments as if there were never anything to do for them that was worthy – to call worthy – of the personal relation. (23, 314)

In his essay on "The Future of the Novel," James laments what he sees as a "tremendous omission" in English fiction: "the great relation between men and women, the constant world-renewal" (*LC*, 1:107). And as long as Maggie resides in a realm free of the necessity of choice, where nothing requires renewal because nothing is ever lost, she will remain herself "unworthy" and incapable of mature intimacy and passion. The terrible irony is that if Maggie's failure to choose between her husband and her father vitiates her marriage to the former, it also trivializes her relationship with the latter. For Maggie and Adam are finally pathetic in their "make-believe renewals of their old life." Having left Amerigo with Charlotte at a grand diplomatic reception, the Princess scurries home to her father; "the two," as Charlotte sarcastically observes,

> were doubtless making together a little party at home. But it was all right . . . there was nothing in the world they liked better than these snatched felicities, little parties, long talks, with 'I'll come to you tomorrow,' and 'No, I'll come to *you*' . . . They were fairly, at times, the dear things, like children playing at paying visits, playing at 'Mr. Thompson' and 'Mrs. Fane,' each hoping that the other would really stay to tea. (*23*, 252)

James's repeated emphasis on the Verver's childishness – "they were good children, bless their hearts, and the children of good children" (*23*, 334) – reminds us that he had characterized Strether's adoption of the desiring mode as in part a rejection of adult authority and responsibility. Strether tries to see the world as through a child's eyes, to grant every object and moment the newness and infinite potentiality which the mature observer, with his preconceptions and *a priori* epistemological assumptions, rarely discerns. But it is the more negative attributes of childhood, the implications of powerlessness, sexual immaturity and vulnerability to manipulation by others, that James is accentuating in his presentation of Adam Verver – "the infant king" (*23*, 324) – and the Princess. Indeed, father and daughter seem to have regressed beyond mere childishness to something very much like a state of infancy, where Maggie is unable to differentiate herself from her parent. Like a baby which cannot distinguish where its self ends and the other (the mother) begins, or perhaps even like a foetus in the womb which cannot exist independently of the mother, Maggie has no sense of an identity apart from her father. When she returns home from church one Sunday morning to find Adam cornered by the romantically aggressive Mrs. Rance, Maggie's real shock is her discovery that she is separate from her father:

> when till this moment, had she shown a fear, however dumbly, for his individual life? They had had fears together, just as they had had joys, but all of hers, at least, had been for what equally concerned them. Here of a sudden

was a question that concerned him alone, and the soundless explosion of it somehow marked a date. He was on her mind, he was even in a manner on her hands – as a distinct thing, that is, from being, where he had always been, merely deep in her heart and in her life; too deep down, as it were, to be disengaged, contrasted or opposed, in short objectively presented. But time finally had done it; their relation was altered. (*23*, 154)

At this point, however, Maggie is still unwilling to allow the intrusion of time and change into her felicitous, all-too-perfect world; she is not yet "able not to mind – not to mind what became of [Adam or], without anxiety, to let him go his way and take his risk and lead his life" (*24*, 81). And so she proposes for her father a marriage as meaningless as her own, so that they might be again as they were.

The Oedipal overtones of this father–daughter relationship have not escaped the notice of James's critics. And for the most part, commentators have been justifiably cautious in applying Freudian structures to a novel published in 1904. Matthiessen, for example, argues that "James occupies a curious border line between the older psychologists like Hawthorne or George Eliot, whose concerns were primarily religious and ethical, and the post-Freudians" (*The Major Phase*, 92–3). When James has Maggie speak of "being married" to her father (*23*, 172), he is undoubtedly unaware of the implications of incestuous sexual desire which we, as contemporary readers, cannot help but notice. But James surely apprehends the life-denying failure to mature, morally *and* psychologically, that stands behind Maggie's "guileless idea" of marrying the Prince "while still having her father, of keeping him fast" (*23*, 393). And when he calls our attention to the way in which Adam supplants the Prince, not only for Maggie, but for the Principino – "it was of course an old story and a familiar idea," he tells us, "that a beautiful baby could take its place as a new link between a wife and a husband, but Maggie and her father had, with every ingenuity, converted the precious creature into a link between a mamma and a grandpapa" (*23*, 156) – James presents us with a frightening image of the Oedipal fantasy hallucinated into fulfillment.

In his study of Freud, Paul Ricoeur points out that

the essence of the oedipal drama is itself fantasy: it is a drama enacted and dreamed. Yet it is all the more serious a drama, for it stems from an impossible request on the part of desire. Desire began by wishing for the impossible (. . . the son wishes to have a child by his mother, and the daughter by her father); because it wished the impossible, desire was necessarily disappointed and wounded. Hence the path to reality is not only lined with lost objects but with forbidden and refused objects as well. (273–74)

Maggie, however, has never been obliged to travel "the path to reality"; she exists – for she doesn't yet know how to *live* – in a hermetically-sealed world figured by her own desire, a world where nothing is "lost" or "forbidden" or "refused," and where the "impossible" finds a magical realization, as if in a dream. Indeed, this world *is* a dream, an illusory presence that is really a fundamental absence, a massive projection of the might-have-been which constituted Strether's essential abode. In Freud's view, the failure to resolve and move beyond the Oedipal crisis leaves the ego under the domination of the pleasure principle, able to "do nothing but wish" ("The Two Principles of Mental Functioning," 12:223), dependant on what Ricoeur calls "the short circuit between desire and hallucination" for its vain satisfactions. This "pleasure-ego" is characterized by modalities which, as we have seen, distinguish the Jamesian desiring consciousness: "*exemption from mutual contradiction, primary process* (mobility of cathexes, *timelessness,* and *replacement of external by psychical reality*)" ("The Unconscious," 14:187). And it would thus appear that Maggie Verver, in the perfection of her felicity, has achieved what James's desiring protagonists had always sought: an alternative, imaginary world, which exists in "entire disregard of reality-testing," where "reality of thought" is equated with "external actuality, and wishes with their fulfillment – with the event – just as happens automatically under the dominance of the ancient pleasure principle" (12:225).

"Every neurosis," Freud asserts, "has as its result, and probably therefore as its purpose, a forcing of the patient out of real life, an alienating of him from reality" (12:218). And in her attachment to her father, Maggie comes very close to embodying this definition of the neurotic. Yet with the help of the strange shopkeeper who exposes the cracks in her golden world, Maggie finds her way back to reality, and learns that she can and must part from Adam. In Freud's terms, the dissolution of the Oedipus complex coincides with the supercession of the pleasure principle by the reality principle:

it was only the non-occurrence of the expected satisfaction, the disappointment experienced, that led to the abandonment of [the] attempt at satisfaction by means of hallucination. Instead of it, the psychical apparatus had to decide to form a conception of the real circumstances in the external world and to endeavour to make a real alteration in them. A new principle of mental functioning was thus introduced; what was presented in the mind was no longer what was agreeable but what was real, even if it happened to be disagreeable. This setting-up of the reality principle proved to be a momentous step. (12:219)

The new "reality-ego" accepts the inevitability of negation and contradiction, and defines itself within the context of time. It "strive[s]," as Freud puts it, "for what is useful" (12:223), and "endeavours to make a real alteration" in "the external world," not merely to imagine illusory alternatives to it. But Freud insists that "actually the substitution of the reality principle for the pleasure principle implies no deposing of the pleasure principle, but only a safeguarding of it. A momentary pleasure, uncertain in its results, is given up, but only in order to gain along the new path an assured pleasure at a later time" (12:223). This is what Strether fails to grasp in his wholesale rejection of Woollett's utilitarian vision, and what James himself unconsciously obscures when he depicts Strether's imaginative and Woollett's active principles as mutually exclusive. The reality-ego transforms imagination into action, and so reaches the fulfillment of which the desiring pleasure-ego can only dream.

There is, writes Ricoeur, "an element of 'evil infinitude' in desire; the reality principle − even when stated in the seemingly philistine form of the utility principle − basically expresses the loss of the 'evil infinitude,' the reconversion to the finite" (275). This is what Freud means when he says that acceptance of the reality principle involves "the conversion of freely displaceable cathexes into 'bound' cathexes" (12:221). In Strether, the excessive mobility of cathexes defines itself as an inordinate responsiveness to everyone and everything: in Maggie, as an inability to choose between her father and her husband. But Strether refuses the "binding" implied by Maria Gostrey's offer of marriage, whereas Maggie learns to choose, and to allow her desire to die in the satisfaction of a specific want. It is this successful "reconversion to the finite" that marks this Princess as the true heir to Milly Theale. Through experiencing the loss of her illusory "everything," Maggie gains the limited but concrete possibility of "something beautiful."

As I have already noted, Maggie begins to discern "realities looming through the golden mist" (24, 31) even before her encounter with the sure knowledge embodied in the golden bowl. And the fact that her first tentative efforts at reality-testing coincide with the opening of the novel's second book suggests the brilliance of the structure James has created for *The Golden Bowl*. In the first part of the novel, Maggie is the only major character through whose consciousness the action is never perceived – a device which serves to emphasize her incapacity for life, as well as the degree to which her identity is subsumed in her father's. Our sudden, total immersion in Maggie's consciousness at the beginning of the second book thus reflects something of the shock she herself undergoes when the Prince returns from Matcham. More importantly, however, James plunges us into the interior process of the Princess's desiring imagination at precisely that moment when she emerges for the first time as an actor on the stage of life – a fusion of impulses which goes to the heart of the novel's themes. Maggie's initial testing of the waters of reality takes the form of a realization that she had "done, a little, something she was not always doing," that she has "made . . . a difference in the situation so long present to her as practically unattackable" (*24*, 3). Like James emerging from the self-destructive myth of his "thematic doom" – for the novelist too is doing something different here – Maggie begins to doubt her perfect world:

so it was that their felicity had fructified; so it was that the ivory tower . . . had risen stage by stage. Maggie's actual reluctance to ask herself with proportionate sharpness why she had ceased to take comfort in the sight of it represented accordingly a lapse from that ideal consistency on which her moral comfort almost at any time depended. (*24*, 6)

So begins the process by which Maggie abandons her "ideal consistency," and with it any reliance on mere "safety" or "moral comfort." Gradually, she learns to accept contradiction and danger and difficulty – the essential crudity of experience – and to confront "the hard glare of nature," the "gleam of a bare blade." She learns as well the necessity of sometimes giving pain, to oneself, but also to others. Her acknowledged vision of "one's paying with one's life" (*24*, 4) suggests the distance she has come from her earlier state of suffocating fear in which she "had made anxiety her stupid little idol" (*24*, 81); it marks as well her fall from that illusory paradise where nothing ever had to be paid for. Maggie thus fulfills Fanny's prediction by opening her spirit to the "awful mixture in things," to the knowledge that, as the Prince puts it, "everything's terrible . . . in the heart of man" (*24*, 349).

But the Princess's acceptance of the real should not be misread as a denial of desire; rather, it represents a first step towards the realization of desire. And her knowledge of the truth does not preclude the exercise of her imagination. Like Strether, Maggie possesses an intensely desiring consciousness. She in fact continues to rely heavily on the modes of perception and experience which James explores in *The Ambassadors*. Maggie follows in the footsteps of Woollett's wayward pilgrim by rejecting *a priori* definitions and rigid moral structures; by trying "always to have some imagination of the states of others – of what they may feel deprived of" (*24*, 258); and by becoming a "mistress of shades" (*24*, 142) and fine discriminations, by learning to appreciate "the possible heroism of perfunctory things" (*24*, 288). Like Strether, she remains open to the multiplicitous possibilities inherent in every moment. But whereas Strether's process of desire seeks only its own perpetual continuation in the wanting of more wants, Maggie's imaginative activity is ultimately bound by and directed towards the completion of a specific end. When she feels herself "dancing up and down, beneath her propriety, with the thought that she had at last begun something" (*24*, 51), she has reached a point of origin that is wholly transitive in nature. Far from abandoning the figurative freedom of desire – she is in fact responsible for some of the most elaborate and extended metaphorical flights in all of James – Maggie learns to fuse that freedom with the limiting concreteness of purpose in a syntax of the true pleasurable. She speaks the sentence of love through to its concluding and consummatory embrace.

Maggie thus becomes, as James tells us in the Preface to *The Golden Bowl*, "an actor in the offered play" (*AN*, 329). And like Milly Theale in her palazzo in Venice, Maggie "acts" in a sense that is simultaneously histrionic – she pretends, performs, lies – and existential, in that she is literally forging an identity for herself:

Maggie went, she went – she felt herself going; she reminded herself of an actress who had been studying a part and rehearsing it, but who suddenly, on the stage, before the footlights, had begun to improvise, to speak lines not in the text. . . Preparation and practice had come but a short way . . . and she invented from moment to moment what to say and to do. (*24*, 33)

But if Maggie now knows that she must define herself through what she says and does, she discovers as well that she can, as Freud says, "make a real alteration" in the world she inhabits. She begins "to speak lines not in the text," and then, with her new and empowering consciousness of "possessing the constructive, the creative hand" (*24*, 145), to author a text which she willfully imposes on everything and everyone around her. The culminating moment in Maggie's progress towards a full assumption of creative power comes in the extraordinary scene at Fawns, as she stands on the terrace, gazing through a window at her gathered companions:

they might have been . . . figures rehearsing some play of which she herself was the author; they might even, for the happy appearance they continued to present, have been such figures as would by the strong note of character in each fill any author with the certitude of success, especially of their own histrionic. They might in short have represented any mystery they would; the point being predominantly that the key to the mystery, the key that could wind and unwind it without a snap of the spring, was there in her pocket. . . She walked to the end and far out of the light; she returned and saw the others still where she had left them; she passed round the house and looked into the drawing-room, lighted also, but empty now, and seeming to speak the more in its own voice of all the possibilities she controlled. Spacious and splendid, like a stage again awaiting a drama, it was a scene she might people, by the press of her spring, either with serenities and dignities and decencies, or with terrors and shames and ruins, things as ugly as those formless fragments of her golden bowl she was trying so hard to pick up. (*24*, 235–36)

James always sees his protagonists as figures for the artist. But if Strether represents the *writer* in James, the artist of desire, who can do nothing but imagine illusory alternatives to a fated and ugly reality, then Maggie is clearly the *author*, the artist of the real, for whom art is no longer a vain protest against life, but a powerful act of life.

The action of the novel's second book thus defines the heroine's progress from little Maggie Verver to magnificent Princess; it shows a woman slowly becoming "worthy" of "the personal relation." Maggie emerges from the undifferentiated, womblike sphere of her desire into an almost joyful sense of the specific pleasures available through human relationship, and comes to place her highest valuation on "the flower of participation . . . the idea, so absurdly obscured, of her *sharing* with [Amerigo], whatever the enjoyment, the interest, the experience might be" (*24*, 26). Her quest for love begins, after all, with a small but direct appeal to the Prince's imagination, with "the freshness of relation produced by her having administered to her husband the first surprise to which she had ever treated him. It had been a poor thing, but it had been all her own . . ." (*24*, 10). The Prince's affair with Charlotte, though based on a once-genuine passion, is revived largely as a result of a default on Maggie's part. Wrapped with Adam in her enormous and smothering felicity, Maggie has given nothing of herself to Amerigo – except perhaps her father's money. But more importantly, she has not allowed the Prince to give anything to her other than his beautiful, sterile antiquity. It is only when she becomes willing to face danger, to try and test herself in an imperfect world, that Maggie can effectively "change" her husband in order to find out "how many pounds, shillings and pence he had to give." By declining to take the simple path of exposing her knowledge to Adam and Charlotte, Maggie provokes in Amerigo a creative response and allows him to "change" her in return. Having embraced her own condition of human neediness, she discovers as well

the possibility, richer with every lapsing moment, that her husband would have, on the whole question, a new need of her. . . It struck her truly as so new that he would have felt hitherto none to compare with it at all; would indeed absolutely by this circumstance be *really* needing her for the first time in their whole connexion. (*24*, 186)

"It was as if she had passed, in a time incredibly short," she muses elsewhere, "from being nothing to him to being all" (*22*, 228). Maggie and Amerigo are finally joined together in a partnership of imagination and action; his lie to Charlotte – he tells her that Maggie knows nothing –

had given [the Princess] something to conform to, and she hadn't unintelligently turned on him, "gone back on him," as he would have said, by not conforming. They were together thus, he and she, close, close together. . . The heart of the Princess swelled, accordingly, even in her abasement; she had kept in tune with the right, and something, certainly, something that might be like a rare flower snatched from an impossible ledge, would, and possibly soon, come of it for her. (*24*, 250)

Like Adam and Eve cast out of the garden, the Prince and Princess learn to "strive/ In offices of love, how we may lighten/ Each other's burden in our share of woe" (*Paradise Lost*, x.959–61).

Yet if Maggie finally chooses to love her husband, she also manages to recreate her relationship with her father, not in their old desiring mode, where the "stupid little idol" of fear for their illusory happiness was allowed to dominate, but on a new, mature basis of mutual respect and genuine love. Maggie learns that by clinging to the might-have-been, she has come perilously close to destroying her real chances for life; but she also comes to recognize that her failure to define herself apart from her father has deprived *him* of the opportunity to explore the full range of his own potentiality. The whole disastrous situation comes about, she realizes, because she has been unwilling "to let him go his way and take his risk and lead his life" (*24*, 81), and what she now seeks is "the possibility of some understanding between them in consequence of which he should cut loose" (*24*, 82). By not running to Adam with her terrible secret, by leaving him alone to "take his risk and lead his life," Maggie arrives at a transforming re-vision of her father. No longer a mere extension of herself, he is now, like Amerigo, an other. By ceasing to protect both herself and Adam, Maggie discovers that he too is capable of life, and perhaps even of love:

Before she knew it she was lifted aloft by the consciousness that he was simply a great and deep and high little man, and that to love him with tenderness was not to be distinguished, a whit, from loving him with pride. . . The sense that he wasn't a failure, and could never be, purged their predicament of every meanness. . . It was like a new confidence. . . (*24*, 274)

Adam, James hints, has learned the terrible secret, and has found the "path to reality" on his own. And Maggie's revelation continues as she perceives that her father, in his turn, has tested and found new value in *her*:

Wasn't it because now, also, on his side, he was thinking of her as his daughter, was *trying* her . . . as the child of his blood? Oh then, . . . what was she but strong enough too? It swelled in her fairly; it raised her higher, higher: she wasn't in that case a failure either – hadn't been, but the contrary; his strength was her strength, her pride was his, and they were decent and competent together. (*24*, 274–75)

Maggie thus escapes the necessity for separation and avoids succumbing to the "deeper treachery . . . in recoveries and reassurances" (*24*, 72). She leaves behind the illusory past, and in so doing is able to repossess it in a truer form. For unlike Charlotte, who attempts to repeat the past with Amerigo and loses everything, the Princess and Adam are left with the knowledge that "they *had*, after all, whatever happened, always and ever each other; each other – that was the hidden treasure and the saving truth – to do exactly what they would with: a provision full of responsibilities" (*24*, 255). In memory they will always be capable of "remounting the stream of time and dipping again . . . into the contracted basin of the past' (*24*, 258). But their accepted loss of each other is real, moving, genuinely painful, and despite Maggie's success in restoring her marriage there is a bittersweet quality to the final pages of *The Golden Bowl*. One catches here an echo of *The Tempest*, where the triumph of Prospero's reintegrative vision is balanced by a deep sadness at the need to give up his beloved Miranda.

In choosing the loss of her father, Maggie experiences the death of desire. But for the first time in James, desire also dies into the consummation of love. Maggie gives up the false past – the illusory might-have-been – in order to gain a true one; and in so doing she also gains a future that reaches beyond the endless present of the desiring mode. What does that future hold? As she waits for her husband to return from seeing Charlotte and Adam to their carriage – they are leaving for America – Maggie attempts to define the nature of her achievement:

Yet *this* above all – her just being there as she was and waiting for him to come in, their freedom to be together there always – was the meaning most disengaged: she stood in the cool twilight and took in all about her where it lurked her reason for what she had done. She knew at last really why – and how she had been inspired and guided, how she had been persistently able, how to her soul all the while it had been for the sake of this end. Here it was then, the moment, the golden fruit that had shone from afar; only what *were* these things in fact, for the hand and for the lips, when tested, when tasted – what were they as a reward? Closer than she had ever been to the measure of her course and the full face of her act, she had an instant of the terror that, when there has been suspense, always precedes, on the part of the creature to be paid, the certification of the amount; he still held it, and the delay in his return, making her heart beat too fast to go on, was like a sudden blinding light on a wild speculation. She had thrown the dice, but his hand was over the cast. (*24*, 367)

The uncertainties expressed in this passage, as well as the feelings of "pity and dread" (*24*, 369) with which Maggie submits to Amerigo's final embrace, have caused many of James's critics to doubt the value of the consummation at which, after so long, he has arrived. But such doubts suggest that the critics have fallen victim to the same error which had prevented Henry James from speaking the sentence of love; like the desiring hero of "The Beast in the Jungle," who eschews "the mere usual and normal human adventures" – including the adventure of love – while he awaits "a translation into bliss sublime". (*AN*, 246), they expect too much, and want the impossible rather than the attainable.

In terms that echo Maggie's recognition of the "wild speculation" implicit in her act, Denis de Rougemont asserts that "once we ask ourselves what is involved in choosing a man or a woman *for the rest of one's life*, we see that to choose is to wager" (303). For de Rougemont, marriage – which he defines as "the institution in which passion is 'contained,' not by morals, but by love" (315) – is an active commitment by two persons in which "everything depends on a decision":

It must lie in that irrational event, a decision that we venture upon in spite of everything and that lays the foundation of a new life in being a consent to take new chances.
Let me forestall any misunderstanding. "Irrational" in no way means "sentimental." To choose a woman for wife is not to say to Miss So-and-So: "You are the ideal of my dreams, you more than gratify all my desires, you are the Iseult altogether lovely and desirable . . . of whom I want to be the Tristan." For this would be deceit, and nothing enduring can be founded on deceit. Nobody in the world can gratify me; no sooner were I gratified than I would change! To choose a woman for wife is to say to Miss So-and-So: "I want to live with you just as you are." For this really means: "It is you I choose to *share* my life with me, and that is the only *evidence* there can be that I love you." If anybody says, "Is that all?" – and this is no doubt what many . . . people will say, having been led by virtue of the myth to expect goodness knows what divine transports – he must have had little experience of solitariness and dread, little experience indeed of solitary dread. (305)

If James is affirming love in marriage in *The Golden Bowl* – and I think he is – it is on this existential basis alone: as an absurd yet world-renewing commitment by two human wills, not a falling-in-love, but a making of it through the enactment of desire.

De Rougemont tells us that a commitment requires a prior experience of "solitariness and dread." And if Maggie's act of love follows from her acceptance of the world's "evil," which is to say its limitations and imperfections, then James's own act in telling this remarkable love story issues from the tragic recognition he had embraced in *The Wings of the Dove*. In his last novel, James moves beyond tragedy to attain an affirmative, tragicomic vision, its essential message being, in Robert Langbaum's words, "that we lose in order to recover something greater, that we die in order to be reborn to a better life" (*The Modern Spirit*, 188). And I think Gore Vidal is right in seeing this final incarnation of Henry James as a "magician who, unlike Prospero, breaks not his staff but a golden bowl" (8). For in breaking the bowl, and in providing Maggie Verver with the empowering knowledge it contains, James is also breaking with the seductive yet ultimately sterile magic of his desiring art. Like Prospero's, James's "charms are all o'erthrown"; he no longer has "spirits to enforce, art to enchant" (*The Tempest.* "Epilogue"), and must rely on his own strength – his own power to choose and to act – in creating what is now a wholly human art, conceived as an act of life. James scoffed at the notion that *The Tempest* in any way represented Shakespeare's farewell to the stage, at the idea that he "could so, at a given moment, announce his intention of capping his divine flame with a twopenny extinguisher, and who then, the announcement made, could serenely succeed in carrying it out" (*LC*, 1:1215). And to be sure, the "divine flame" of James's writing would finally be extinguished only with his death. But the author of *The Golden Bowl* never completed another long fiction, and one is tempted to interpret *that* human choice as a sign that James himself believed his long career had been, like Maggie's ordeal, all "for the sake of this end." We inevitably recall the strange Bloomsbury shopman, handling with "tenderness" and "ceremony" the gilded drinking vessel, precious, we know, for its flaw as well as for its beauty: " 'My Golden Bowl,' he observed – and it sounded, on his lips, as if it said everything."

NOTES

1 Introduction: Desire, love and the question of Henry James

1 The most notable dissenter from Matthiessen's high valuation of the late fiction is F.R. Leavis (*The Great Tradition*, 154–172).

2 This period is usually taken to include James's work between 1895 and 1901.

2 *The Ambassadors* (I): Strether, James, and the figuration of desire

1 Strether's relationship to Chad can be linked to René Girard's concept of "triangular desire" (*Deceit, Desire, and the Novel*, esp. 1–52). Desire, in Girard's structural scheme, is never original; it is always "desire *according to another*" (4). The individual does not choose the object of his own desire, but instead imitates the desire of a "mediator," whom he envies. "The object is only a means of reaching the mediator. The desire is aimed at the mediator's *being*" (53). Girard's characterization of the way in which great novelists ultimately recognize, expose, and transcend this unconscious "triangulation of desire" offers an illuminating parallel to my own analysis of James's movement from desire to love in the late novels.

2 There is, of course, much in James to support the opposite conclusion: that the novelist saw himself as having *failed* to live, precisely because of his devotion to his art. James's profound ambivalence about these questions – Does the artist really live? Or is he inevitably cut off from life? – is central to my concerns in the pages that follow. As my argument will make clear, I think – despite the passage quoted from the *Notebooks* – that the James who wrote *The Ambassadors* was still convinced that the artist's career and "real" living were somehow incompatible, and that he himself, like Strether, was a "man who ha[d]n't, 'lived,' ha[d]n't at all."

3 Weinstein ultimately sees this distinction as representing a dichotomy that James was incapable of bridging. In my own view, however, James succeeds in fusing direct and imaginative experience in *The Golden Bowl*. Weinstein's excellent study – a constant reference point for my approach to

200

James – is flawed by his tendency to see *The Ambassadors* as a prescriptive model for all of James's novels.

4 In his Preface to *The Portrait of a Lady*, James admiringly quotes George Eliot's encomium to her young female protagonists – "in these frail vessels is borne onward through the ages the treasure of human affection" – as a way of locating Isabel Archer in the tradition of Hetty Sorrel, Maggie Tulliver, and Gwendolen Harleth (*AN*, 49). Strether too can be seen as a direct descendant of George Eliot's heroines, and as an illustration of her belief that the novelistic protagonist, as opposed to the masculine hero of classical epic and tragedy, is *essentially* feminine. Another passage from *The Mill on the Floss* – again a contrast between Tom and Maggie Tulliver – is suggestive in this regard:

> While Maggie's life-struggles had lain almost entirely within her own soul, one shadowy army fighting another, and the slain shadows forever rising again, Tom engaged in a dustier, noisier warfare, grappling with more substantial obstacles, and gaining more definite conquests. So it has been since the days of Hecuba, and of Hector, tamer of horses: inside the gates, the women with streaming hair and uplifted hands offering prayers, watching the world's combat from afar, filling their long, empty days with memories and fears: outside, the men, in fierce struggle with things divine and human, quenching memory in the stronger light of purpose, losing the sense of dread and even of wounds in the hurrying ardour of action. (V. ii.)

Like George Eliot, James saw the increasing interiorization of character in the novel as a movement towards the feminine.

5 Patricia Tobin discusses the importance of this trend at some length (29–53). Tobin characterizes late nineteenth-century novelists as intent on "subverting the father" (29), and analyzes the theme as it is manifested in Samuel Butler's *The Way of All Flesh*. Malcolm Bradbury also examines these issues briefly (4–5). In a passage from *A Small Boy and Others*, James describes his own childhood envy of some parentless cousins:

> Parentally bereft cousins were somehow more thrilling than parentally provided ones. . . I think my first childish conception of the enviable lot, formed amid these associations, was to be so little fathered or mothered, so little sunk in the short range, that the romance of life seemed to lie in some constant improvisation. . . My first assured conception of true richness was that we [James and his siblings] should be sent separately off among cold or even cruel aliens in order to be there thrillingly homesick. (*SBO*, 14–15)

Elsewhere in the same volume James explains that he saw the orphaned state of his cousin Albert as "a setting necessarily more delightful than our father'd and mother'd one," and that he ascribed to Albert "an air of possibilities that were none the less vivid for being quite indefinite" (*SBO*, 120–21).

6 See, for example, *What Maisie Knew, In the Cage, The Turn of the Screw,* and *The Awkward Age.* Edel's discussion of this phenomenon is helpful (*The Treacherous Years*, 260–67).

7 It is significant that the one metaphor of relationship *not* applied to Strether and Maria Gostrey is that of mature romantic love. Strether's ultimate rejection of Maria's offer of marriage suggests the real limits that are an inevitable part of the figurative "freedom" he discovers in their relationship.

8 Bachelard's distinction between masculine and feminine is derived in part from the Jungian concepts of *animus* and *anima.* Naomi Schor has recently offered an extended and persuasive argument for linking the feminine with modernity's "privileging of the detail" – its "pervasive valorization of the minute, the partial, and the marginal." "The detail," she insists, "is gendered and doubly gendered as feminine" (3–4).

9 It hardly needs to be said that James's idealization of his mother embodies assumptions about gender roles which are extremely retrogressive. Carren Kaston remarks on James's presentation of his mother as "an expert at what one might call selfless or evacuated selfhood" – an "image of a mirror-self, a selfless self" – and goes on to point out that

> his image of the self as a reflector, of consciousness as a mirror, receiving its identity from outside of itself, closely resembles and helps us to understand the stereotypical feminine self scrutinized by feminists. The image beautifully articulates the paradox that seems to define female identity – that women are more sensitive, more conscious than men, but that these assets often fail to give them an advantage. Because of them, in fact, women are generally less able to bring a personal self into existence. (68)

10 For another discussion of masculine and feminine elements in James, see Lisa Appignanesi (20–80). Appignanesi argues that James's later work moves progressively towards a triumph of the feminine – a view with which I cannot agree.

11 In the introductory chapter to her study of James's American girl, Virginia Fowler points suggestively to the novelist's persistent use of embroidery metaphors to figure his art. Fowler concludes that "James identifies his novelistic art as a feminine art" (6–7).

3 *The Ambassadors* (II): The point where the death comes in

1 In his celebrated discussion of metaphor and metonymy, Roman Jakobson in fact posits an affinity between the metonymic mode and nineteenth-century realistic fiction (*Fundamentals of Language*, 91–92).

2 Foucault uses the term "author" to refer to the whole context of historical and ideological determinations which restrict the infinite possible meanings

of the text. But as Edward Said has pointed out, Foucault's thinking lends itself to a discussion of the ethics of individual authorship ("An Ethics of Language").

3 Barthes's categories – "work" and "Text" – overlap in many ways with my own terms, *author* and *writer*. In opposition to the work, which "closes itself on a signified," the Text is "dilatory" and "plural," practising "the infinite deferral of the signified" (76–77). Barthes's association of the work with a "myth of filiation" is suggestive in light of James's own ambiguous feelings about paternal authority:

> The work is caught up in a process of filiation. Three things are postulated here: a *determination* of the work by the outside world (by race, then by history), a *consecution* of works among themselves, and an *allocation* of the work to its author. The author is regarded as the father and owner of his work. . . The Text, on the other hand, is read without the father's signature . . . [It] can be read without the father's guarantee. . . It is not that the author cannot "come back" into the Text, into his text; however, he can only do so as a "guest," so to speak . . . his signature is no longer privileged and paternal, the locus of genuine truth, but rather, ludic. (78)

4 See, for example, Ruth Bernard Yeazell (21).

5 Barthes also considers the attractions of delay, both in the sentence and in the narrative, in *S/Z* (75–76).

6 James's own antipathy to the "art" of modern advertising finds expression in his "London Notes" for June 1897, where he makes little effort to disguise his disgust at the "gross defacement of London" – complete with "screaming advertisements" – occasioned by Queen Victoria's Jubilee (*Notes on Novelists*, 428–33).

7 Carren Kaston defines Strether's failure in more specific terms: Strether, she argues, is unable to embody his love for Madame de Vionnet "in any permanent or material form, to make a reciprocally *lived* fiction out of it, because he is bound by his 'only logic,' " renunciation. The result of this logic, Kaston continues, "is a continuing commitment to acts of substitution" – such as "Strether's substitutive concern with Chad's behaviour" – in which

> the interests of the self can only be expressed decenteredly, through an interest in what is outside the self. The strenuousness of Strether's language to Chad reveals an effort to impose a fiction on the book that will enact his own attachment to Madame de Vionnet without his having to experience it himself. But his absence from the design that he wishes to promote, which follows inevitably from his absence from his own desires, means that he cannot be accountable for what finally will happen to Madame de Vionnet. Only Strether's presence could secure Marie de Vionnet from abandonment. (107–08)

4 *The Wings of the Dove* (I): The contracted cage

1 *The Wings of the Dove* was published in 1902, *The Ambassadors* in 1903 – in reverse order of their composition.

2 Richard Hocks offers what is perhaps the boldest challenge to the unity of the "major phase" novels when he suggests that there is "an argument to be made for *The Wings of the Dove* and *The Golden Bowl* constituting a departure from *The Ambassadors* as significant on its side as the three novels together from those . . . of the nineties." In Hocks's scheme, *The Wings of the Dove* initiates a new phase in James's career marked by an increasing emphasis on spiritual questions and "supernatural agencies" at the expense of the more "humanistic and secular" concerns of *The Ambassadors* (190–95). Hocks's reading of *The Wings of the Dove* as a Jamesian ascent into "supernatural or quasi-supernatural" realms seems to me as far-fetched as Quentin Anderson's earlier attempt to interpret the novel as Swedenborgian allegory (207–80). Nevertheless, Hocks's redefinition of the major phase – his belief that *The Ambassadors* belongs more properly with the novels that precede it, and that *The Wings of the Dove* embodies a new impulse – seems to me richly suggestive.

3 The "young man from Texas" was Stark Young.

4 Leon Edel has examined James's tendency, in the "experimental fiction" of the 1890s, to use little boys and little girls as protagonists. Edel sees the pattern as evidence of an "imaginative self-therapy" through which James was "intuitively questioning his unconscious experience, reliving the long-ago 'education' of his emotions" (*The Treacherous Years*, 26–67 and *passim*).

5 Chad Newsome (*The Ambassadors*) and Sir Claude (*What Maisie Knew*) – like other characters in the fiction of the 1890s – are, of course, "sexually potent," even sexually active. Indeed, in many respects the fiction of this period is obsessed with sex. But James never employs these sexually active characters as centers of consciousness; the main protagonists are Strether and Maisie, and it is only through the "blocked" sexuality of these central reflectors that we approach the experience of the young men. Densher is the first young adult male character since Nick Dormer to serve as a center of consciousness, and thus as a protagonist in any real sense.

6 See the *Notebooks*, especially pages 169–76. James indicates that he had been thinking about his subject for *The Wings of the Dove* for several years before he made his initial *Notebook* entry.

7 Edel also links *The Wings of the Dove* to James's relationship with the American novelist, Constance Fenimore Woolson. James's failure to respond to Miss Woolson's romantic overtures was, as Edel indicates, a reprise of his failure to love Minny Temple. Miss Woolson committed suicide in Venice, the scene of Milly Theale's death (*The Middle Years*, 386–87).

8 "On a parlé vers la mort et contre elle, pour la tenir et la détenir."

Foucault's original essay, "Le Language à l'infini," appeared in *Tel Quel*, 15 (Autumn 1963).

9 In his chapter on "Realism and the Fear of Desire," Bersani discusses the inevitable contradiction between individual desire and realism's "prior imagination . . . of ends."

10 For another discussion of the end-perspective of classical realism, see Lukács (33–39).

11 James gave this advice in a letter to the Duchess of Sutherland, dated December 23, 1903. Like many readers since, the Duchess was apparently daunted by the intricacies of James's late style and center of consciousness technique.

12 Leo Bersani has argued that the distinction between single and multiple-consciousness form in late James is moot, since all the centers of consciousness are "merged with the narrator," and "assimilated into his point of view on the story." Bersani's argument rests largely on his observation that "stylistic distinctions between narrator and centers of consciousness [are] difficult to perceive" ("The Narrator as Center in 'The Wings of the Dove,' " 131). While Bersani's comments on the stylistic elision between narrator and centers of consciousness are not wholly unjustified, his wholesale dismissal of the novel's dramatic textures seems to me extreme. As my own argument will suggest, I believe Bersani pays too much attention to the style in which the characters think and talk, and not enough to the substance of what they say and do.

13 J.A. Ward relates *The Wings of the Dove* to the structural pattern Francis Fergusson (*The Idea of a Theater*) discovers in the agon of the Greek tragedy: the progression from "purpose" through "passion" to "perception" (*The Search for Form*, 186–89). See also King (127–57).

5 *The Wings of the Dove* (II): Choosing, acting and the chance for love

1 Sallie Sears, for example, has argued that Milly's story, like Strether's, is "one of resisting until too late, and in spite of reiterated warnings, knowledge that she should have accepted; a story of not seeing" (79–82). Milly is undoubtedly emotionally susceptible to being deceived about the nature of Kate and Densher's relationship. Nevertheless, there is nothing in *The Ambassadors* to match the repeated, deliberately false assertions – made by Kate, Mrs. Lowder, and even Mrs. Stringham – that Kate does not love Densher.

2 Many critics have read Milly's bequest as an act of spiritual or even religious transcendence. Quentin Anderson (278–79) and R. W. B. Lewis (188ff.) have offered explicitly Christian interpretations of her act. Dorothea Krook is more circumspect, but essentially in agreement. Milly, she argues, injects into the world "its first knowledge of an order of

goodness and power greater than any this world by itself can show." Although Krook's reading of the novel is informed throughout by the vocabulary of Christian moral hierarchies, she still believes that James's vision in *The Wings of the Dove* is brought only "to the edge of the religious. If in the end it remains on this side of the dividing line, the parallels with the religious are nonetheless striking." Milly thus represents "the power of the good" to answer "the power of the world" with "forgiveness, loving-kindness and sacrificial death" (220–21, 195–231 *passim*). Other critics, while eschewing specifically religious interpretations, have adopted related approaches. Philip Sicker sees Milly's legacy as a "telepathic communication" from the "transmigrating spirit" of Milly – a character he sees as "sublimely spiritual" – to Densher (139–40). Richard Hocks tries to link *The Wings of the Dove* to James's ghost stories, and finds "supernatural" intimations in Milly's act, as well as elsewhere in the novel (191–94). My own convictions are clearly expressed by Alwyn Berland, when he argues that "James's eyes were fixed firmly on finite and mortal men living in a finite social world," and that the novelist's vision "was altogether secular and mundane" (9).

6 *The Golden Bowl* (I): The resumption of authority

1 For other negative judgments of *The Golden Bowl*, see Leavis (159–61) and Weinstein (165–94).

2 Yeazell herself contrasts the ending of *The Golden Bowl* to what she sees as the "undefined futures" projected by the conclusions of *The Ambassadors* and *The Wings of the Dove* (100–01).

3 Girard's broader discussion of the importance of novelistic conclusions – he sees the conclusion as "the stationary axle around which the wheel of the novel turns" (307) – is relevant here (290–310, *passim*).

4 James also employs the multiple-consciousness form in *The Ivory Tower*, the unfinished novel which follows *The Golden Bowl*.

5 J.A. Ward, for example, sees the novel as offering "a more symmetrical version of the scheme of *The Wings of the Dove*" (*The Search for Form*, 203).

6 "Thel's Motto," from "The Book of Thel" (*The Poetry and Prose of William Blake*, 3). The complete text of "Thel's Motto" is as follows:

> Does the Eagle know what is in the pit?
>   Or wilt thou go ask the Mole:
> Can wisdom be put in a silver rod?
>   Or love in a golden bowl?

7 "That allegorical description of Hermes [that God is a circle whose circumference is nowhere and whose center is everywhere] pleaseth me beyond all the metaphysical definitions of divines" (*Religio Medici*, 12).

8 Although he does not discuss its significance for *The Golden Bowl*, Wein-

stein has explored the pattern of "open windows and closed doors" in James, seeing in it a "metaphor [that] penetrates deeply into the world of James's novels." Weinstein points out that "windows are customarily seen through; doors walked through. With some figurative extension, the open windows are meant to signify the multifold visions, the expansive panoramas so characteristic of the Jamesian hero's imagination, while the closed doors suggest the fate of a certain kind of experience in James's world; the stifled nature of intimate or passionate relationships that, balked, either do not come to fruition, or do so only behind closed doors" (6).

9 For a suggestive discussion of the bowl's multitudinous symbolic possibilities, see Holland (348–49).

10 James himself once wrote that the artist is "in every page of every book from which he sought so assiduously to eliminate himself" (quoted in Edel, *The Conquest of London*, 300). The whole question, in James, of the author's presence or absence in his work is explored at length by William Goetz in his recent book on the novelist.

11 As John Carlos Rowe has pointed out, "James's criticism of Trollope is troubling when we consider how often he himself exposes the illusion of his art. . . " Rowe argues that in addition to James's "inveterate use of the first-person narrator," and his frequent use of "narrative asides, in which the omnipotence of that [narrator] is generally manifested," there is

> a less tenuous and more pervasive sense in which James always exposes his fiction, and that is in the fundamental assumption of the *textuality* of experience. . . James's characters are always involved in theatrical, fictional, *artistic* situations, so much so that the perceptiveness and intelligence of his characters are most often measured in terms of their sensibilities for the "arts" of society. In this regard, James is, even more than Trollope, perpetually tipping his hand to the reader, exposing the fictive foundations for his "illusion" of the real. (70–71)

12 Jacques Barzun, Leo Levy, and Peter Brooks offer the most useful discussions of James's melodramatic tendencies.

13 Many critics appear to have assumed that James was singling out *The American* as a romantic aberration in a realistic *oeuvre*. James himself suggests that *The American* was rather a less successful version of the romantic novel he had been writing all his life. "The art of the romancer," James argues, "is, 'for the fun of it,' insidiously to cut the cable" which ties "the balloon of experience," and its attached "car of the imagination," to the earth, to cut it "without our detecting him" (*AN*, 33–34). James catches himself cutting the cable in *The American* – hence his estimation of the novel as problematic.

14 James himself usually dated the injury as of 1862 – a slip which Edel sees as significant (*The Untried Years*, 175–76).

15 Edel summarizes the history of these speculations about James's supposed

sexual incapacity in *The Untried Years* (176). He includes among the perpetrators of this "theory" such critics as Glenway Westcott, Stephen Spender, F.O. Matthiessen, R.P. Blackmur, and Lionel Trilling.

16 The way in which James's negative myth of fate inevitably becomes a self-confirming prediction of defeat and disaster is illuminated by Freud's concept of "moral masochism" ("The Economic Problem of Masochism," 19:161). According to Freud, the masochistic ego, disturbed by "an unconscious sense of guilt," seeks "punishment, whether from the super-ego or from [other] parental powers outside" the psyche. "The dark power of Destiny" – a force, Freud remarks, "which only the fewest among us are able to look upon as impersonal" – is really "the last figure in the series [of punishing authority figures] that began with the parents." And the moral masochist clings to this "parental view of fate," thereby expiating his guilt over his self-conceived shortcomings through his suffering, as James would say, at the hands of "nature and fortune." But masochism also "creates a temptation" to fail, for failure invites the desired

> chastisement from the great parental power of Destiny. In order to provoke punishment from this last representative of the parents, the masochist must do what is inexpedient, must act against his own interests, must ruin the prospects which open out to him in the real world and must, perhaps, destroy his own real existence. (19:168–70)

According to Freud, masochism in its more primary forms usually involves an unconscious wish to be castrated (19:162). And while this point can easily be overemphasized, its relevance to the strange history of James's "obscure hurt" cannot be ignored. In any case, the concept helps to explain James's "wish that the hurt might endure."

17 James's relationship with the naturalists has received some attention. See Phillip Grover, Lyall Powers, and especially Joseph Firebaugh's suggestive article on *The Princess Cassimassima*. More recently, Mark Seltzer has offered a limited but valuable comparison of James and Zola (passim).

7 *The Golden Bowl* (II): For the sake of this end

1 The scene recalls in particular that moment in *The Ambassadors* when Strether wonders whether he has not in fact been "fantastic and away from the truth. . . Did he live in a false world, a world that had grown simply to suit him" (22, 80–81)? The governess in *The Turn of the Screw* and the narrator of *The Sacred Fount* are repeatedly overwhelmed by this kind of self-doubt.

WORKS CITED

Allott, Miriam, ed. *Novelists on the Novel*. New York: Columbia University Press, 1959

Anderson, Quentin. *The American Henry James*. New Brunswick: Rutgers University Press, 1957

Appignanesi, Lisa. *Femininity and the Creative Imagination: A Study of Henry James, Robert Musil and Marcel Proust*. London: Vision Press, 1973

Aristotle. *Poetics*. Trans. S.H. Butcher. New York: Hill and Wang, 1961

Armstrong, Paul. *The Phenomenology of Henry James*. Chapel Hill: University of North Carolina Press, 1983

Bachelard, Gaston. *The Poetics of Reverie: Childhood, Language, and the Cosmos*. Trans. Daniel Russell. Boston: Beacon Press, 1969

Barthes, Roland. "From Work to Text" in *Textual Strategies: Perspectives in Post-Structuralist Criticism*, ed. Josué V. Harari. Ithaca: Cornell University Press, 1979, 73–81

A Lover's Discourse: Fragments. Trans. Richard Howard. New York: Farrar, Straus and Giroux, 1978

The Pleasure of the Text. Trans. Richard Miller. New York: Farrar, Straus and Giroux, 1975

S/Z: An Essay. Trans. Richard Miller. New York: Farrar, Straus and Giroux, 1974

Barzun, Jacques. "Henry James, Melodramatist" in *The Question of Henry James*, ed. F.W. Dupee. New York: Henry Holt and Company, 1947, 261–73

Berland, Alwyn. *Culture and Conduct in the Novels of Henry James*. Cambridge University Press, 1981

Bersani, Leo. *A Future for Astyanax: Character and Desire in Literature*. Boston: Little, Brown and Company, 1969

"The Narrator as Center in 'The Wings of the Dove.'" *Modern Fiction Studies*, 6 (1960): 131–44

Blackmur, R.P. *Studies in Henry James*, ed. Veronica A. Makowsky. New York: New Directions, 1983

Blake, William. *The Poetry and Prose of William Blake*, ed. Daniel V. Erdmann. New York: Doubleday, 1970

Bosanquet, Theodora. *Henry James at Work*. The Hogarth Essays. London: The Hogarth Press, 1924 (?)

Bradbury, Malcolm. *The Social Context of English Literature*. New York: Schoeken, 1971

Brooks, Peter. *The Melodramatic Imagination: Balzac, Henry James. Melodrama and the Mode of Excess*. New Haven: Yale University Press, 1976

Brooks, Van Wyck. *The Pilgrimage of Henry James*. New York: E.P. Dutton, 1925

Browne, Sir Thomas. *Religio Medici*, ed. F.L. Huntley. New York: Appleton-Century-Crofts, 1966

Crews, Frederick C. *The Tragedy of Manners: Moral Drama in the Later Novels of Henry James*. Hamden, Connecticut: Archon Books, 1971 [1957]

Dewey, John. *Art as Experience*. New York: Minton, Balch and Company, 1934

Dupee, F.W., ed. *The Question of Henry James*. New York: Henry Holt and Company, 1945

Edel, Leon. *Henry James*. vol. 1: *The Untried Years. 1843–1870*; vol. 2: *The Conquest of London. 1870–1881*; vol. 3: *The Middle Years. 1882–1895*; vol. 4: *The Treacherous Years. 1895–1901*; vol. 5: *The Master. 1901–1916*. New York: Avon Books, 1978

   ed. *Henry James: A Collection of Critical Essays*. Englewood Cliffs, N.J.: Prentice-Hall, 1963

Eliot, George. *The Mill on the Floss*, ed. Gordon S. Height. Boston: Houghton Mifflin Company, 1961

Felman, Shoshana. "Turning the Screw of Interpretation" in *Literature and Psychoanalysis. The Question of Reading: Otherwise*, ed. Shoshana Felman. Baltimore: Johns Hopkins University Press, 1982, 94–207

Fergusson, Francis. *The Idea of a Theater: A Study of Ten Plays, The Art of Drama in Changing Perspective*. Princeton University Press, 1968

Firebaugh, Joseph J. "A Schopenhaurian Novel: James's *The Princess Casamassima*." *Nineteenth-Century Fiction*, 3 (December 1958): 177–97

Foucault, Michel. "Language to Infinity" in *Language, Counter-Memory, Practice: Selected Essays and Interviews*, ed. Donald F. Bouchard. Trans. Donald F. Bouchard and Sherry Simon. Ithaca: Cornell University Press, 1977, 53–67

   "What is an Author?" in *Textual Strategies: Perspectives in Post-Structuralist Criticism*, ed. Josué V. Harari. Ithaca: Cornell University Press, 1979, 141–60

Fowler, Virginia C. *Henry James's American Girl: The Embroidery on the Canvas*. Madison: University of Wisconsin Press, 1984

Freud, Sigmund. *Complete Psychological Works of Sigmund Freud (Standard Edition)*, ed. James Strachey, 24 vols. London: Hogarth Press, 1953

Frye, Northrop. *Fools of Time: Studies in Shakespearian Tragedy*. University of Toronto Press, 1967

Gard, Roger, ed. *Henry James: The Critical Heritage*. London: Routledge and Kegan Paul, 1968

Garis, Robert. "The Two Lambert Strethers: A New Reading of *The Ambassadors*." *Modern Fiction Studies*, 7 (Winter 1961–62): 303–21

Gass, William H. *Fiction and the Figures of Life*. Boston: Nonpareil Books, 1971

Geismar, Maxwell. *Henry James and the Jacobites*. New York: Hill and Wang, 1961

Girard, René. *Deceit, Desire, and the Novel: Self and Other in Literary Structure*. Trans. Yvonne Freccero. Baltimore: The Johns Hopkins University Press, 1965

Goetz, William R. *Henry James and the Darkest Abyss of Romance*. Baton Rouge: Louisiana State University Press, 1986

Graham, Kenneth. *Henry James: The Drama of Fulfillment*. Oxford: Clarendon Press, 1975

Grover, Philip. *Henry James and the French Novel: A Study in Inspiration*. New York: Barnes and Noble, 1973

Hocks, Richard A. *Henry James and Pragmatist Thought: A Study in the Relationship between the Philosophy of William James and the Literary Art of Henry James*. Chapel Hill: The University of North Carolina Press, 1974

Holland, Laurence B. *The Expense of Vision: Essays on the Craft of Henry James*. Princeton University Press, 1964

Hollington, Michael. "Svevo, Joyce, and Modernist Time" in *Modernism: 1890–1930*, ed. Malcolm Bradbury and James McFarlane. Harmondsworth: Penguin, 1976

Homer. *The Iliad of Homer*. Trans. Richard Lattimore. University of Chicago Press, 1961

Hutchinson, Stuart. *Henry James: An American as Modernist*. London: Barnes and Noble, 1982

Jakobson, Roman, and Halle, Morris. *Fundamentals of Language*. The Hague: Janua Linguarum, Mouton, 1956

James, Henry. *The Art of the Novel: Critical Prefaces by Henry James*, ed. R.P. Blackmur. New York: Scribner's, 1934

The Bostonians. New York: Modern Library, 1956

The Complete Tales of Henry James, ed. Leon Edel, 12 vols. Philadelphia: Lippincott, 1964

The Ivory Tower. New York: Scribner's, 1923

Letters, ed. Leon Edel, 4 vols. Cambridge, Mass.: Harvard University Press, 1984

Letters to A.C. Benson and Auguste Monod, ed. E.F. Benson. London: Elkin Matthews and Marrot, 1930

The Novels and Tales of Henry James, 24 vols. New York: Scribner's 1907–9

The Notebooks of Henry James, ed. F.O. Matthiessen and Kenneth B. Murdock. Chicago University Press, 1981 [1947]

Notes and Reviews. Cambridge: Dunster House, 1921

Notes of a Son and Brother. New York: Scribner's, 1914

Notes on Novelists. With Some Other Notes. New York: Scribner's, 1916

The Sacred Fount. New York: Grove Press, 1953

A Small Boy and Others. New York: Scribner's, 1913

Kaston, Carren. *Imagination and Desire in the Novels of Henry James.* New Brunswick: Rutgers University Press, 1984

Kermode, Frank. *The Sense of an Ending: Studies in the Theory of Fiction.* New York: Oxford University Press, 1978

King, Jeannette. *Tragedy in the Victorian Novel: Theory and Practice in the Novels of George Eliot, Thomas Hardy and Henry James.* Cambridge University Press, 1967

Kristeva, Julia. *Desire in Language: A Semiotic Approach to Literature and Art,* ed. Leon S. Roudiez. Trans. Thomas Gora, Alice Jardine, and Leon S. Roudiez. New York: Columbia University Press, 1980

Krook, Dorothea. *The Ordeal of Consciousness in Henry James.* Cambridge University Press, 1962

Langbaum, Robert. *The Modern Spirit: Essays on the Continuity of Nineteenth and Twentieth Century Literature.* New York: Oxford University Press, 1970

The Poetry of Experience: The Dramatic Monologue in Modern Literary Tradition. New York: Norton, 1957

Leavis, F.R. *The Great Tradition.* New York University Press, 1964

Lebowitz, Naomi. *The Imagination of Loving: Henry James's Legacy to the Novel.* Detroit: Wayne State University Press, 1965

Levy, Leo. *Versions of Melodrama: A Study of the Fiction and Drama of Henry James, 1865–1897.* Berkeley: University of California Press, 1957

Lewis, R.W.B. *Trials of the Word.* New Haven: Yale University Press, 1965

Lukács, Georg. *The Meaning of Contemporary Realism.* Trans. John and Necke Mander. London: Merlin Press, 1963

Man, Paul de. *Blindness and Insight: Essays in the Rhetoric of Contemporary Criticism,* 2nd edn, revised. Minneapolis: University of Minnesota Press, 1983

Matthiessen, F.O. *Henry James: The Major Phase.* New York: Oxford University Press, 1944

Ortega y Gasset, José. *On Love: Aspects of a Single Theme.* Trans. Toby Talbot. New York: Meridian Books, 1957

Plato. *The Symposium.* Trans. Walter Hamilton. Harmondsworth: Penguin, 1951

Poirier, Richard. *A World Elsewhere: The Place of Style in American Literature.* New York: Oxford University Press, 1966

Poulet, Georges. *Studies in Human Time.* Trans. Elliot Coleman. Baltimore: The Johns Hopkins Press, 1956

Powers, Lyall M. *Henry James and the Naturalist Movement.* East Lansing, Michigan: Michigan State University Press, 1971

Ricoeur, Paul. *Freud and Philosophy: An Essay on Interpretation.* Trans. Denis Savage. New Haven: Yale University Press, 1971

Rilke, Rainer Maria. *Letters to a Young Poet.* Trans. M.D. Herter Norton. New York: Norton, 1954

Rimmon, Shlomith. *The Concept of Ambiguity – the Example of James.* University of Chicago Press, 1977

Rougemont, Denis de. *Love in the Western World,* revised and augmented edn. Trans. Montgomery Belgron. Princeton University Press, 1983

Rowe, John Carlos. *The Theoretical Dimensions of Henry James.* Madison: University of Wisconsin Press, 1984

Said, Edward. *Beginnings: Intention and Method.* Baltimore: Johns Hopkins University Press, 1975

"An Ethics of Language." *Diacritics: A Review of Contemporary Criticism,* 4 (1974), 28–37

Sartre, Jean-Paul. *Being and Nothingness: An Essay on Phenomenological Ontology.* Trans. Hazel E. Barnes. New York: Philosophical Library, 1956

Schor, Naomi. *Reading in Detail: Aesthetics and the Feminine.* New York: Methuen, 1987

Sears, Sallie. *The Negative Imagination: Form and Perspective in the Novels of Henry James.* Ithaca: Cornell University Press, 1968

Seltzer, Mark. *Henry James and the Art of Power.* Ithaca: Cornell University Press, 1984

Sicker, Philip. *Love and the Quest for Identity in the Fiction of Henry James.* Princeton University Press, 1980

Spender, Stephen. *The Destructive Element: A Study of Modern Writers and Beliefs.* Boston: Houghton Mifflin, 1936

Stendhal. *Love.* Trans. Gilbert and Suzanne Sale. Harmondsworth: Penguin, 1975

Stevens, Wallace. *The Palm at the End of the Mind,* ed. Holly Stevens. New York: Alfred A. Knopf, 1971

Thackeray, W.M. *Letters and Private Papers.* ed. G.N. Ray, II. Cambridge, Mass.: Harvard University Press, 1945

Tobin, Patricia. *Time and the Novel: The Genealogical Imperative.* Princeton University Press, 1978

Todorov, Tzvetan. *The Poetics of Prose.* Trans. Richard Howard. Ithaca: Cornell University Press, 1977

Trilling, Lionel. "Freud and Literature" in *The Liberal Imagination.* New York: Vintage, 1950

Vidal, Gore. "Return to 'The Golden Bowl.' " *The New York Review of Books,* 30 (January 1984): 8–12

Ward, J.A. *The Imagination of Disaster: Evil in the Fiction of Henry James.* Lincoln: University of Nebraska Press, 1961

The Search for Form: Studies in the Structure of James's Fiction. Chapel Hill: The University of North Carolina Press, 1967

Weinstein, Philip M. *Henry James and the Requirements of the Imagination.* Cambridge, Mass.: Harvard University Press, 1971

Wells, H.G. *Boon. The Mind of the Race. The Wild Asses of the Devil, and the Last Trump.* New York: G.H. Doran, 1915

Winters, Yvor. *In Defense of Reason.* New York: Swallow Press, 1947

Yeazell, Ruth Bernard. *Language and Knowledge in the Late Novels of Henry James.* University of Chicago Press, 1976

INDEX